Organising Neoliberalism

Organising Neoliberalism

Markets, Privatisation and Justice

Edited by
Philip Whitehead and Paul Crawshaw

ANTHEM PRESS
LONDON · NEW YORK · DELHI

Anthem Press
An imprint of Wimbledon Publishing Company
www.anthempress.com

This edition first published in UK and USA 2014
by ANTHEM PRESS
75–76 Blackfriars Road, London SE1 8HA, UK
or PO Box 9779, London SW19 7ZG, UK
and
244 Madison Ave. #116, New York, NY 10016, USA

First published in hardback by Anthem Press in 2012

British Library Cataloguing-in-Publication Data
A catalogue record for this book is available from the British Library.

Library of Congress Cataloging-in-Publication Data
The Library of Congress catalogued the hardcover edition as follows:
Organising neoliberalism : markets, privatisation and justice / edited
by Philip Whitehead and Paul Crawshaw.
p. cm.
Includes bibliographical references and index.
ISBN 978-0-85728-533-1 (hbk. : alk. paper)
1. Neoliberalism. I. Whitehead, Philip, 1952– II. Crawshaw, Paul.
HB95.O74 2012
320.51–dc23
2012022746

ISBN-13: 978 1 78308 314 5 (Pbk)
ISBN-10: 1 78308 314 X (Pbk)

This title is also available as an ebook.

CONTENTS

Chapter 1   Introduction: A Preliminary Mapping of the Terrain   1
Philip Whitehead and Paul Crawshaw

Chapter 2   Neoliberalism and Crime in the United States and
the United Kingdom   23
Mark Cowling

Chapter 3   Neoliberalism, Prisons and Probation in the United States
and England and Wales   45
Michael Teague

Chapter 4   The Neoliberal Wings of the 'Smoke-Breathing Dragon':
The Cigarette Counterfeiting Business and Economic
Development in the People's Republic of China   81
*Anqi Shen, Georgios A. Antonopoulos, Marin K. Kurti and
Klaus von Lampe*

Chapter 5   A Neoliberal Security Complex?   105
Georgios Papanicolaou

Chapter 6   The Influence of Neoliberalism on the Development
of the English Youth Justice System under New Labour   135
Raymond Arthur

Chapter 7   Institutionalising Commercialism? The Case of Social
Marketing for Health in the United Kingdom   155
Paul Crawshaw

Chapter 8   Neoliberal Policy, Quality and Inequality in
Undergraduate Degrees   179
Andrea Abbas, Paul Ashwin and Monica McLean

Chapter 9   Religion and Criminal Justice in Canada, England
and Wales: Community Chaplaincy and Resistance
to the Surging Tide of Neoliberal Orthodoxy   201
Philip Whitehead

Chapter 10 Markets, Privatisation and Justice: Some
                Critical Reflections   229
                Philip Whitehead and Paul Crawshaw

Notes on Contributors   242

Index   245

Chapter 1

INTRODUCTION: A PRELIMINARY MAPPING OF THE TERRAIN

Philip Whitehead and Paul Crawshaw

> The global capitalist system is approaching an apocalyptic zero-point.
> (Žižek 2011, x)

Introduction

As the long history of the twentieth century drew to a close, a series of political events took place which, although initially local to nation states, changed the landscape of global politics in a fundamental and seemingly irrevocable way. The revolutions which marked the demise of the Eastern communist blocs, which had so defined the political dialectic of the second half of the twentieth century, were said to herald the end of history (Fukuyama 1992) and the inevitable end point of political and economic tensions which had begun some fifty years earlier. The doctrinal dominance of the free market had finally been established, which signalled the end of ideological contestations and the creation of a new global capitalist order without national or international boundaries. These Eastern convulsions followed a steady retreat from Keynesian polity, located within the policies of Western governments, which had begun with the economic crisis of the 1970s. Where the post-war period in nations such as the United States and the United Kingdom had been defined by a general consensus around the provision of welfare and a form of managed capitalism of greatest benefit to ordinary workers and their families, this earlier crash brought finance to the fore in a previously unprecedented manner and prepared the ground for a new form of politics based upon the championing of free-market capitalism and an overt attack upon established forms of social organisation. A new hegemony of finance emerged under the direction of powerful ideologues such as President Reagan in the United States and Mrs Thatcher in the United Kingdom, both of whom entered power with explicit mandates to roll back the state, quash unionisation and promote Hayekian free-market economics as the only route to growth and prosperity (Hayek 1944). These changes fundamentally altered the landscape of political economies at national, regional and global levels, leading to the hegemony of free-market ideologies and the promotion of competitive capitalism as the orthodox means of economic organisation within late-modern societies. Although most clearly identifiable in the Global North, particularly in the Western post-industrial nations, the effects are not limited to these regions with significant direct and indirect impacts upon other economies, apparent in both the burgeoning capitalist markets of China and other parts of East Asia and the continuing inequalities manifest in the Global South.

A key contention of this collection is that the effects of neoliberalism are not observable only at the level of macro-political decision making and economic shifts. Rather, we and our colleagues in the chapters which follow argue that one of the most important ways in which neoliberalism must be understood is in its escalating institutionalisation within diversely mutating organisational domains, from crime and the criminal justice sector to health and education. We contend that the micro level of organisational structures which we explore are indicative of what Harvey (2010, 131) has described as the new 'mental conceptions of the world' which neoliberalism has engendered. In other words, it is within these organisational reconfigurations that we can observe how the neoliberal dynamic is played out in a range of shifting operational structures and discourses which are fundamental in shaping social life, including our day-to-day experiences and encounters with each other and the wider social world. As Harvey notes,

> Neoliberalism…has pervasive effects on ways of thought to the point where it has become incorporated into the common sense way many of us interpret, live in, and understand the world. (Harvey 2005, 3)

Harvey (2005) echoes Althusser's (1971) conception of ideology which operates not only in the classically Marxist sense of inculcating dominant social relations and a fixed social order, but more insidiously in the way it becomes existentially lived out in the material, ideological and cultural practices of everyday life. Neoliberalism and its myriad effects thus become an unchallenged commonplace, a veritable ontological and epistemological orthodox ordering within contemporary Western societies while being simultaneously proposed as a model for the 'developing' world. As Žižek has argued, 'in a given society, certain features, attitudes and mores are no longer perceived as ideological but as "neutral", as a non-ideological or common sense way of life' (2006, xiii).

Further, Read (2009, 2) argues that neoliberalism represents not merely a new ideology, but a transformation of ideology, as it is generated not from the state or a dominant social class, but from the experience of buying and selling commodities from the market which is then extended across other social spaces – 'the market place of ideas' – to become a paradigmatic image of society. It is this embedding of neoliberalism as an unchallenged force within contemporary political economies, its manifestation in diverse organisational spheres, along with its morally questionable impacts and social effects that are to be the recurring motifs in the discussions which follow.

Accordingly, the purpose of this book, in its theoretical and empirical, national and international dimensions, is to present diverse accounts of the operationalisation of the neoliberal dynamic in a range of organisational fields. It is intended that the chapters contained within this collection explore and critically interrogate the impacts of neoliberalism upon political, social, economic and organisational structures from the late twentieth century onward. To achieve this, we pursue different and yet overlapping perspectives on how they are both complicit in, actively maintain and promote neoliberal doxa. These enquiries require us to interrogate how organisational structures associated with crime control, probation, prisons, criminal justice and penal policy, drugs policy, state and policing, youth justice, the voluntary sector and faith organisations, health and education, have come to reproduce and reinforce neoliberalism as a dominant mode of social and political organisation. Our proposition is that neoliberalism as the selected path for governmental reason to pursue (Foucault 2008), draws into its orbital sphere the values, norms, ideas and operational dynamics of diverse organisations in a mutually reinforcing line dance.

Our intention is most certainly not to argue that these reformulated organisational structures slavishly adhere to neoliberal parameters in an inevitable or deterministic way (notwithstanding the lingering whiff of the functionality of dominant neoliberal economic doctrine and subservient organisational expression representing a contemporary dalliance with the base-superstructure metaphor). Rather, the state and its affiliated organisational structures can be understood as a site of contradiction and contestation; not inevitable collusion but containing the potential threat of collision, protest and perhaps even resistance to its blandishments. These thematics will emerge in the following chapters. Prior to dilating upon the dynamics and differential effects of neoliberal hegemony, including the scope for resistance within the operating framework of *institutionalising neoliberalism in diverse organisational spheres*, we proceed initially with a necessary historical excursion into the emergence of capitalism. Discussion begins in the United Kingdom and introduces conceptual lines of enquiry which are explored further in subsequent chapters where their international salience is illuminated. Once the parameters of our theoretical and empirical terrain have been mapped out, we progress towards our central concerns, which begin in Chapter 2. However, the following pages offer some general comments on the rise of industrial capitalism, nineteenth-century liberalism and challenges offered by Keynesianism during the middle years of the twentieth century, before moving on to the rise of neoliberalism, which has been described as the latest phase of capitalist formation (Duménil and Lévy 2004; also 2011 for a deeper contemporary analysis of globalisation and financialisation).

Historical Dynamics of Nineteenth-Century Industrial Capitalism

The historical schematisation adumbrated by Marx identifies four different types of social organisation: primitive communism, ancient or slave society, feudalism and then, emerging in sixteenth- and seventeenth-century Europe, the tracings of capitalist formation.[1] Capitalism, an economic system rationally geared to the accumulation of profit (indubitable economic benefits) alongside which there are profound moral effects (questionable social costs), is composed of a number of identifiable elements whose longevity can be enumerated as follows:

- Private ownership of the means of production, distribution, and exchange
- The creation of goods and services (commodities) that are produced, bought, and sold in a free and competitive national and increasingly global marketplace
- The owners of capital and those who sell their labour provide the time, skills and resources to make the capitalist system function, the latter receiving a wage that is not tantamount to the value of their labour resulting in alienation and exploitation
- Capital resources (the raw materials and tools required for the production process) create the consumer goods (from cars to computers and the latest ephemeral gadgets) which are then bought and sold for money with a specific exchange value
- Finally money currency within a money-dominated economy is the measure of all things, the definitive standard of value by which all things are judged, as well as making the world spin on its capitalist axis.

The emergence and historical development of capitalism, which Arrighi (2010) traces to its formative period within Italian city-states of the fifteenth century, may well have progressed through numerous transformations – free market and the ideal-type laissez-faire variant, the social market, corporate capitalism and the mixed economy of social democracy – but it remains fundamentally a capitalist system. Moreover, notwithstanding a history of attempts at ameliorative modifications, it has robustly persisted throughout repeated threats and crises, so much so that it currently pervades the global sphere. Regardless of its arguable benefits (the most efficient way of making money), corresponding adverse effects (poverty, unemployment and inequality), the spikes of temporary crises (the most recent being the banking crisis since 2007), it possesses a remarkable facility to persist, recover, even thrive; its penetrative reach, its blessings and curses, strike into the lives of all individuals, families, communities, countries and even organisational spheres which provide the empirical focus for this collection. Seemingly everyone and everything is defined by this phenomenon.

During the early nineteenth century, as industrial capitalism flexed its muscles in England, it was coterminous with the Industrial Revolution of the early Victorian era.[2] During this period the expansion of industrial production began to displace (not without opposition) the small-scale cottage industries. This signalled major changes in the political, social and economic structures of England as the first industrial country. Ian Morris (2010) set himself the task of explaining Western domination or more precisely, why the West rules (for now). Morris advances the position that it has not been inevitable that the West has dominated for as long as it has (over 200 years), rather than China in the East. It is conceivable to speculate that the course of history could have turned out differently, even though a complex yet fortuitous combination of biology, sociology, accidents of geographical location, specific decisions and activities pursued by the intelligentsia as well as bungling idiots, including the part played in historical formation by contingency and sheer dumb luck, combined to produce specific outcomes. Discussing the Industrial Revolution, Morris (2010) argues that it occurred where and when it did because of coal, steam, the entrepreneurial spirit, factories and railways, as well as brute force exercised by prowling gunboats. Accordingly, the West rules, and the Industrial Revolution occurred in England because of social development, the ability to get things done in the way factors of the revolution 'shape their physical, economic, social, and intellectual environment to their own ends' (Morris 2010, 24). But none of this was historically inevitable; the end of the process was not built-in at the beginning in conformity with some Hegelian dialectical teleology. As Morris makes clear, he is not operating with a *lock-in theory* of historical development. Rather, the outcomes which have occurred were only made more likely by the combination of such features being found in one place rather than another. Concomitantly, the development of capitalism was not inevitable; the West was not inexorably moving forward to inculcate this economic system to the exclusion of other possibilities. Rather, it constitutes a human invention which relied upon, among other things, an act of will, this decision rather than that, these choices rather than others, the salience of material (Marx) but also cultural factors (Weber 1904–5). Where the latter is concerned, it is Weber who draws our attention to the role of religion, specifically Protestant asceticism, in the emergence and historical development of capitalism in Western Europe.

The transition from a feudal economy and its cottage industries to industrial capitalism from around the 1780s, along with its deleterious effects, continued later in the operations of unfettered markets, is traced sociologically in Polanyi ([1944] 1957). Correspondingly, this transition has been illuminated within a more literary mode of expression by Uglow (1987) when writing about the context for the life and art of George Eliot. During the early nineteenth century, for the purpose of illustration, the county of Warwickshire was characterised by farms and fields, canals and coach roads. This was the environment which shaped the formative years of George Eliot and about which she wrote in her novels. However, by the time she came to write *Felix Holt* in 1865, the landscape was already changing, if not permanently vanishing.

> The pace of life had accelerated, the railway had pierced provincial seclusion, the traditional political patterns had vanished with the 1832 Reform Act, and the old economic base of farms and market towns was crumbling with the development of the mines and rise of the factory system, which was already throwing hand-loom weavers out of work when she was a girl. (Uglow 1987, 13)

Consequently, the emergence and historical progress of industrial capitalism, the effects and disruptions created by the Industrial Revolution in the nineteenth century, initially occurred in England which was rapidly becoming the most industrialised country in the world (Sabine 1948, 564). In fact, Hobsbawm (1977) argues the point that by 1848 the British economy was industrialised to such an extent that it dominated the world, but that during the 1840s the United States and parts of Europe were also on the brink of capitalist industrialisation.

Dominant Liberalism and Victorian Ideology

Victorian capitalism, particularly during the early to middle periods (Harrison 1971 and 1990; Best 1979), was dominated by the governmental reason of liberalism (see Cowling, this volume),[3] which promoted an ideology comprising three substantive features: classical laissez-faire economics, utilitarianism and evangelical religion. Sabine (1948, 564) states that only in England, which during the nineteenth century was the most industrialised country in the world, did 'liberalism achieve the status of a national philosophy and a national policy'. The first constituent feature of this liberal triumvirate, classical laissez-faire capitalism, extolled the virtues of a free and competitive economic system that eschewed state interference. Under the tutelage of this system, the market attained hegemonic cogency to such an extent that its moral and social effects remained beyond the purview of the state. The second complementary limb, utilitarianism, defined human beings as rational calculators (Mack 1962) who, imbued with a copious dose of Kantian Enlightenment rationality, deliberately weighed the costs and benefits, pleasures and pains, of human action. Martin Wiener provides a succinct explanation of nineteenth-century utilitarianism by stating that

> calculation meant gauging consequences or looking to the future. The Benthamite calculator was a man whose attention was habitually focused upon distant consequences. Utilitarianism thus sought to habituate men to consequential thinking, which did not come naturally or easily, that required and promoted impulse control. (Wiener 1994, 39)

Accordingly, the argument is extrapolated that the control of impulsiveness, a pressing issue for liberal policy directed towards the lower orders during the early Victorian era, was a unifying discourse which the state, voluntary societies and philanthropic movements could endorse. This also included the third feature of evangelical religion, because to master impulsiveness required the development of character through scripture readings, exhortatory tracts, church attendance, Sunday Schools, the assimilation of spiritual homilies, thus clinging to the eternal verities provided by religion.[4] Therefore, the trinitarian complex of laissez-faire, utilitarianism, and evangelical religion formed the staple diet of Victorian ideology that facilitated individual responsibility, impulse control, moral restraint and behavioural orthodoxy, which in turn shaped the minds, attitudes and disciplined bodies required by the civilised person within a capitalist order. It is within this context that the Nietzschean-inspired sociological and philosophical reconstructions of social science produced by Foucault, and the latter's musings on the function of religion, constituted systems of domination required by specific social and economic arrangements (Carrette 2000). Additionally, and this is worthy of comment at this juncture, Garland (1985), in Marxist mode, argues there was a 'strategic fit' between Victorian liberalism and circuits of capitalist production,[5] the trinitarian elements of Victorian ideology and, as an example, the contours of penal policy manifested in prison regimes. In other words, this analysis is offered as an example of, and a case study in, the Marxist base-superstructure metaphor at work during the nineteenth century.

Impacts, Effects and Critiques of Capitalism

Harrison (1971) argues that as early as the 1830s and 1840s government select committees, Bluebooks, royal commissions, government publications, statistical enquiries, as well as social-problem novels, addressed what had become the 'Condition of England' question. Too many hours spent at the workplace, debilitating living conditions in the burgeoning towns and cities, equally difficult conditions in factories and mines, indiscriminately deleterious impacts upon men, women, children, and the precariousness of family life, elicited critical questions which aroused the moral and aesthetic sensibilities of Carlyle, Ruskin and Morris, just as much as the political and economic ire of Marx (Berlin 1948). Even though during the mid-Victorian period (1851–75) there were parliamentary interventions in the enforcement of minimum standards for hours of work and health and safety preoccupations, the casualties of the Victorian political economy were scattered throughout the social landscape and reproduced in a lexicography of vagrancy, criminality, want, destitution, poverty and pauperism. It has been concluded that 'there can well have been, through the fifties and sixties, at least as much painful poverty as Booth and Rowntree proved to exist in the nineties: i.e. affecting about 30 per cent of the population' (Best 1979, 144).

If we retrospectively gaze through the lens of nineteenth-century social problem novels that addressed the Condition of England question,[6] the formative influences upon and traumatic childhood of Dickens (1812–70) shaped the multifaceted insights, passions, and sensibilities of his fiction. For the purpose of illustration, one can refer to the exploitation of the poor, the deleterious impacts upon children, and workhouse conditions recounted in Oliver Twist (1837–38). Blamires alludes to the social conscience, subtle characterisation, emotional power, humour and poetry in his work by recounting that

> his suspicion of institutions, his hatred of harsh and mean vices, and his high valuation of the gentler virtues, give him a strong appeal today. We know what decent people are up against, in the Dickensian world, though it wears different masks in different novels. (Blamires 1984, 304)

When turning from a literary to a more sociological lens by which to access the impacts, effects and critiques of capitalist reason, Marxist analyses draw our attention to industrial conflict, class divisions, an alienated proletariat, the destruction of familial-social bonds, the brutalising of human life attendant upon capitalist organisation of the economy, the sheer misery and discontent created by the unequal contest between man and machine. As Sabine comments,

> As with his historical studies, the novel and distinctive characteristic of Marx's treatment was his stress upon the social repercussions of industrialisation, its tendency to weaken primary social groups like the family, and therefore upon the human problems that it created. The upshot was the conclusion that capitalism is essentially parasitic and devours the human substance of society. (Sabine 1948, 655)

The 1880s and 1890s: Towards Modifications

Even though the Condition of England question was raised as early as the 1830s and 1840s, the question was revived during the 1880s (Gilbert 1966; Harris 1984). There was a discernible shift in intellectual and moral perspectives which enabled poverty to be conceptualised as a symptom of a capitalist political economy, rather than an individual condition caused by sin, idleness, and the malfunctioning utilitarian rational calculator deliberately choosing irresponsibility. This discernible shift in perspective is illustrated, specifically within a London context, by Stedman Jones in *Outcast London* (1971). Stedman Jones argues that prior to the 1880s, Victorian ideology explained poverty non-sociologically by abstracting human problems from their political, social, and economic location shaped by industrial capitalism. By contrast, from the 1880s and into the early years of the twentieth century, the nexus of market forces, the forces and relations of production, level of state intervention, the liberal notion of individual responsibility, were reconfigured from the moral inadequacies of sinful individual practices into the demonstrable effects of capitalist-structural organisation that required amelioration. This was the period when Booth in London and Rowntree in York surveyed the realities of poverty which precipitated a set of transformational dynamics associated with socialist working class agitation, thus providing an impetus to developments in the trade union movement and labour representation. It was at this time that, according to the analysis of Garland (1985), numerous political and social *changes* created a *crisis* which, in turn, elicited a number of *responses* during 1906–14 when a reforming Liberal government both modified and mitigated the effects of capitalism. Therefore,

> Over the twenty-five years from 1883 the concern which had begun as an enquiry into the housing question and then extended into an investigation

into poverty, broadened into an inquest into social policy as a whole. The assumptions and certainties of mid-Victorian individualist, laissez-faire society were challenged and new possibilities of collective and state action were aired. (Harrison 1990, 191)

As a consequence of the surveys of Booth and Rowntree, the Condition of England question during the early part of the Victorian period became the social question towards the end of the nineteenth century. As Peter Clarke comments,

Whether the Rowntrees were to blame, or their workers, or the capitalist system, or Free Trade, was a matter on which Tories, temperance activists, socialists and Tariff Reformers naturally had different opinions, which they sought to support by bandying selective findings from Rowntree on their different platforms in subsequent years. (Clarke 2004, 42)

Clarke expands his analysis of the twentieth century by saying that notwithstanding the social reforms introduced by the Liberal government of 1906–14, life remained hard in Britain at the beginning of the First World War. Subsequently, 1926, the year of the General Strike, was the worst year for industrial disputes in British history and that the period from 1929 to 1937 was marked by economic blizzards in both the United Kingdom and the United States. Economic depression became an emerging global pattern, the ravages and uncertainties created by cyclical unemployment amounted to the discrediting of the capitalist system during the 1930s and culminated in another world war only twenty years after the last (Duménil and Lévy 2011).

Into the Twentieth Century: Emergence, Decline and Fall of Keynesianism

Eric Hobsbawm (1977, 1997, 1994a) has boldly claimed, with supporting evidential legitimacy that reaches back to 1789, that capitalist economic systems do not run smoothly. In fact 'fluctuations of various lengths, often very severe, are integral parts of this way of running the affairs of the world' (1994b, 86). The economic slump of 1929–33 and interwar economic blizzards provide credence for this analysis (as does the analysis of Arrighi 2010). In fact, the economic cataclysm of the 1930s was so severe that it 'destroyed economic liberalism for half a century' (1994b, 94–5), which created the conditions for the post-1945 reforms in the United Kingdom and the United States under the guiding tutelage of Keynes who displaced (but did not deliver the coup de grace to) the liberal economic theories located within the tradition of Smith, Ricardo, Hayek and Friedman. Subsequently, the challenges of Keynesian interventionist policies from the 1930s to the 1970s produced a new form of governmental rationality which, according to Foucault (2008 and specifically the lecture of 1 January 1979), constituted a 'crisis of liberalism', which in the United States created more interventionist political, social, economic arrangements. These Keynesian state arrangements were reflected in Roosevelt's New Deal, later built upon by the Democratic administrations of Truman, Kennedy and Johnson within the confines of the Big Society (Hardt and Negri 2001, 241). Correspondingly, in the United Kingdom the Keynesian–Beveridge welfare social-state was committed to a society of full employment, social security for all and protections against the unpredictable excesses of capitalism. Accordingly, the Keynesian-led post-war settlement, which in the late 1950s and early 1960s allowed Macmillan to exclaim that 'we'd never had it so good', proved to offer a comforting glaze that was extinguished all too quickly. By the 1970s economic blizzards returned with a vengeance. If the Keynesian social democratic consensus established a new social contract between capital and labour (capitalism with a human face), this was put into reverse during the 1970s, which saw the fighting back of capitalism and accompanying liberal doctrines to restore its global hegemony in the guise of neoliberalism.

Resurgent Neoliberalism

Hobsbawm (1994b, 403) describes the 1970s and 1980s as the *crisis decades* of economic dislocation which experienced the mounting bile of economic insecurity as the state abandoned its Keynesian-inspired post-war policy of citizen security through full employment. The problems had become noticeably acute by the recession of 1973, precipitating industrial disputes, rising unemployment, balance of payments deficits, the enveloping gloom of inflation and out-of-control government spending. The 1970s began with a Conservative government under Edward Heath and ended with the election of another under Margaret Thatcher in 1979. The Thatcher period, ideologically complemented by the Reagan Republicans during the 1980s in the United States, reconfigured what David Harvey has described as the 'state-finance nexus' (2010, 131). Accordingly, the period following the 1979 general election in the United Kingdom is described by Clarke as the implementation of a government programme of economic liberalism (2004, 379) which turned back the clock to the nineteenth century, in marked contrast to the policies and practices pursued during the Keynesian interregnum. Thus the neoliberal formation determined that the control of inflation was the central economic priority through the implementation of strict financial and market disciplines, not the fact that by the autumn of 1981 unemployment stood at 2.8 million, rising during the winter of 1982–83 to 3.3 million and accompanied by inner-city riots which flared up again during August 2011. Moreover, the new economic policy exerted the levers of control over public expenditures, imposed cash limits and raised the value added tax to reduce the budget deficit. Government seemed prepared to live with generating insecurities caused by economic restructuring, deemed necessary to restore confidence in the operational effectiveness of capitalist markets and restore economic and market freedoms.

Birch and Mykhnenko (2010) clarify, as Foucault (2008, 216) did previously, that the phenomenon of neoliberalism can be traced to the 1930s as a response to the threat posed by Fascist totalitarianism. By the 1970s the conditions were propitious to allow the revivalist economic project to emerge, which is considered in numerous texts to have five steering principles:[7] privatisation of state assets, liberalisation of trade, monetarism and the control of inflation, the deregulation of labour and the marketisation of society through public–private partnerships and commodification. Additionally, Colin Crouch (2011, 167), when reflecting upon some of the impacts and effects of neoliberalism which include the promotion of market solutions within an increasingly competitive market place, prosecutes the view that the neoliberal political project is to transform social institutions such as universities and hospitals, which are placed 'under an obligation to behave as though they were business corporations'. This pertinent insight resonated with Leys (2003) when he expatiated upon the commercialisation and marketisation of everyday life, a theme taken forward within the chapters of this book.

At the time of building the materials to construct this introductory chapter, it is thematically pertinent to record that on 12 July 2011 the National Association of Probation Officers (which emerged in 1910) responded with concern to the latest government proposal for probation services to be put out to competitive tender.[8] The following week the National Health Service was once again attracting media attention because of the professional and social implications of expanding market competition which would encourage more private sector involvement, and this continued to fester into the early months of 2012. Furthermore, universities are currently entering the commercialised marketplace where a university degree is constructed as a product – a veritable commodity – to be sold by universities and purchased at the right price by students. Coincidentally, on 25 July 2011 academics in the United Kingdom received correspondence from Greek colleagues expressing their concern at 'reforms' to the Greek university sector which is being transformed from a public good and civil right into a marketised commodity. They asked for help from the European academic community to respond to these concerns in the form of a signed petition. Then in the *Times* newspaper on Monday, 1 August 2011 there was a report on care homes for the elderly being run as businesses, which elicited the comment that the drive to turn a profit from the plight of the needy is deplorable. Later that week, again in the *Times* (Wednesday, 3 August 2011, 59) journalist Matthew Syed provided a critique of football in which he lamented its transformation from a game that facilitated community spirit and drew its players from the local community, into nothing short of a capitalist enterprise replete with the accompanying language of business, market, profit and commodity. Syed commented that 'Where once the club was represented by players and owners who were also fans, it is now a cog in the machine of capitalism'. Accordingly, by such developments it is argued that state-controlled public services located within the public sector, formerly constructed and operated as a public good (in addition to other domains such as sport), are being herded up and driven forward into a competitive and commercialised marketplace and thus integrated into the circuits of capitalist production as a site of profit generation. If it is the case that a capitalist economy 'must expand continually if it is not to collapse' (Tyfield 2010, 61), then these illustrative shifts exemplify the extension of the neoliberal dynamic into the last frontier of organisational domains not previously subjected to market rationality, which elucidates our collective preoccupations within this book.

Back in the 1980s there were wave after crashing wave of privatisations and the political, social, and economic landscape was positively transformed or negatively blighted depending upon the perspective adopted and vested interest pursued.[9] The neoliberal-inspired political debates of this period even forced the hand of the social democratic 'old' Labour Party to pitch its lot in with the enveloping orthodoxy, rebranding itself as modernised 'New' Labour during the 1990s to secure electoral legitimacy; if you can't beat them, might as well join the club! Accordingly, from a neoliberal Thatcherite standpoint there were considerable victories in the United Kingdom, as there were for the Reagan Republicans. However, veritable successes were achieved at a 'terrible cost' (Clarke 2004, 400) manifested by beggars walking the streets and sleeping in inner-city shop doorways, in addition to prising open the door onto a more unequal and unjust society. Both liberalism in the nineteenth century and the pursuit of neoliberal doctrine during the closing decades of the twentieth century, along with its uneven developments throughout the world order (Harvey 2005 refers to the situation in the US, the UK, China, Mexico, Argentina, South Korea), have inflicted a heavy price upon human lives: economic freedom nurtured by a dark and brooding heart which threatens life itself; the trapdoor into social insecurity unlocked (Brook 2007); and neoliberalism indicted at the bar of justice for committing social murder, generating anomie, facilitating social and moral dislocations as well as extending the range of poverty and inequality (Chernomas and Hudson 2007; Dorling 2010; Wilkinson and Pickett 2009). It is also currently imposing its deleterious effects within organisational domains, where millions of people continue to earn their living, in addition to countless others who come into contact with these organisations as service users, or should we more accurately say customers? As we will see in succeeding chapters, institutionalising neoliberalism within diverse organisational formations creates new opportunities for capital expansion. However, this is at the expense of organisational integrity and the merciless shelling of ethical and axiological debates which attempt to put the interests of people, rather than profit, first.

Chapter Summaries

This book is structured as follows: Chapter 2 by Cowling begins with a historical evaluation of liberalism before expatiating on the rise of neoliberalism in the United States and the United Kingdom, but it also alludes to its differential impacts and effects in other countries. This chapter considers the extent to which the prevailing tenets of neoliberalism are an inevitable feature of globalisation, as well as a hegemonic project promoted by some academic and political elites. Accordingly, this substantive chapter expands upon those areas of concern delineated in our introduction prior to considering the themes of the material foundations of neoliberalism in association with ideology, knowledge production, information technology and communication through the Internet. As the chapter proceeds, Cowling turns his questioning gaze to the links between neoliberalism and incarceration by considering alternative accounts such as political decisions, electoral strategies, legislative changes, and transformations which are internal to the culture of the criminal justice system itself. Finally, he turns to explore the linkages between neoliberalism and crime. Accordingly, Cowling begins to dilate upon some of our introductory themes, thus preparing the ground for a more detailed exploration of crime and specifically, prisons and probation services, in the next chapter.

In Chapter 3, Teague proceeds to analyse the impacts of neoliberalism on the criminal and community justice systems in the United Kingdom and the United States, drawing particular attention to the prison and probation systems in these two countries. He explores the way in which the neoliberal operating environment has prioritised punitiveness, competition, marketisation and the pursuit of profit over criminal and social justice within these two organisational configurations. Under neoliberal governments in the United Kingdom, the prison population has expanded from 43,600 in 1993 to over 87,000 by early 2012. This pales into insignificance when one compares the situation within the United States, which has made a concerted bid towards carceral growth on an industrial scale. There are currently 7.3 million Americans on probation, incarcerated or on parole, which is 1 of every 31 adults. The country's 5,000 prisons and jails hold 2.3 million inmates, with race being a significant analytic. The phenomenon of private prisons is also considered, alongside the concepts of the prison–industrial complex (Goldberg and Evans 2009), which asserts the position that features of the criminal justice system are now integrated into the circuits of capitalist production to secure profit rather than enhance the cause of justice. What is more, probation services in England and Wales could be heading in the same direction, because in July 2011 the future configuration of what was formerly a state-run and public-sector organisation could be put out to competitive tender. In other words, probation will be removed from the state sector (to save costs for the coalition government) and entered into the private sector (for profit). It remains to be seen what the balance will be like between the public, private and voluntary sectors in years to come. Nevertheless, a key political-neoliberal driver is to widen competition beyond the current private sector involvement in bail accommodation, support services such as cleaning, and community payback schemes.

Chapter 4 by Shen, Antonopoulos, Kurti and von Lampe broadens the notion of organisation. China is believed to be the main source of counterfeit cigarettes worldwide because, according to recent estimates, up to 400 billion counterfeit cigarettes are produced in China every year. There is also a perception that cigarette counterfeiting in China has been increasing and that no part of the mainland has remained immune from such activity. Furthermore, since the 1990s a large quantity of this product has penetrated illegal markets around the world, thus rendering China an important node in the global illegal tobacco trade. Critically, China's leading role in cigarette counterfeiting cannot be understood without considering the broader social and economic importance of tobacco in the country as well as the wider neoliberal operating environment. Accordingly, the illegal cigarette business in general and counterfeiting in particular must be analytically located within a transformational socio-economic context facilitated by the dynamics of neoliberalism: entrepreneurship, market forces, privatisation and the relentless application of the profit motive regardless of the economic and social consequences. Pertinently, the final paragraph of the chapter states that 'Overall cigarette counterfeiting in China, and by extension the rest of the world, appears to be an integral part of the neoliberal marketplace jigsaw in the country', underpinned and associated as it is with state planning, local government competition and the search for profit, human greed, consumption and need, as well as market dynamics, which are forces released by the global reach of neoliberalism.

In Chapter 5, Papanicolaou trains a critical, materialist eye on the functioning of the state's police force during periods of economic crisis engendered by neoliberal policies and practices by utilsing Nicos Poulantzas's analyses of authoritarian statism. Neoliberalism therefore constitutes the prevailing context and active dynamic within which to analyse discernible transformations in police responses in crisis situations which require new forms of social discipline and population control. The following elements are brought together in this account of policing the neoliberal state: the prevailing material context, economic crisis and class divisions, followed by the response of the state's police. Accordingly, Papanicolaou advances a historical, materialist approach which meshes Marxist state theory and radical criminology. Specifically, he applies this theoretical framework to four major incidents that resonate in the imagination: public order and *containment* through the police tactic of 'kettling'; undercover policing as *deceit*, *collusion* between the state, police, and the media; riots on the streets of London and *exclusion*. This analysis reveals how contemporary policing is becoming increasingly severed from traditional paths to accountability, as well as other ways that could meaningfully involve citizens and communities in the production of security in everyday life.

Next, in Chapter 6 Arthur turns to examine how the brave new world of neoliberalism has impacted upon and consequently reshaped the youth justice system in England and Wales. Neoliberal conceptions of the market and the vagaries of international capital have encouraged the formulation of policies based less on principles of social inclusion and more on social inequality, penal expansionism and on the diminution of welfare concerns, resulting in a renewed criminalisation of young people and their families. Less attention is paid to the social determinants of crime and more upon the utilitarian construction of individual, family and community responsibility and accountability (Whitehead and Arthur 2011). The chapter critically examines whether the influence of neoliberalism has led to the development of a contradictory and conflicting imposition of criminal liability upon children and their families. It examines the contention that the state has a moral obligation to protect and promote the welfare of children and prevent youth offending under domestic and international law. It argues that the state, as well as the young person, has a responsibility for juvenile crime and that it can punish young offenders for their offending only to the extent that it has fulfilled its obligations to those young people as members of society. Ideological and cultural features of neoliberalism have impacted upon youth justice over the last two to three decades and in doing so, the differences between the organisation of youth justice and adult criminal justice are being progressively diluted.

It is noted by Crawshaw in Chapter 7 that the publication of one of Michel Foucault's later series of lectures at the College de France, such as the *Birth of Biopolitics* (2008), has invigorated scholarship on the relationship between neoliberalism and governmentality in a number of fields, including critical health studies. Although Foucauldian methods are now well established in this area, the explicitness of his analysis of neoliberalism and its impact upon subjectivity in the second half of the twentieth century has provided a rich resource for continued critical interrogation of the impact of market-driven modes of governance upon the management of the health, welfare and the well-being of populations. A particular focus has continued to be the individualisation of responsibility for the management of well-being through strategies of 'government at a distance' which act upon subjects to produce autonomous and rational healthy citizens capable of reflexively monitoring their own behaviours and health within capitalist economic structures that privilege freedom, choice and self determination. The chapter draws on *The Birth of Biopolitics* and a range of recent scholarship which it has inspired, to interrogate the use of social marketing strategies as part of newer modes of health governance within contemporary Western liberal democracies. Social marketing mimics the methods of commercial marketing by attempting to influence health and other behaviours among diverse audiences and range of contexts and settings. It is argued that through constructing health behaviours as another field within the neoliberal marketplace, these methods are indicative of the continued hegemony of neoliberal models of governance which have moved beyond the realms of the market to infiltrate all aspects of everyday experience. This supports Foucault's contention that under such conditions, *Homo economicus* has become the dominant form of human subjectivity. Theoretical discussions will be illustrated with reflections upon qualitative interview data (17 interviews) collected with key professional stakeholders working in health-related organisations in the United Kingdom.

Chapter 8, by Abbas, Ashwin and McLean, explores the field of higher education (i.e. the university sector) predominantly in England and they introduce the argument that the neoliberal default approach could paradoxically increase social inequality. The authors explore a range of governmental policy documents which advocate that higher education marketisation is essential to promoting quality and that students from disadvantaged backgrounds would prefer to pursue degrees that focus on employment training rather than social science academic disciplines. By contrast, the findings of empirical research undertaken by the authors of social science students from diverse social backgrounds at four universities indicate that they value engaging with disciplinary knowledge(s) because it changes them personally for the better and is empowering, as well as preparing them for work. In other words, an academic education delivers personal, social and employability benefits. These two perspectives or 'framings' of current educational debates – what governmental policy documents state students want and should get by way of a university education, and what students would like gleaned through empirical research – are evaluated through the lens of 'pedagogic rights' in the work of Basil Bernstein (1974, 1990, 2000). This chapter, just like others in this collection, draws attention to the neoliberal culture within which university education is being located. This means that developments in the direction of private provision and marketisation, thus mirroring the United States, is turning knowledge production and the experience of university into a commodity to be sold and bought and the university degree reduced to a product in the global educational marketplace. But could this development increase inequality rather than reduce it?

In the penultimate Chapter 9, Whitehead returns to the criminal justice domain, but from a different perspective. Even though the neoliberal analytic can be questioned in its application to the field of criminal justice (see the chapters by Cowling and Teague in this volume), there is little doubt that criminal justice approaches have become more managerial, bureaucratic and expressively punitive. What is more, this trajectory seems set fair to continue during the next few years. This is the prevailing context for the construction of the chapter, which explores the scope for the voluntary sector in general, but the faith sector in particular, to critique and directly challenge the surging tide of neoliberal orthodoxy. This is achieved by introducing the phenomenon of community chaplaincy which began in Canada during the early 1980s before migrating to England and Wales in 2001. Importantly, this chapter is illuminated by original research facilitated by the author's visit to Ottawa in September 2010 (followed by a further visit in the fall of 2011). The voluntary and faith-based sectors may well be encouraged to become an essential component of the Big Society and contribute to the rehabilitation revolution in England and Wales. But in doing so, opportunities are being presented, paradoxically, that could mount a radical challenge to the prevailing orthodoxy by reintroducing ethical- and value-orientated debates that inform the pursuit of criminal and social justice in the face of the neoliberal agenda. In other words, can community chaplaincy, which primarily works with offenders as they exit the prison system, become a catalyst for change in criminal justice in Canada, England and Wales, and other neoliberal countries? Finally, the concluding Chapter 10 returns to explore the impacts of markets and privatisation, but also to pursue the search for alternatives to the current terrain dominated by neoliberal ideology and culture, and to reflect on the perilous future which is awaiting these organisational domains.

Notes

1 Giovanni Arrighi (2010, the new and updated version) *The Long Twentieth Century: Money, Power and the Origins of our Times*. Even though the word capitalism was only introduced into the social science vocabulary in the twentieth century (Arrighi 2010, 20) this text recounts the historical formation of capitalism from its formative period in the fifteenth century. It begins with an analysis in Venice, Genoa, Milan and Florence, proceeding to incorporate the Dutch period before turning to Great Britain in the nineteenth century and the United States in the twentieth. Accordingly, Arrighi traces the trajectory from Italian city-states to the creation of a global capitalist system with periodic disruptions and crises along the way. Arrighi states that the development of 'historical capitalism as a world system has been based on the formation of ever more powerful cosmopolitan-imperial (or corporate-national) blocs of governmental and business organisations endowed with the capability of widening (or deepening) the functional and special scope of the capitalist world economy' (2010, 225). Moreover, Crouch (2011) addresses the way in which neoliberalism and corporations have combined to transform the state, politics, the operations of big corporations, and the media; our collection extends the scope of the analysis into diverse organisational spheres.

2 For a detailed exposition of the Industrial Revolution within its wider historical context see the following works by Hobsbawm: *The Age of Revolution: Europe 1789–1848* (1977); *The Age of Capital 1848–1875* (1997); *The Age of Empire 1875–1914* (1994a) which are all texts published by London: Abacus. The final book in the quartet is *Age of Extreme: The Short Twentieth Century 1914–1991* (1994b) London: Michael Joseph.

3 Michel Foucault (2008) *The Birth of Biopolitics: Lectures at the College De France 1978–1979*. In this text Foucault turns to discuss nineteenth-century liberalism (2008, 69) as a form of governmental reason; Keynesian policies from the 1930s which produced what he called in his lecture of 24 January 1979 a 'crisis of liberalism' which in turn produced a reaction in the form of a neoliberal political economy in the United States from the 1970s. Thus, neoliberal reformulation was defined by reactions to Roosevelt's New Deal state interventionism, and the later Democratic administrations of Truman, Kennedy and Johnson. Foucault (2008, 131) makes a distinction between eighteenth- and nineteenth-century liberal free markets and 1970s neoliberalism which is 'how the overall exercise of political power can be modelled on the principles of the market economy', and he proceeds to discuss the application of neoliberalism to objects 'which were not market forms of behaviour or conduct: they attempt to apply economic analysis to marriage, the education of children, and criminality, for example' (quoted in the lecture of 28 March 1979, page 268). This theme is pursued as follows: 'Marketisation involves the obligation on all social institutions to comply with the obligation to re-model themselves on the private market, adopt market disciplines and ways of calculating value' (Coleman et al. 2009, xviii, which is a quotation from Stuart Hall).

4 See Hobsbawm's analysis of religion in chapter 12 of *The Age of Revolution: Europe 1789–1848* (1977), London: Abacus.

5 Professor Garland's argument contained in *Punishment and Welfare* (1985), taken forward in *The Culture of Control* (2001) is that penal and criminal justice policies are formed by social movements which exist within the constraints of larger political, social, and economic structures. The work borrows Marxist and Foucauldian analytical categories to suggest that a changing mode of production towards the end of the Victorian period reformulated penal and social policy. By contrast, it is explained how earlier nineteenth-century penality was

rooted in classical criminology and utilitarian ideology which endorsed a view of the offender as a free and responsible agent. These ideas are, in turn, located within Victorian laissez-faire economic philosophy, the doctrine of a minimalist liberal state, individual freedom and responsibility within a market driven society, that resonates with what has occurred since the 1970s. Accordingly, this analysis suggests that 'penality was, to a large extent, structured by its social context' (Garland 1990, 127). In other words, there is coherence, a strategic fit, between the contours of penal and social policy, and political, social, economic structures. Additionally Cavadino and Dignan (2006, 13) state that a 'society's penal ideology and culture will be greatly shaped by (and to some extent will also shape) the more general ideology and culture of the society, as well as by its material conditions'.

6　Further examples of the 'Condition of England' and social problem novels are: Mrs Gaskell (1810–65) *Mary Barton* (1848) and *North and South* (1854–5); Benjamin Disraeli (1804–81) *Sybil: or the Two Nations* (1845); Charles Kingsley (1819–75) *Alton Locke* (1850); George Elliot (1819–80) *Felix Holt* (1866).

7　Texts on capitalism and neoliberalism which can be consulted are: Arrighi (2010); Bell (2011); Birch and Mykhnenko (2010); Coleman, Sim, Tombs and Whyte (2009); Crouch (2011); Dorling (2010); Duménil and Lévy (2004 and 2011); Garland (2001); Hall, Critcher, Jefferson, Clarke and Roberts (1978); Hardt and Negri (2001); Harvey (2005, 2010); Wacquant (2009); Williams and Elliott (2010); Wilkinson and Pickett (2009).

8　In 2002 Patrick Carter was asked to review correctional services which resulted in the document *Managing Offenders, Reducing Crime: A new approach* (2003). Subsequently, the National Offender Management Service was established which provided new impetus to the pursuit of effectiveness, better performance and achieving targets, through a process described as contestability (or competition) located within an increasingly marketised economy of offender services (Whitehead 2010). In 2007 the Ministry of Justice was created and the Offender Management Act furthered the cause of contestability by making it possible for the public, private, and voluntary sectors to compete against each other for the business of delivering offender services. Subsequently, the green paper on *Breaking the Cycle* (Ministry of Justice 2010a) and the accompanying *Business Plan 2011–15* (Ministry of Justice 2010b) state that the intention of government is to create a functioning market to reduce state costs, but also to enable the private sector to make a profit. This direction of travel culminated in the proposal to put the probation service to competitive tender in July 2011.

9　Some examples of privatisations during the 1980s in England and Wales are: bus and coach companies; British Airways and British Aerospace; British Railways; electricity, gas, and water supplies; London Airports; Telecommunications; Rolls Royce and British Steel. The first flowering of neoliberal privatisations occurred during the 1980s; then a second wave of mounting contestability between government inspired public, private, and voluntary sector organisations followed, more recently, by a third phase of expanding capitalist market mentality which is considered in the various chapters of this book.

References

Althusser, L. 1971. 'Ideology and Ideological State Apparatuses'. In *Lenin and Philosophy and other Essays*, edited by L. Althusser. New York: Monthly Review Press.

Arrighi, G. 2010. *The Long Twentieth Century: Money, Power and the Origins of Our Times*. London and New York: Verso.

Bell, E. 2011. *Criminal Justice and Neoliberalism*. London: Palgrave Macmillan.

Berlin, I. 1948. *Karl Marx: His Life and Environment*, 2nd ed. London and New York: Oxford University Press.

Bernstein, B. B. 1974. *Theoretical Studies Towards a Sociology of Language*. London: Routledge and Kegan Paul.

———. 1990. *The Structuring of Pedagogic Discourse*. London: Routledge.

———. 2000. *Pedagogy, Symbolic Control and Identity: Theory, Research, Critique*. Lanham, MD and Oxford: Rowman and Littlefield.

Best, G. 1979. *Mid-Victorian Britain 1851–75*. London: Fontana Press.

Birch, K. and V. Mykhnenko (eds). 2010. *The Rise and Fall of Neoliberalism: The Collapse of an Economic Order*. London and New York: Zed Books.

Blamires, H. 1984. *A Short History of English Literature*, 2nd ed. London and New York: Methuen.

Brook, D. 2007. *The Trap: Selling Out to Stay Afloat in Winner-Take-All America*. New York: Times Books, Henry Holt and Company.

Carrette, J. 2000. *Foucault and Religion: Spiritual Corporality and Political Spirituality*. London and New York: Routledge.

Carter, P. 2003. *Managing Offenders, Reducing Crime: A New Approach*. London: Home Office Strategy Unit.

Cavadino, M. and Dignan, J. 2006. *Penal Systems: A Comparative Approach*. London: Sage.

Chernomas, R. and I. Hudson. 2007. *Social Murder and Other Shortcomings of Conservative Economics*. Winnipeg: Arbeiter Ring Publishing.

Clarke, P. 2004. *Hope and Glory: Britain 1900–2000*. London: Penguin Books.

Coleman, R., J. Sim, S. Tombs and D. Whyte. 2009. *State Power Crime*. London: Sage.

Crouch, C. 2011. *The Strange Non-Death of Neoliberalism*. Cambridge: Polity Press.

Dorling, D. 2010. *Injustice: Why Inequality Persists*. Bristol: The Policy Press.

Duménil, G. and D. Lévy. 2004. *Capital Resurgent: Roots of the Neoliberal Revolution*, translated by Derek Jeffers. Cambridge, MA: Harvard University Press.

———. 2011. *Crisis of Neoliberalism*. Cambridge, MA: Harvard University Press.

Foucault, M. 2008. *The Birth of Biopolitics: Lectures at the College De France 1978–1979*. London: Palgrave Macmillan.

Fukuyama, F. 1992. *The End of History and the Last Man*. London: Penguin.

Garland, D. 1985. *Punishment and Welfare: A History of Penal Strategies*. Aldershot: Gower.

———. 1990. *Punishment and Modern Society: A Study in Social Theory*. Oxford and New York: Oxford University Press.

———. 2001. *The Culture of Control: Crime and Social Order in Contemporary Society*. Oxford: Oxford University Press.

Gilbert, B. B. 1966. *The Evolution of National Insurance in Great Britain: The Origins of the Welfare State*. London: Michael Joseph.

Goldberg, E. and L. Evans. 2009. *The Prison Industrial Complex and the Global Economy*. PM Press Pamphlet Series No. 0004. Oakland: PM Press.

Hall, S., C. Critcher, T. Jefferson, J. Clarke, and B. Roberts. 1978. *Policing the Crisis: Mugging, the State and Law and Order*. Basingstoke: Macmillan.

Hardt, M. and A. Negri. 2001. *Empire*. Cambridge, MA and London: Harvard University Press.

Harris, J. 1984. *Unemployment and Politics: A Study in English Social Policy 1886–1914*. Oxford: Oxford University Press.

Harrison, J. F. C. 1971. *Early Victorian Britain 1832–51*. London: Fontana Press.

————. 1990. *Late Victorian Britain 1875–1901*. London: Fontana Press.

Harvey, D. 2005. *A Brief History of Neoliberalism*. Oxford and New York: Oxford University Press.

————. 2010. *The Enigma of Capital and the Crises of Capitalism*. London: Profile Books.

Hayek, F. A. 1944. *The Road to Serfdom*. Chicago: The University of Chicago Press.

Hobsbawm, E. 1977. *The Age of Revolution: Europe 1789–1848*. London: Abacus.

————. 1994a. *The Age of Empire 1875–1914*. London: Abacus.

————. 1994b. *Age of Extremes: The Short Twentieth Century 1914–1991*. London: Michael Joseph.

————. 1997. *The Age of Capital 1848–1875*. London: Abacus.

Leys, C. 2003. *Market-Driven Politics: Neoliberal Democracy and the Public Interest*. London and New York: Verso.

Mack, M. P. 1962. *Jeremy Bentham: An Odyssey of Ideas 1748–1792*. London: Heinemann.

Ministry of Justice. 2010a. *Breaking the Cycle: Effective Punishment, Rehabilitation and Sentencing of Offenders*. London: Ministry of Justice.

————. 2010b. *Business Plan 2011–2015*. London: Ministry of Justice.

Morris, I. 2010. *Why the West Rules – For Now: The Patterns of History and What They Reveal about the Future*. London: Profile Books.

Polanyi, K. [1944] 1957. *The Great Transformation: The Political and Economic Origins of Our Time*. Boston: Beacon by arrangement with Rinehart and Company.

Read, J. 2009. 'A Genealogy of Homo Economicus: Foucault, Neoliberalism and the Production of Subjectivity'. In *A Foucault for the 21st Century: Governmentality, Biopolitics and Discipline in the New Millennium*, edited by S. Binkley and J. Capetillo. Newcastle: Cambridge Scholars Publishing.

Sabine, G. H. 1948. *A History of Political Theory*. London: George G. Harrap and Co. Ltd.

Stedman Jones, G. 1971. *Outcast London: A Study in the Relationship between Classes in Victorian Society*. Oxford: Clarendon Press.

Tyfield, D. 2010. 'Neoliberalism, Intellectual Property and the Global Knowledge Economy'. In *The Rise and Fall of Neoliberalism: The Collapse of an Economic Order*, edited by K. Birch and V. Mykhnenko. London and New York: Zed Books.

Uglow, J. 1987. *George Eliot*. London and New York: Virago Pantheon.

Wacquant, L. 2009. *Punishing the Poor: The Neoliberal Government of Social Insecurity*. Durham, NC and London: Duke University Press.

Weber, M. 1904–5. *The Protestant Ethic and the Spirit of Capitalism*. London and New York: Routledge.

Whitehead, P. 2010. *Exploring Modern Probation: Social Theory and Organisational Complexity*. Bristol: The Policy Press.

Whitehead, P. and R. Arthur. 2011. '"Let no one despise your youth": A sociological approach to youth justice under new labour 1997–2010'. *International Journal of Sociology and Social Policy* 31 (7–8): 469–85.

Wiener, M. 1994. *Reconstructing the Criminal: Culture, Law, and Policy in England, 1830–1914*. Cambridge: Cambridge University Press.

Wilkinson, R. and K. Pickett. 2009. *The Spirit Level: Why More Equal Societies Almost Always Do Better*. London: Allen Lane.

Williams, R. and L. Elliott. 2010. *Crisis and Recovery: Ethics, Economics and Justice*. London: Palgrave.

Žižek, S. 2006. *Interrogating the Real*. London: Continuum.

————. 2011. *Living in the End Times*. London and New York: Verso.

Chapter 2

NEOLIBERALISM AND CRIME IN THE UNITED STATES AND THE UNITED KINGDOM

Mark Cowling

Introduction

This chapter begins to develop the theme of the rise of neoliberalism in the United States of America, the United Kingdom, and other countries alluded to in the introductory chapter. It considers the extent to which neoliberal ideologies are an inevitable consequence of globalisation and to what extent they are a hegemonic project of some academic and political elites. It then goes on to consider the link between neoliberalism, crime and the criminal justice system.

The Historical Evolution of Liberalism

Historically, liberalism has been associated with the demise of the doctrine of the divine right of kings and its replacement by the concept of a written constitution and the gradual expansion of electoral democracy. Probably the most important fundamental text of liberalism is John Locke's *Second Treatise on Government*. Locke wrote this in order to justify the Glorious Revolution of 1688, in which William of Orange was invited by British political notables to replace James II. William of Orange arrived with a large army and a printing press, which turned out pamphlets indicating that his intentions were peaceful and that he wanted his monarchy to function pretty much as a rubber stamp to Acts of Parliament.[1] William's political success can be seen as the foundation of the modern British constitutional settlement in which the monarchy is basically decorative rather than absolutist and the state is republican in all but name. The British monarchy has subsequently evolved into an enduring soap opera, of which the April 2011 marriage of Prince William and Kate Middleton is but the latest episode. The basic ideas expounded in the *Second Treatise* which formed the foundations of liberalism are that (1) the state of nature which would exist without a social contract leading to the establishment of a state would be neither alarming, as in Thomas Hobbes' (2007) notion that life in the state of nature would be 'solitary, poore, nasty, brutish and short', nor idyllic, as in Rousseau's conception (Rousseau 1997), but (2) that a constitutionally run society would offer benefits compared to the state of nature. The constitution is held to involve a contract between the sovereign and the people, such that if the sovereign is not doing what he is contracted to do, then he is eligible to be replaced. The application of this to James II is obvious, and Locke's doctrine also provided the basis of the American Declaration of Independence and subsequently, of the Constitution of the United States.

The fundamental ideas of liberalism have come to be embedded in the constitutions and political systems of virtually all leading capitalist states, and the principles also underwrite the European Declaration of Human Rights and thus the United Kingdom Human Rights Act (1998). They include a series of ideas which are so fundamental that they are simply part of the assumed currency of politics in Britain and other European countries. They start with the idea that there must be a written constitution which is a framework of higher laws which lay down the principles governing day-to-day legislation and which require special procedures, such as a referendum or a two-thirds majority in parliament if they are to be altered. Of course, Britain lacks a written constitution, but a series of conventions and precedents essentially serve the same function. Thus, for example, it is safe to assume that David Cameron will not be announcing that he is prime minister for life. The written constitution forms the basis of a parliamentary democracy. An important purpose of this form of the state is to preserve human rights or natural rights, such as the rights to life, liberty and property and freedom of religion. In order to preserve these it is necessary to have an independent judiciary. A series of other rights are necessary for this type of polity to function: freedom of assembly and of forming political parties; freedom of speech and, particularly, a free press. The armed forces and civil service must basically do the bidding of the elected government, subject to the constitution. Governments defeated in general elections must accept the verdict of the people rather than staging coups. These doctrines spread across Europe in the years after the French Revolution of 1789, were advocated in Britain by the Liberal Party, notably under Gladstone during the nineteenth century, and also spread to Latin America, the white-dominated countries of the British Empire and other countries, most notably India, which ceased being white-dominated upon its eventual independence.

A huge range of issues is raised by the above simplistic summary. One of the most fraught is the role of property. The initial rise of liberalism was associated with the defence of private property, chiefly on the grounds that its possession gave the individual independence from the state, thus providing a foundation for other liberal rights which could otherwise be endangered by state action. Linked to this principle were ideas about property qualifications for voting and, more generally, the defence of private property of poor people who might be attracted to schemes of redistribution. The checks and balances written into the Constitution of the United States were intended to avoid radical redistributive policies. This defence of property was consonant with classical economic ideas. Adam Smith, particularly, wrote in *The Wealth of Nations* that something counter-intuitive had happened following the breakdown of feudal society. Feudal society worked to an economic plan with the feudal lord organising the major features of agriculture and the guilds regulating urban manufacturing and trade. One would imagine that a system where lots of independent enterprises produced goods for an open market would lead to chaos, breakdown, gluts and famines. However, Smith observed that in areas where the market was well developed, such as the south of Scotland where Smith himself lived, the seemingly chaotic and competitive system of capitalism led to much greater prosperity than hitherto. It was as if a 'hidden hand' underlay the market and somehow managed to bring harmony out of chaos (Smith 2004, 7889). This in turn proceeded to a series of ideas about the defence of free markets, to which we shall return shortly. An alternative set of views about property was put forward by social liberals, otherwise known as new liberals, towards the end of the nineteenth century and subsequently: in order to be able to engage meaningfully in freedom of speech, one needs not to be starving, to have a certain level of education, be reasonably healthy and to have some sort of access to resources. Thus, everyone might be free to publish whatever they like, but Rupert Murdoch is in a much better position to promote his views than is the average citizen. These views chimed in with the growth of socialist doctrines and widening of the franchise, both of which were major issues in the late nineteenth and early twentieth centuries (for a helpful set of readings on new liberalism, see, Simhony and Weinstein 2001).

The interwar years of the twentieth century saw liberalism increasingly challenged from the left by socialism and on the right by fascism. Socialists were divided between social democrats such as the British Labour Party or the German Sozialdemokratische Partei Deutschlands (SPD), whose socialism was reasonably compatible with liberal values, and communists. Any respect that the latter had for liberal values tended to evaporate in the desperate circumstances of the Soviet Union.[2] Fascism was decisively seen off by the combined efforts of the Soviet Union and the liberal democracies, and in the immediate post-war years the liberal democracies adopted to one degree or another a settlement which combined a welfare state which fulfilled the aspirations of social liberals and social democrats, underpinned by Keynesian economics, which smoothed out the business cycle and appeared to avoid the horrendous depression of the 1930s. In Britain, the Liberal Party itself was marginalised because the Labour Party and the Conservative Party both accepted the fundamentals of liberalism, and because the major liberal reforms needed to turn Britain into a model liberal democracy had been enacted by around the end of the First World War. Thus the liberals were squeezed between two parties that offered something different from them, while respecting their major ideas. The fundamentals of liberal democracy were also accepted following the Second World War in the core Western European states which formed the initial European Community. The typical political cleavage in these states was between social democrats and Christian Democrats. Christian Democrats, while accepting the fundamentals of liberalism, tended to place a stronger emphasis on support for family values and corporatism than did the British Conservatives or the Republicans in the United States (on Christian Democrats, see, Kalyvas 1996; Cowling 1998). The European Community was highly successful economically and acted as a beacon to its neighbouring states, which resulted in the demise of, for example, Francoism in Spain following the death of Franco, as well as the demise of the Greek colonels. Communists in Western Europe tended to become Eurocommunists, accepting the fundamentals of 'bourgeois democracy'.

The Rise of Neoliberalism

Seen against this background, the intellectual progenitors of neoliberalism were eccentric voices in the wilderness. One leading figure was Milton Friedman, a leading economist at the University of Chicago, who questioned the merits of the Keynesian approach to the great depression of the 1930s by arguing that there was a natural rate of unemployment. He stressed the importance of free markets, advocated deregulation and floating exchange rates, and predicted that the Keynesian consensus would lead to stagflation. He was widely read and two of his books, *Free to Choose* and *Capitalism and Freedom*, were highly influential. His ideas had an initial outing in Chile following Pinochet's coup against the elected government of Salvador Allende on 11 September 1972. Once the dictatorship had established itself in power by torturing and killing some 3,000 leftists, it adopted the policies of the Chicago school. These led ultimately to prosperity, but also to serious inequality. Once neoliberalism gained political ascendancy in the United States with the presidency of Ronald Reagan, Milton Friedman became an adviser to the government. A second major figure was Friedrich Hayek, an Austrian economist and political theorist who came to Britain as a refugee from the Nazis. During the Second World War he published *The Road to Serfdom*, which advocated a free-market system and was critical of centralised planning. Mrs Thatcher famously slammed this book on the Cabinet table at the first Cabinet meeting after the 1979 general election stating 'this is what we believe'.

In Britain, the combination of a welfare state and Keynesian economics delivered a degree of social harmony and prosperity in the post-war period of the 1950s and early 1960s. Towards the end of the 1960s the weakness of the British economy was increasingly exposed. Levels of productivity were seriously behind those in Europe and the United States; trade unions were able to negotiate inflationary wage settlements, which led to a series of balance of payments crises. Governments attempted to negotiate a wage agreement, impose a wage freeze, or negotiate a social contract with the unions, but all of this failed for one reason or another. There was also some interest in legislation to curb union power and reduce the amount of unofficial strike action, most notably Barbara Castle's *In Place of Strife* (1969) and Ted Heath's Industrial Relations Act (1973). However, the former was never the basis of legislation because of opposition inside the Labour Cabinet, and the latter was abandoned when it became clear that it would involve imprisoning trade unionists. Heath famously performed a U-turn and moved from attempting legislation to attempting to negotiate a wage policy. This also failed, thanks to a highly successful miner's strike which produced such a reduction in the amount of coal being delivered to power stations that the government was forced to implement a three-day workweek. Early in 1974 Heath went to the country with the slogan 'Who Rules Britain?' and received the answer that although the result was a hung Parliament, *he* definitely didn't. Harold Wilson then formed a government and commissioned the Bullock Report (1977) which proposed that the trade unions should be given a significant role in governing industry, with equal numbers of trade unionists and shareholders' representatives on the boards of companies, mediated by some agreed outsiders. It was perhaps no surprise that industrialists on the commission should have reservations about this, but trade unionists also generally opposed the principles in the report, holding that managers had a duty to manage. Opponents notably included Ken Coates of the Institute for Workers Control and Arthur Scargill (see Coates 2011). This ended an attempt to introduce a version of the highly successful German system of *Mitbestimmung* (co-determination), which formed the basis of Rhineland capitalism in Britain. Finally, the trade unions successfully resisted yet another attempt at a social compact or contract under the government of Jim Callaghan which succeeded that of Harold Wilson. Public sector workers went on strike in the 1978–79 Winter of Discontent leaving dustbins unemptied and the dead unburied. Britain's problem was summed up in the term 'stagflation', meaning a combination of high rates of inflation and stagnant economic growth. This is not supposed to happen within the Keynesian economic framework under which Britain was being governed. There is supposed to be either growth with a mild tendency to inflation, or contraction with a mild tendency to deflation, and the role of government is to stop either of these tendencies from getting out of hand. In the 1970s, however, inflation, shown by the British Consumer Price Index, was alarmingly high, initially pushed forward by the OPEC oil price increase of 1973: in 1974 it was 15.99 per cent; in 1975, 24.11 per cent; 1976, 16.77 per cent; 1977, 15.89 per cent; 1978, 8.2 per cent; 1979, 13.35 per cent (Inflation. eu 2011). There was actually a recession of about 3.5 per cent between 1973 and 1975, and economic growth thereafter was relatively slow. Stagflation also occurred in United States, initially caused by the government printing dollars to help pay for the Vietnam War and exacerbated by the Nixon shock of 15 August 1971, in which he imposed temporary price and wage freezes and a 10 per cent imports surcharge and, most importantly, ended the convertibility between the dollar and gold, leading to the collapse of the Bretton Woods system of managed convertibility of currencies and then subsequently leading to the current system of free-floating currencies. This was followed by the failure of the Peruvian anchovy fishery in 1971 (a major US agricultural feedstock) and then the OPEC oil price increase of 1973 (Wikipedia 2011a and 2011b).

By this time, enough of the British electorate had become tired of the activities of the trade unions for Mrs Thatcher to be elected and to introduce neoliberalism to Britain. Although there had been some moves in the direction of legislation to curb trade union power (see above) and some flirtation with monetarism under Denis Healy as chancellor of the exchequer (see, for example, Davies 2006 105), Mrs Thatcher applied neoliberal ideas with a determination and ruthlessness not seen before or since. The Conservatives fought the 1979 general election using the classic Saatchi & Saatchi slogan 'Labour isn't working'. Unemployment at that stage was a post-war record of around 700,000 and the neoliberal policy response was initially described as monetarism. The central idea of monetarism is that inflation is caused by an excessive supply of money in circulation, so that if this is reduced, then inflation will fall. However, the Thatcher government used a series of different definitions of money supply, and the doctrine is perhaps best thought of as bringing down inflation while not worrying unduly about unemployment. The result of this policy was that by January 1982 unemployment rose to over 3 million, the highest it had been since the 1930s, despite some 31 changes in the definition of unemployment, all of which were directed towards reducing the overall figure, which would probably have been somewhat over 4 million without the changes. Although some unemployment was disguised by allowing the unemployed to be shifted onto incapacity benefit, a legacy which continues to haunt government today, the general approach to unemployment was summarised in Norman Tebbit's injunction to 'get on your bike'.[3] A series of measures were introduced with the intention of making unemployment less comfortable and reducing public expenditure on Social Security: the earnings-related supplement was abolished; unemployment benefits became taxable; statutory indexation of unemployment benefit was suspended for a time; the unemployed were vigorously described as 'scroungers' and strenuous measures were taken to find and prosecute benefits fraud, whereas one of Mrs Thatcher's first measures was to reduce the staff investigating tax evasion; the disqualification period for voluntary redundancy was increased; the minimum contribution period for getting unemployment benefits was extended from one year to two; mortgage interest was treated less favourably; the entitlement of 16- and 17-year-olds was essentially removed; the period before school leavers could apply for Social Security was extended; claimants had to pay more of a contribution to rates or the poll tax; grants for exceptional needs were replaced by loans (Blanchflower and Freeman 1993, Appendix A, 35). The overall effect was that between 1978–79 and 1991–92 unemployment benefits declined from about a quarter of median male earnings to about a fifth (Blanchflower and Freeman 1993, 6). Unemployment particularly afflicted areas dependent on large-scale manufacturing, which was seriously devastated by the Thatcher government's measures. Over the Thatcher years, manufacturing declined from 25.8 per cent to 22.5 per cent of British output. However, the decline continued in the 12 years of Labour governments which followed, sinking to 12.4 per cent by 2007 (Giles 2009). The decline in manufacturing employment was particularly devastating in the Thatcher years, going from 7.1 million to 4.4 million between 1979 and 1993, whereas job losses under Labour have amounted to about 1.4 million. The job losses were particularly severe in northern areas. Surprisingly, Britain remains the world's seventh-largest manufacturer with 2.6 per cent of world manufacturing output, but the manufacturing is largely in niche areas requiring a relatively small labour force of about 3 million (Marsh 2010; Department for Business, Innovation and Skills 2010).

Neoliberal ideology requires a properly working labour market, and the powerful British trade unions which Mrs Thatcher inherited in 1979 were a significant obstacle to this. She particularly wanted vengeance on the miners who had brought down her predecessor, Edward Heath, which resulted in a series of bitter confrontations between the government and public-sector unions. The first major battle was with the steel workers who undertook their first national strike in 50 years for 14 weeks starting on 2 January 1980. The strike was eventually settled with a 16 per cent pay rise linked to significant productivity agreements (BBC 2005). The government believed that the steel industry was overmanned and brought in a macho Canadian manager, Ian MacGregor, with the specific brief to render British Steel profitable and ready for privatisation. By the end of his tenure the workforce had been scaled down from around 166,000 to 71,000 and losses reduced from about £1.8 billion per year to about £256 million (Wikipedia 2011c). The remaining workers at the large and modern steel plant at Redcar, England, commented how empty the place felt now that their friends had been made redundant, and some of the working practices imposed on the remaining workforce were alarming, involving riding by bicycle from one end of a large steel works to the other in order to control a process involving molten steel (interview with author).

Mrs Thatcher had a good sense of strategy in staging confrontations with the unions. A water workers strike which would have led to raw sewage rising up the nation's toilets instead of going down them was quickly and generously settled. However, a great deal of planning went into her centrepiece confrontation with 'the enemy within', the National Union of Mineworkers led by Arthur Scargill. Ian MacGregor was moved from being in charge of British Steel to being in charge of coal mining. Scargill was provoked into calling a series of local strikes, which virtually added up to a national strike in 1984, by the government announcing plans to close 20 pits with the loss of 20,000 jobs. Because he failed to hold a national ballot, miners in the Nottingham area worked through the strike, although they adhered to an overtime ban which had been nationally agreed to. Stocks of coal were at a record high, whereas they had been very low at the beginning of the successful strike which brought down Mr Heath during the early 1970s. Although the miners heroically remained on strike for a year, they were eventually starved back to work. The strike was a milestone: Arthur Scargill had alleged that the government was intending to close very many more of the less efficient pits, something which they were able to do easily when dealing with the beaten men who returned to work. Other unions saw that they faced a ruthless opponent and industrial action in the public sector diminished massively. The nineteenth-century liberalism which Mrs Thatcher cited as her inspiration typically calls for a 'night watchman state', and she herself talked of rolling back the frontiers of the state. However, the role of the police in the miners' strike belies this approach: the police were politicised by their involvement in battles with the pickets, most notably at the Orgreave coking plant, and in stopping the freedom of movement of miners at locations well away from industrial action. The police also played a major role in the most significant industrial battle in the private sector. This was triggered by media mogul

Rupert Murdoch, who decided to take on the powerful print unions. He moved his newspapers' operations away from Fleet Street to a warehouse in Wapping in London Docklands where journalists engaged in electronic single-stroke copy-editing in which there was no role for skilled printers. When his printers went on strike, he dismissed 6,000 of them. They proceeded to picket his Wapping operation, leading to battles with the police who were encouraged to take a firm line by Mrs Thatcher's government. Murdoch in turn was supportive of Mrs Thatcher, most notably through his mass-market, red-top newspaper the *Sun*. The defeat of the print unions encouraged a general toughening of management attitudes towards industrial relations in the private sector. The Thatcher government also took major legislative action against the trade unions, passing four Acts of Parliament and preparing a fifth which was passed under John Major. Legislative measures included: a ban on secondary picketing so that, for example, striking miners could not pickct railway workers to encourage them to strike in support of the miners; limiting numbers of pickets so that coercive mass picketing became illegal; compulsory ballots prior to taking industrial action; making unofficial strikes illegal; compelling elections for union leaderships; and compelling periodic ballots on the political levy through which trade unions support the Labour Party with the obvious intention of weakening the main electoral opposition to the Conservatives. Various other pieces of Conservative legislation also had a weakening effect on organised labour and the general position of working people. Wage councils which had set minimum wages in various low-paid sectors of the economy were abolished, so that there was no minimum wage; councils and hospitals were forced to open their contracts for cleaning and services to outside agencies rather than just employing their own workforces, with the effect that the unions which organised cleaners, home helps and direct labour organisations to repair council houses, for example, became much weaker. Employees in these areas experienced a significant reduction in pay and worsening of conditions set against a background of heightened job insecurity. The overall effects of this are illustrated in Polly Toynbee's (2003) book *Hard Work* in which she went to live for a few months in a sink estate and tried to make ends meet by working at low-paid jobs. She concluded that even somebody as resourceful, temperate and well educated as herself could not survive in these conditions.

Another feature of neoliberalism is the running of tight fiscal policy, which means that governments should aim to balance the books except for short-term measures during recessions. The aim should be to repay the public debt, and the Thatcher government was quite successful in this respect. In early budgets, Geoffrey Howe, the chancellor of the exchequer, raised income tax, national insurance, value added tax (VAT) and duty on petrol and cigarettes. He was thus taking money out of the economy and exacerbating a recession. This approach reduced the public sector borrowing requirement from 5 per cent of GDP to 2.7 per cent by 1983 (see, for example, Jones 2010). Later on in the Thatcher years the achievement was undermined by Nigel Lawson who as chancellor in his budgets of 1987 and 1988 cut income tax from 29 per cent to 25 per cent, and cut the top rate of taxation to 40 per cent with the idea that this would demonstrate that the Conservatives were a party of low taxation. However, the aim of reducing the public sector borrowing requirement led to another policy which has come to be associated with neoliberalism – privatisation. Mrs Thatcher did not initially come to power promising to engage in privatisation and seems to have discovered the idea as she went along. Overall, she privatised a large part of the public-sector enterprises, notably British Telecom, British Gas, much of the electricity industry, a large part of the aerospace industry, the water boards and a variety of other enterprises. Many of these were sold off at bargain prices to small shareholders, thus – she hoped – enhancing her popularity. She also sold council houses to sitting tenants, some of whom got excellent bargains at the expense of other people who might need social housing, while others were conned into buying their flats in tower blocks, which let them in for expensive repairs. Britain was a pioneer in this respect and other neoliberal governments followed suit. Another major neoliberal policy is deregulation and cutting of red tape. Mrs Thatcher engaged in some of this, notably of buses, express coaches, telecommunications and professional monopolies such as conveyancing.

Advocates of neoliberalism such as Samuel Brittan (2011) tend to argue for a high degree of personal freedom, which draws a clear dividing line between them and traditional conservative philosophy with its belief that people are prone to do evil unless suitably restrained. Mrs Thatcher was capable of saying things which sounded much more like a traditional conservative, such as that producers of sadomasochistic pornography should be 'very severely punished', said with great relish. However, she did not actually pursue these views with any great enthusiasm. Her major initiatives in this direction were bringing video nasties within the film classification system, consigning pornography to the top shelf in newsagents, and the notorious Section 28 which prohibited local governments from advocating homosexuality. This last initiative was popularly thought to apply to school sex education, but in fact, the Department of Education announced the day after the clause became law that it did not apply to schools. In sharp contrast to traditional conservatism with its championing of the family, Mrs Thatcher's policies had the effect of undermining the family, and the illegitimacy rate increased significantly during her term in office. The overall effect of the Thatcher years was a considerable growth of inequality and child poverty, with the very rich becoming richer; a marked decline in the membership and influence of trade unions; a decline in large-scale manufacturing industry; a consequent growth of a pool of long-term unemployed people concentrated in particular areas of Britain; and a shift rightward in the Labour Party in order to try to render itself electable. There is a real sense in which Labour under Blair and Brown and the coalition government under Cameron and Clegg all operate within an inherited Thatcherite framework. Blair and Brown managed to raise spending on schools and hospitals considerably, which was a welcome change from the relative neglect these had suffered under Mrs Thatcher. However, they made much use of private finance initiative (PFI), which gave large amounts of money to the public sector, for example, in building new hospitals. They also persisted with the deregulated regime for the city, particularly banking, which had been instituted under Mrs Thatcher with particularly evil consequences.

A broadly similar pattern applied in the United States under Ronald Reagan. His attack on the welfare state, historically more limited in the United States, was more brutal. His confrontation with the unions involved firing striking air traffic controllers, a bold and ultimately successful move which encouraged private employers to declare open season on the unions. He practised what came to be known as Reaganomics and, in particular, he slashed taxation on the rich. When he came into office, the top rate of federal taxation was 70 per cent and the bottom rate was 14 per cent. When he left office, the top rate was 28 per cent and the bottom rate was 15 per cent. He claimed that the effect would be a 'trickle-down' in which the rich would expand businesses and provide employment for people at the bottom of society. The experience of those at the bottom, however, was basically of reduced welfare payments and a general feeling that they were neglected. Reagan raised the defence budget by 40 per cent, which was a major factor in the budget deficit which he bequeathed: the deficit rose from just under US$1 trillion to US$2.8 trillion. Another feature of Reagan's economic policy was his freeing up of the supply side, basically interpreted as a policy of deregulation. Additionally, neoliberal policies have been applied in many other countries and although the results are frequently broadly similar, the exact effect depends considerably on the pre-existing arrangements. Four examples need to be briefly mentioned.

- Iceland applied a vigorous version of neoliberalism which went very well until the banking crisis which saw Iceland go bankrupt, its citizens now being burdened with massive debts.
- Denmark also took on board a surprising amount of neoliberal policies for a Scandinavian country.
- The Washington Consensus, meaning a set of neoliberal policies, was imposed on many Third World countries through the medium of Structural

Adjustment Programs imposed by the International Monetary Fund and the World Bank. These tend to have very bad effects on poor people, involving the curtailing of what was already a minimal educational and welfare system; quite often any benefits to be gained from packages of aid are siphoned off by corrupt political elites (for a critique from a former head of the World Bank, see Stiglitz 2003).

• Finally, in terms of countries applying neoliberal policies there is neoliberalism with Chinese characteristics which can be expanded as follows:

Having managed to defeat the Gang of Four following the death of Mao, Deng Xiaoping put forward the slogans 'it is glorious to be rich' and 'it does not matter whether a cat is black or white provided it catches mice'. The point of the slogans was that China should use the most effective methods of economic development and that Deng's judgement was that a limited reintroduction of capitalism, starting with light industry and with a stress on exports together with the use of special economic zones, was the most effective way forward. The result of this change, which started in 1978, has been staggering, because the Chinese economy has grown at around 10 per cent per annum. However, some of the standard drawbacks of neoliberalism have also been present, in particular, the condition of many peasants has worsened. In the Cultural Revolution years China developed a system of barefoot doctors, meaning peasants with a limited level of medical knowledge who engaged in a mixture of public health education and healing. Under the new dispensation, the barefoot doctors had either to become properly medically qualified, in which case they would charge for their services, or give up practising. This has left many peasants without any medical help whatsoever. At the village level, the socialist system which prevailed under Mao, in which villages were given a target to produce and production beyond the target brought little reward, was replaced in 1981 with the household-responsibility system in which the quotas were very small and the bulk of a peasant household's work went into private production for the market. Overall, this was highly successful, but was less good if you had the misfortune to be a less-efficient peasant. Many of China's state-owned enterprises, which tend to be overmanned and inefficient, have been wound down. This has involved 'breaking the iron rice bowl' which conveys the meaning that their employees no longer get the package of employment for life, medical care and pensions to which they were originally entitled. However, if they are enterprising, then there are also better opportunities. Much of modern China's booming economy is based on poorly paid migrant labour. Migrant labourers do not receive the package of benefits enjoyed by established urban workers. Although China has become the second-largest economy in the world in the years since 1978, it has also become much more unequal. Hu Jintao may be thought of as somewhat like a Chinese version of Blair, although, thankfully, without the relish for imperialist adventures. He has inherited a system with rampant neoliberal features, but is attempting to introduce an improved Chinese welfare state and is placing greater emphasis on developing the relatively backward western China.

Neoliberalism can thus be seen to be a major feature of many countries, including some not so far mentioned here such as Canada, Mexico, New Zealand and Australia. Neoliberal ideas are also influential in reforms sought elsewhere, notably by Nicolas Sarkozy in France and Angela Merkel in Germany. An important question, thus, is what accounts for its spread and influence? Are we looking at an intellectual fashion, perhaps because other countries frequently imitate trends in the United States? Or is it that neoliberal policies have been so successful in some places that others naturally want to imitate them? Or perhaps political and economic elites advocate neoliberalism out of personal interest, hoping to get rich?

The Material Foundations of Neoliberalism

All the above factors doubtless have some influence, but another significant possibility is that neoliberalism is bound up with globalisation. Exactly what is involved in globalisation is a controversial issue far too complex to be considered within the scope of this chapter, but typically it is an argument that it includes rapid communication, rapid financial flows, significant outsourcing of production, a global intermingling of culture dominated by the United States and increased movement of people from one part of the world to another. This, it is argued, leads to the spread of increased inequality within the advanced countries, matched by increased global inequality, power exerted over thousands of people in one continent by decisions made in another and the triumph of neoliberalism (see, for example, Held and McGrew 2001, 4; McGrew 1997, 8; Giddens, Jameson and Wallerstein severally quoted in Beynon and Dunkerley 2000, 4; Gill 1995, 406). Arguably, what is involved in globalisation is more than the neoliberal projects of politicians such as Thatcher and Reagan. A plausible way of looking at it is that it has a material foundation in the development of information technology and the Internet. Manuel Castells presents this case in his trilogy *The Information Age: Economy, Society and Culture* (Castells 1996, 2000, 2004). His basic idea is that in the last thirty years or so of the twentieth century there was a fundamental shift in the way in which the capitalist mode of production operates. This new social structure he terms informationalism (Castells 1996, 14). In the industrial mode of development, the main source of productivity lies in introducing new energy sources or using them in different places. In the informational mode of development, the source of productivity lies in knowledge generation, processing and communication. Information processing is focused on improving the technology of information processing. There, the chief aim is the production of knowledge (Castells 1996, 17). Informational capitalism has two fundamental distinctive features: it is global, and it is structured to a large extent around a network of financial flows. Capital works globally as a unit in real time (Castells 1996, 471).

> Financial capital needs…for its operation…knowledge and information generated and enhanced by information technology. This is the concrete meaning of the articulation between the capitalist mode of production and the informational mode of development. (Castells 1996, 472)

This new form of society is based on networks, which 'are the fundamental stuff' of which new organisations are and will be made' (Castells 1996, 168). The networked enterprise is 'that specific form of enterprise whose system of means is constituted by the intersection of segments of autonomous systems of goals' (Castells 1996, 171). Additionally, the 'network enterprise makes material the culture of the informational/global economy: it transforms signals into commodities by processing knowledge' (Castells 1996, 172). Castells proceeds to argue that the phenomena which others attribute to neoliberalism or globalisation are fundamentally the product of informationalism. He looks at a variety of ways in which different social actors and countries try to come to terms with the new realities. Neoliberalism fits very well with informationalism, but there are other possibilities and he specifically describes Finland as a state where an excellent welfare state has been constructed in such a way as to be compatible with the new informational realities (Castells and Himanen 2004). If Castells is right, then we are dealing with something much more fundamental than a transient ideological fashion. Deciding whether or not he is right obviously requires much more space than is available here.

Incarceration and Neoliberalism

Let us turn to a brief introductory discussion of criminal justice systems and neoliberalism. Almost certainly, there are some connections to be made and the issue will be discussed in much more detail in the next chapter (Teague, Chapter 3 in this volume). Here, I simply want to suggest that rates of imprisonment are determined by factors beyond neoliberal explanations. It is tempting to regard the United States, the world leader in high rates of imprisonment and also a society very much run on neoliberal lines, as demonstrating that neoliberalism leads to high rates of imprisonment with about 743 prisoners per hundred thousand of population (see Wikipedia 2011d for this and other prison statistics). However, Iceland, which is so integrated into the global economy that it went bankrupt in 2010 – thanks to the behaviour of its banks – has 59 prisoners per hundred thousand of population; Denmark, which has assimilated many neoliberal features, has 71 prisoners per hundred thousand. Both these states are at the low end of imprisonment figures around the world. Russia, which suffered horribly from neoliberalism immediately after the collapse of the Soviet Union, has reverted to a set of arrangements somewhat more reminiscent of communist times and has a high rate of imprisonment, with 577 prisoners per hundred thousand – doubtless a hangover from the real Stalinist gulag. There is clearly a regional element to rates of imprisonment, so that Scandinavian countries have low rates, while Caribbean countries have high rates, whether they are communist like Cuba or capitalist. We also, clearly, need to be looking at specific features of particular criminal justice systems. In the United States, there is the effect of the Republican 'southern strategy', which involved generating fear of crime and associating crime with black people in order to attract white southern voters who had traditionally voted for Dixiecrat Democrats, but whose politics were more aligned with the Republicans. This worked in the South and was then extended to other areas of the United States (see Parenti 1999, 6–7; Chambliss 2001; Wood 2011). The Democrats responded by trying to demonstrate that they, too, were tough on crime, resulting in increasingly harsh penal policies from both parties. There were some additional factors, one of which was a move towards truth in sentencing, meaning that judges had little discretion over the length of sentences. A particularly pernicious variant on this was the 'Three Strikes and You're Out' laws enacted by several states, resulting in extremely long sentences for very minor offences. The war on drugs has seen numerous small dealers imprisoned. There has also been a tendency for probation officers to be more ready to return offenders to prison for breaching their parole conditions. Private companies with an economic interest in building, equipping and supplying prisons, as well as running them, have not been the cause of the expansion, but their lobbying has certainly been in the direction of more rather than less imprisonment. Finally, there has been the expansion of zero-tolerance policing which is liable to cause more minor offenders to be incarcerated, backed up by the manipulation of criminal statistics by the FBI (see Chambliss 2001).

In Scandinavia, by way of contrast, the public has been willing to allow professionals to run the prison system and these professionals have generally favoured minimising the size of the prison estate. The case of Finland is particularly instructive. Finland emerged from the Second World War with a much higher rate of imprisonment than other Scandinavian countries. People who were influential in the criminal justice system decided that it should be made clear that Finland was a Scandinavian country rather than a part of Russia, and that its rate of imprisonment should be reduced as far as possible. Finland today has a rate of imprisonment similar to the other Scandinavian countries (on this, see Christie 2000, 53; Tonry 2004; Pratt 2008). Curiously, some of the countries with the lowest rate of imprisonment are African countries, which have tended to be left on one side by the onward march of globalisation and neoliberalism, but which have suffered from corrupt and kleptocratic governments.

Neoliberalism and Crime

We turn finally to the link between neoliberalism and crime. Four types of linkage need to be explored. The first relates to what were traditional industrial areas of countries which have acquired neoliberal governments. Both in Britain and in the United States, much of the former industrial base has gone out of business or moved to other parts of the world such as Mexico, Turkey, India, China or Indonesia, where labour is much cheaper. The consequence has been persistent high unemployment, particularly for men who were engaged in Fordist mass production and for their sons. To the extent that they exist, replacement jobs tend to be minimum wage, insecure and in the service sector. This has had an effect on family life in that jobs of this sort fit better with a female pattern of employment, punctuated with periods at home looking after children, than they do with a stereotypically male career. At the least, some men in former industrial areas of this sort turn to crime, for example, drug dealing, or engage in work in the black economy. Exactly what is going on in these areas is a matter of controversial debate, but the empirical research and theorisation of authors in North East England (Hall and Winlow 2005 and 2007; Hall, Winlow and Ancrum 2008), draw attention to neoliberalism in association with the visceral drives of envy and greed. In other words, neoliberalism inverts traditional humane values (social responsibility, mutuality, personalism, care, altruism) by stimulating inverted axiological orientations associated with competitive individualism located within a marketised economy. Consequently, the more entrepreneurial among us, imbued with the spirit of the neoliberal age, look for ways to bypass the injunctions of traditional values by hitching oneself to our neoliberal inspired competitors. Accordingly, both offenders and those offended against become the victims of the same economically driven impulses. It is also pertinent to refer to other complementary work undertaken within similar localities (MacDonald 1994, 2006, 2008 and 2009; MacDonald and Marsh 2005; MacDonald and Shildrick 2010; MacDonald, Webster, Shildrick and Simpson 2009; Shildrick 2008; Shildrick and MacDonald 2008; Shildrick, MacDonald and Blackman 2009).

A second linkage concerns corporate crime. Neoliberal deregulation has been responsible for some spectacular frauds, notably the savings and loan scandals occurring after Reagan's deregulation of the banking sector. The losses incurred in these bankruptcies amounted to about US$1 trillion, which has had to be made up by US taxpayers. The frauds were so spectacular that they could not have occurred outside the G-7 countries, because there simply is not enough money to steal anywhere else (see Calavita, Pontell and Tilman 1999). There were also a series of frauds and 'financial restatements' under George W. Bush. The most spectacular frauds were Enron and WorldCom. Implicated in these was the Arthur Andersen accountancy firm, which was closed down. A good starting point for investigating these neoliberal triumphs is Paul's Justice Page (http://www.paulsjusticepage.com/RichGetRicher/fraud 2004.htm); and apart from ruining numerous innocent people, the frauds have helped produce a burgeoning criminological literature (most notably, Gray, Frieder and Clark 2005; Michalowski and Cramer 2006; Rosoff, Pontell and Tillman 2006).

A third type of linkage is arguably based on the limitations of neoliberalism – governments have been reluctant to permit free trade in certain areas with the result that criminals step in to facilitate things. A first and obvious matter is that the neoliberal free circulation of goods and money around the globe does not extend to people, so that there is a significant role for 'people smuggling'. Even minimum wage jobs in the advanced countries pay much better than their equivalent in the Third World, so that there is every incentive for economic migration. Estimates of the scale of this activity vary, but a reasonable judgment would probably be that of Thoraya Ahmed Obaid, executive director of UNFPA (the United Nations Population Fund) that the value of the global trade in people trafficking – which probably includes people smuggling – is US$8–12 billion annually (Obaid 2005). This is even more true of activities which first world governments wish to discourage, such as sex work. Governments also have their reservations about free trade in recreational drugs, works of art and antiquities, firearms and body parts, so these form the basis of lucrative smuggling enterprises. In 2005 the United Nations estimated the global retail value of illegal drugs sold amount to about US$321.6 billion. This was higher than the GDP of 88 per cent of countries (United Nations 2005). In more recent years the United Nations World Drugs Report estimates that the general picture is of the trade in drugs having stabilised, but also that the 40-year-long war on drugs started by President Nixon in 1971 has ended in failure; the drugs have won (United Nations 2011). Much of the money made from these activities, once laundered, increases the instability of the global financial system.

The fourth and final linkage is more political and concerns resistance to aspects of globalisation, most spectacularly by Al Qaeda but also by other resistance movements. Various forms of terrorism are undertaken in order to resist what is seen as US imperialism and these are criminal in themselves, involving murder and destruction of property, and may also involve crimes linked to financing terrorism. Terrorism has generated a huge literature in recent years and Castells conceptualises it in terms of his analysis of informationalism and its link to globalisation (Castells 2004, 81–142).

A Final Reflection

Much of what has been discussed concerns neoliberalism working against the interests of ordinary people and generating crime. However, it has to be said that by adopting neoliberal policies, China has managed to bring enormous numbers of its population out of extreme poverty, so that between 1981 and 2005 some 600 million people escaped from poverty, defined as earnings of under US$1.25 a day, and perhaps the same achievement is open to other countries, notably perhaps India (see Shah 2011). It also needs to be said that over-regulation can also generate crime. The most spectacular example is probably the Soviet Union (see, for example, Anderson 1995). The effect of having a command economy in which enterprises were given targets, with inputs supplied by the state planners, was that all kinds of goods had the same contraband status that illegal recreational drugs have in our society. Thus, a factory that wanted to acquire extra machine tools needed to get them from the black market, which provided opportunities for what has come to be known as the Soviet Mafia. Neoliberalism may be generally pretty bad, but it's not all bad!

Notes

1 For a thrilling account of these events from the historical rock star of his era see Macaulay, *The History of England*, vol. 4.
2 Thus, Lenin, who portrayed British Labour Party leaders such as Henderson as being basically the same as the Mensheviks in Russia, said, 'I want to support Henderson in the same way as the rope supports a hanged man' (Lenin 1920). The Mensheviks were subject to considerable interference following the Bolshevik revolution and were eventually made illegal in 1921. Lenin's approach to the Mensheviks at this time can be seen in the famous quotation, 'permit us to put you before a firing squad for saying that' (Lenin 1922, 283).
3 This was Norman Tebbit's response in 1981 to a Young Conservative who suggested that rioting was a natural response to unemployment.

References

Anderson, A. 1995. 'The Red Mafia: A Legacy of Communism'. In *Economic Transition in Eastern Europe and Russia: Realities of Reform*, edited by P. Edward. Stanford, CA: The Hoover Institution Press.

BBC. 2005. 'On This Day: 1980: Steel Workers Strike over Pay'. Available at http://news.bbc.co.uk/onthisday/hi/dates/stories/january/2/newsid_2478000/2478393.stm (accessed April 2011).

Beynon, J. and D. Dunkerley (eds). 2000. *Globalisation: The Reader*. New York: Routledge.

Blanchflower, D. G. and R. B. Freeman. 1993. 'Did the Thatcher Reforms change British Labour Market Performance? CEP/NIESR Conference: Is the British Labour Market Different?' Available at www.dartmouth.edu/~blnchflr/papers/Thatcher.pdf. (accessed April 2011).

Brittan, S. 2011. There are numerous articles at http://www.samuelbrittan.co.uk. (accessed April 2011).

Bullock, A. 1977. *Report of the Commission on Industrial Democracy*. London: HMSO.

Calavita, K., H. N. Pontell and R. Tillman 1999. *Big Money Crime: Fraud and Politics in the Savings and Loans Crisis*. Berkeley: University of California Press.

Castells, M. 1996. *The Rise of the Network Society*, The Information Age: Economy, Society and Culture Volume One. Oxford: Blackwell.

————. 2000. *End of Millennium*, The Information Age: Economy, Society and Culture Volume Three, 2nd ed. Oxford: Blackwell.

————. 2004. *The Power of Identity*, The Information Age: Economy, Society and Culture Volume Two, 2nd ed. Oxford: Blackwell.

Castells, M. and P. Himanen. 2004. *The Information Society and the Welfare State: The Finnish Model*. Oxford: Oxford University Press.

Chambliss, W. J. 2001. *Power, Politics, and Crime*. Boulder, CO: Westview Press.

Christie, N. 2000. *Crime Control as Industry: Towards GULAGS, Western Style*. London: Routledge.

Coates, K. 2011. Institute of Workers Control Pamphlet 56. Available at http://thecommune.co.uk/ideas/workers-control-a-reply-to-arthur-scargill/ (accessed April 2011).

Cowling, M. 1998. 'What is Christian Democracy?' *Labour and Trade Union Review* 75 (May): 11–14.

Davies, H. 2006. *The Chancellors' Tales: Managing the British Economy*. Cambridge: Polity.

Department for Business, Innovation and Skills 2010. Press release, 29 September.

Friedman, M. 2002. *Capitalism and Freedom*. Chicago: University of Chicago Press.

Friedman, M. with R. Friedman. 1990. *Free to Choose*. Andover: Tomson Learning.

Giles, C. 2009. 'Lofty ideals give way to thwarted hopes'. *Financial Times*, 3 December.

Gill, S. 1995. 'Globalisation, market globalisation and disciplinary neo-liberalism'. *Millennium, Journal of International Studies* 24 (3): 399–423.

Gray, K. R., L. A. Frieder and G. W. Clark. 2005. *Corporate Scandals: The Many Faces of Greed, the Great Heist, Financial Bubbles, and the Absence of Virtue*. St Paul, MN: Paragon Press.

Hall, S. and S. Winlow. 2005. 'Anti-Nirvana: Crime, culture and instrumentalism in the age of insecurity'. *Crime, Media, Culture* 1 (1): 31–48.

————. 2007. 'Cultural Criminology and Primitive Accumulation: A formal introduction for two strangers who should really become more intimate'. *Crime, Media, Culture* 3 (1): 82–90.

Hall, S., S. Winlow and C. Ancrum. 2008. *Criminal Identities and Consumer Culture: Crime, Exclusion and the New Culture of Narcissism*. Cullompton: Willan.

Hayek, F. A. 2001. *The Road to Serfdom*. London: Routledge.

Held, D. and A. McGrew (eds). 2001. *The Global Transformation Reader*. Cambridge: Polity Press.

Hobbes, T. 2007. *Leviathan* (Amazon Kindle edition) – page references refer to Kindle location.

Inflation.eu. 2011. 'In Great Britain 2011'. Available at http://www.inflation.eu/inflation-rates/great-britain/historic-inflation/cpi-inflation-great-britain-1976.aspx   (accessed April 2011).

Johnston, L., R. MacDonald, , P. Mason, L. Ridley and C. Webster. 2000. *Snakes and Ladders: Young People, Transitions and Social Exclusion.* Bristol: The Policy Press/Joseph Rowntree Foundation.

Jones, R. 2010. 'The Thatcher Blueprint'. *Investors Chronicle*, 17 December.

Kalyvas, S. N. 1996. *The Rise of Christian Democracy in Europe.* London: Cornell University Press.

Lenin, V. I. 1920. 'Left-Wing Communism: An Infantile Disorder'. Available at http://www.marxists.org/archive/lenin/works/1920/lwc/ch09.htm#id35 (accessed April 2011).

———. 1922. 'Political Report of the Central Committee of the RCP (B)'. *Collected Works*, vol. 33. Moscow: Progress Publishers.

McGrew, A. 1997. *The Transformation of Democracy.* Cambridge: Polity Press.

MacDonald, R. 1994. 'Fiddly Jobs, Undeclared Working and the Something for Nothing Society'. *Work Employment and Society* 8 (4): 507–30.

———. 2006. 'Social exclusion, youth transitions and criminal careers: Five critical reflections on "risk"'. *Australian and New Zealand Journal of Criminology* 39 (3): 371–83.

———. 2008. 'Disconnected youth? Social exclusion, the "underclass" and economic marginality'. *Social Work and Society* 6 (2): 236–48.

———. 2009. 'Precarious work: Risk, choice and poverty traps'. In *Handbook of Youth and Young Adulthood: New Perspectives and Agendas*, edited by A. Furlong. London: Routledge.

MacDonald, R. and J. Marsh. 2005. *Disconnected Youth? Growing Up in Britain's Poor Neighbourhoods.* Houndmills: Palgrave.

MacDonald, R. and T. A. Shildrick. 2010. 'The view from below: Marginalised young people's biographical encounters with criminal justice agencies'. *Child and Family Law Quarterly* 22 (2): 186–99.

MacDonald, R., C. Webster, T. A. Shildrick and M. Simpson 2009. 'Paths of exclusion, inclusion and desistance: Understanding marginalized young people's criminal careers'. In *Escape Routes: Contemporary Perspectives on Life after Punishment*, edited by S. Farrall, R. Sparks, S. Maruna and M. Hough. London: Routledge.

Marsh, P. 2010. 'Britain Slips in League Table of Top Global Producers'. *Financial Times*, 20 June.

Michalowski, R. and R. C. Cramer (eds). 2006. *State-Corporate Crime: Wrongdoing at the Intersection of Business and Government.* Piscataway, NJ: Rutgers University Press.

Obaid, T. A. 2005. 'Statement, Panel on International Migration and the Millennium Development Goals'. Available at http://www.unfpa.org/news/news.cfm?ID=685 (accessed April 2011).

Parenti, C. 2009. *Lockdown America: Police and Prisons in the Age of Crisis.* London and New York: Verso.

Pratt, J. 2008. 'Scandinavian Exceptionalism in an Era of Penal Excess, Part 1: The Roots of Scandinavian Exceptionalism'. *British Journal of Criminology* 48 (2): 119–37.

Rosoff, S. M., H. N. Pontell and R. Tillman. 2006. *Profit without Honour: White-Collar Crime and the Looting of America*, 4th ed. Upper Saddle River, NJ: Prentice Hall.

Rousseau, J-J. 1997. *The Social Contract and Other Later Political Writings.* Cambridge: Cambridge University Press.

Shah, A. 2011. 'Poverty around the World'. *Global Issues.* Available at http://www.globalissues.org/article/4/poverty-around-the-world#WorldBanksPovertyEstimates Revised (accessed April 2011).

Shildrick, T. A. 2008. 'Hiding out in the open: Young people and social class in UK youth studies'. *Youth and Policy* 100: 209–17.

Shildrick, T. A. and R. MacDonald. 2008. 'Understanding youth exclusion: Critical moments, social networks and social capital'. *Youth and Policy* 99: 46–64.

Shildrick, T. A., R. MacDonald and S. Blackman. 2009. 'Young People, Class and Place'. *Journal of Youth Studies* 12 (5): 457–66.

Simhony, A. and D. Weinstein (eds). 2001. *The New Liberalism: Reconciling Liberty and Community* Cambridge: Cambridge University Press.

Smith, A. 2004. *The Wealth of Nations* (Amazon Kindle edition) – page references refer to Kindle location.

Stiglitz, J. 2003. 'Challenging the Washington Consensus'. *The Brown Journal of World Affairs* 9 (2) (Winter/Spring): 33–40.

Tonry, M. 2004. 'Why Aren't German Penal Policies Harsher and Imprisonment Rates Higher?' *German Law Journal* 10, 1 October.

Toynbee, P. 2003. *Hard Work: Life in Low-Pay Britain*. London: Bloomsbury.

United Nations Office on Drugs and Crime 2005. 'United Nations World Drugs Report 2005, Executive Summary'. United Nations. Available at http://www.unodc.org/pdf/WDR_2005/volume_1_ex_summary.pdf (accessed April 2011).

United Nations Office on Drugs and Crime 2011. 'United Nations World Drugs Report 2010, Executive Summary'. United Nations. Available at http://www.unodc.org/documents/wdr/WDR_2010/World_Drug_Report_2010_lo-res.pdf (accessed April 2011).

Wikipedia. 2011a. 'Stagflation'. Available at http://en.wikipedia.org/wiki/Stagflation (accessed April 2011).

———. 2011b. 'Nixon Shock'. Available at http://en.wikipedia.org/wiki/Nixon_Shock (accessed April 2011).

———. 2011c. 'IanMacGregor'. Available at http://en.wikipedia.org/wiki/Ian_MacGregor (accessed April 2011).

———. 2011d. 'List of Countries by Incarceration Rate'. Available at http://en.wikipedia.org/wiki/List_of_countries_by_incarceration_rate (accessed April 2011).

Wood, P. J. 2011. 'When Political Science Comes to Town: Positivism, Marxism and Political Change in the American South'. *Studies in Marxism* 12: 165–204.

Chapter 3

NEOLIBERALISM, PRISONS AND PROBATION IN THE UNITED STATES AND ENGLAND AND WALES

Michael Teague

Introduction[1]

> Neoliberalism entails social injustice and thus undermines liberal approaches to criminal justice. (Reiner, quoted in Bell 2011, x)

> Recourse to the prison apparatus in advanced societies is not destiny but a matter of political choices... (Wacquant 2001, 410–11)

The correctional populations of the United States and England and Wales have undergone substantial and relentless expansion over the last forty years.[2] Throughout this period, these countries have also experienced neoliberal governments. This chapter aims to analyse the impact of those governments upon the criminal and community justice systems of the United States and of England and Wales, with a particular focus on prisons, probation and privatisation, and to consider whether neoliberalism has indeed undermined liberal and rehabilitative approaches (Reiner 2007 and 2011). It will consider whether neoliberalism, arguably 'the defining political economic paradigm of our times' (McChesney 1998, 7) but also a cultural system, has become institutionalised and embedded within the penal systems of those countries. Evidence will be assessed to consider the shift by neoliberal governments towards punitive penal and correctional interventions. In particular, this chapter will explore the way in which neoliberalism has prioritised punitiveness, de-prioritised rehabilitation, fostered a growing incarcerated population and engaged in the pursuit of private profit at the expense of social justice within the carceral and probation systems. The phenomenon of private prisons in the United Kingdom and America will also be considered alongside the concept of the prison–industrial complex (prisons integrated into the circuits of capitalist production). In addition, moves linked to the possible privatisation of probation services within England and Wales which are being introduced as part of the Conservative–Liberal Democratic coalition government's much vaunted 'rehabilitation revolution' (officially defined as the establishment of 'an offender management system that harnesses the innovation of the private and voluntary sectors, including options for using payment by results, to cut reoffending') (Ministry of Justice 2010a, 3) will be discussed.[3]

Wacquant (2009b, 1–40) adduces an impressive wealth of evidence to demonstrate linkage between the pre-eminence of neoliberalism and the deployment of punitive penal policies. In their typology of economies and their penal tendencies, Cavadino and Dignan (2005, 15) cite the United States as the archetypal model of a neoliberal political economy. England and Wales are also listed as exemplars of neoliberalism.[4] Neoliberal governments have driven the economic and social policies of the United States and the United Kingdom towards a stance which emphasises the centrality of market processes. Such governments are robustly supportive of privatisation, a process which requires that those sectors previously operated or regulated by the state must be unchained from state involvement, pass to the operational control of the private sector and become deregulated (Harvey, 2007). Competition for the running of criminal and community justice services is an inevitable part of these processes of deregulation and wholesale marketisation. Furthermore, if there happen to be no existing markets, then they must simply be created, even if this requires direct state action (Harvey 2007, 2). However, the link between neoliberal governments and crime control is not always unambiguous; indeed, these links may be 'complex, dialectical and multi-dimensional' (Reiner 2011, ix). Reiner attests that '"freeing" of the economy will engender a strong penal state and policing response to the social dislocation it produces' (Reiner 2011, x). Wacquant (2009b) contends that the predominance of neoliberalism has been paralleled by a shift towards greater punitiveness in order to ensure the maintenance of social order, with the punitiveness of the neoliberal state disproportionately concentrated on members of minority ethnic communities (particularly African-Americans in the United States). Underpinning his work is the idea that the 'downsizing of the social welfare sector of the state and concurrent upsizing of its penal arm are functionally linked, forming, as it were, two sides of the same coin of state restructuring' (Wacquant 2009b, 43). Punishment, and plenty of it, is seen as the solution to problems that may be socio-economic in nature. Indeed, in the United States it seems, on occasion, as if all that is required to solve every criminal justice issue is 'more police, more prisons, more punishment' (Reiman, cited in (Mariani 2001, 3). However, it is also arguable that neoliberalism, in reality, aspires to cost-effective justice solutions rather than an expanding criminal and community justice system, and that such expansion is effectively forced upon neoliberal governments by their own economic policy imperatives which boost unemployment and crime.

Law and order attained prominence as a key political issue in the United States in the late 1960s and in England and Wales in the early 1970s (Reiner 2007, 1). Garland (2001a) convincingly demonstrates the key role played by the neoconservative politics that became prevalent in both the United Kingdom and United States in the 1980s, and the changing way in which societies were organised and structured with particular reference to gender, class and race. This provided a context for developments in criminal and community justice. Cavadino and Dignan (2005) also provide a useful account of changing societies and changing criminal justice systems. Bell (2011) offers persuasive evidence for the shift towards the 'punitive turn'. Her meticulous and reflective account analyses the political economy of neoliberalism and confronts the complexities surrounding the way in which neoliberalism has been the key driving force underpinning the intensification of the punitive capacity of the state. This chapter argues that a punitive outcome is rendered more likely with neoliberal regimes because of the conditions created and fostered by neoliberal policies and their cultural underpinnings (including the marketisation of society, notions of individual responsibility for behaviour, less tolerance, poverty, inequality and discrimination in terms of race and ethnicity). There has, of course, been a significant degree of 'policy transfer' between America and the United Kingdom over the period in question (see, for example, Jones and Newburn 2007; Newburn 2002) which became particularly visible under the respective neoliberal regimes of Reagan and Thatcher and, ideological allegiances notwithstanding, continued under the governments of Clinton and Blair, Bush and Blair (and Brown), and now Obama and Cameron. Newburn has analysed the neoliberal penal-policy complex, which he characterises as 'a set of bureaucratic, political and moral entrepreneurial interests that encourage the adoption of punitive and exclusionary policies in the area of crime control' (Newburn 2002, 180–81). While the imperative to make a profit plays a key role in the penal-policy complex, it is also inextricably interlinked with populist politicians who utilise fear of crime to garner electoral support.

Neoliberal culture – which typically depicts individual offenders as ultimately personally culpable for their offending rather than understanding offending as related to neoliberal social and economic structures – may be linked with a tendency to punish. It may also be associated with increased crime and violence. Whitehead (2010) argues that individual offending behaviour and the penal system's response to it are 'associated largely with the dislocations of labour markets, wider structural processes engendered by the neoliberal economic musculature' (Whitehead 2010, 94). Hall and Maclean (2009) observe that homicide rates are notably higher in countries with neoliberal regimes,[5] citing the spike in the US murder rate following the 'crime explosion' in the late 1980s and early 1990s which trailed the Reagan administration's rapid introduction of free-market policies.[6] They assert that much of the culpability for elevated crime rates can be ascribed to neoliberalism, which breeds a culture supportive of offending and violence by inculcating the conviction that competitive individualism can be stimulated and exploited to create wealth. They observe that 'minimally regulated forms of neoliberal capitalism invariably generate the basic socio-cultural conditions that tend to increase homicide rates' and conclude that our 'hyper-individualist consumer culture' (Hall and McLean 2009, 333) inculcates the notion that life is rendered meaningless without the continuous consumption of expensive consumer goods. The process by which neoliberal culture transforms offending into a seductive lifestyle for those lacking sufficient resources to legitimately purchase those goods is skilfully delineated by Hall, Winlow and Ancrum (2008) in their study of narcissistic consumerism and crime in the United Kingdom.

However, neoliberalism alone does not explain rising crime or increased punitiveness. Nor does the shift towards neoliberalism render a swing towards punitiveness and penal expansionism unavoidable. Both South Africa and Russia, for example, have begun to embrace neoliberalism while simultaneously acting to diminish their prison populations (Bell 2011, 162). As Tonry (2009, 380) points out, the Netherlands – hardly a neoliberal country – had Europe's second-highest imprisonment rate in 2005 (then exceeded only by England and Wales). Alternatively, while Canada's regime may be viewed as neoliberal, it has a relatively low imprisonment rate. Tonry asserts that neoliberalism does not fully explain the differences in individual national criminal justice policies, arguing that such variations can be explained by differing constitutional, structural and cultural values. He judges neoliberalism to be one of a number of 'amorphous and overgeneralized notions' (Tonry 2009, 377) which lack utility in explaining penal policies, and he questions why the French and Italian electorates have long accepted amnesties and pardons of prisoners, citing a mass commutation in 2006 which shrunk the Italian inmate population by 40 per cent. Similar commutations in the United States and England, he speculates, would engender political outrage and widespread opposition (Tonry 2009, 390). In support of this analysis, the authoritative British Crime Survey (BCS) for 2009–10 suggests that two-thirds of the population believe that crime has increased across the country in recent years (Flatley, Kershaw, Smith, Chaplin and Moon 2010, 111). Two-thirds of respondents indicated their belief that crime has increased nationally since the question was first asked in 1996 (BCS evidence that, overall, crime has been falling since 1995, notwithstanding Flatley et al. 2010, 111). Garland's (2001a) hugely influential work has explored the process by which the United States and the United Kingdom have developed into societies which increasingly embrace harsher punishments, regardless of whether actual crime rates are rising. This has been accompanied by the de-prioritisation of rehabilitation and penal-welfare intervention, presaged by the Thatcher regime which came to power in 1979 and the Reagan government which took office two years later.

The Correctional System in the United States: A 'Frenzied and Brutal Lockup Binge'?

Until the late 1960s incarceration was envisioned in the United States as a regrettable necessity, a punishment of last resort. The reports of the President's Crime Commission in the 1960s articulated the conviction that rehabilitative correctional intervention might address the root causes of criminality.[7] This faith in rehabilitation failed to maintain its ascendancy (Walker 1978), and attitudes to imprisonment have altered to the extent that, as Parenti acerbically noted, the United States has been engaged on a 'frenzied and brutal lockup binge' since 1981 (2008, 163). It is now well established that America leads the world in incarceration (Lynch 2007; Pratt 2009; Teague 2008). Though home to just 1 in 20 of the world's people, America's penal–industrial complex currently incarcerates about a quarter of the planet's prison population. The United States' 5,000 state and federal prisons and local jails currently lock up almost 2.3 million inmates (Glaze 2010, 7), thereby bestowing upon the 'land of the free' the dubious honour of the world's highest per capita rate of imprisonment, with no fewer than 1 in 100 of its adult citizens behind bars (Pew Center on the States 2008, 5). The United States imprisons 743 of every 100,000 of its populace (ICPS 2011a). This not only surpasses the much more populous country of China, it is a rate 5–10 times greater than those of other Western industrialised democracies,[8] including England and Wales, which currently incarcerate 154 in every 100,000 (ICPS 2011c).

While these points are common currency amongst criminologists (for example, Bosworth 2010; Clear, Cole and Reisig 2009; Parenti 2008; Pratt 2009), significantly less academic attention has been focused on the staggering increase in the number of Americans supervised under the auspices of the community corrections system.[9] It is not just the totality of those incarcerated in which America leads the world, but also those on probation and parole. No fewer than 1 in 45 US adults is now subject to supervision in the community and the total of American probationers and parolees now stands at over 5 million (Glaze, Bonczar and Zhang 2010), up from 1.6 million nearly 30 years ago.

To quantify this from another perspective, in a nation of 309 million people,[10] no fewer than 1 in every 31 adult American citizens is subject to some form of correctional control, whether this is in the community or behind bars (Glaze 2010, 1).[11] This amounts to almost 7.3 million Americans who are now incarcerated (in state or federal prisons or local jails[12]) on probation or parole.[13] United Nations data indicates that the level of probation supervision in the United States is historically high (as is the level of supervision in England and Wales) (Miethe and Lu 2005, 57).

The level of imprisonment in England and Wales, while significant by European standards, pales into insignificance when compared with the United States' unprecedented industrial scale of imprisonment.[14] Despite extreme pressure on public expenditure, America currently spends an overwhelming $68 billion each year on its penal–industrial complex which includes local, state, and federal correctional systems (Ruiz 2011, 3). The United States' second-largest employer (surpassed only by General Motors) is the prisons industry; about three-quarters of a million people work in corrections. Like England and Wales, the United States has moved away from decades of a relatively stable imprisonment rate to dash towards carceral growth. American incarceration rates have consistently grown since the early 1970s and now lead the rates of other developed nations by a secure margin. Just as had occurred in England and Wales, the US prison population began to climb sharply in the early 1970s (Garland 2001b), having remained relatively static for 70 years.[15] Though the prison population rose by 105 per cent over the half-century prior to 1973,[16] this measured increase in imprisonment simply reflected the growth of the general population. After 1973 the US prison population continued to grow year in, year out. In the 38 years since 1972 the number of prisoners incarcerated in the US state prison system has increased by 708 per cent (Ruiz 2011, 3). Overall American imprisonment rates trebled between 1973 and 1990 (Tonry 2009). Wacquant (2009a, 145) observed that this relentless exponential growth was absolutely unprecedented for a developed democratic country. It is only now, forty years later, that this consistent expansion is beginning to ease; 2009 saw the United States' slowest annual increase in the inmate population of the last ten years.[17] In 1997 the United States had the second-highest recorded imprisonment rate in the world, imprisoning 645 prisoners per 100,000 of population (Barclay and Tavares 1999, 56).[18] Within thirteen years the imprisonment rate had surpassed 700 per 100,000 of the US population before it gradually began to stabilise (Wacquant 2009a, 145). As was the case in the United Kingdom over the same period, the burgeoning inmate population's unremitting growth was not primarily propelled by either escalating crime rates or, indeed, wider social forces outwith governmental control. Rather, it was due to '…sentencing, release and other correctional policies that determine who goes to prison and how long they stay' (Pew Center on the States 2009, 4).

The fact that US imprisonment rates are disproportionately higher for African-American men (Pew Center on the States 2010; Pratt 2009, 6–7) may not come as a surprise in a country which was engaged in civil war over slavery, among other things, only two lifetimes ago. Race is a key analytic in US penality, not least because black males in the United States are incarcerated at a rate of six times that of their white counterparts (Ruiz 2011, 3). Over 2 million African-Americans are currently under the control of the correctional system, whether in custody, on probation or on parole. According to Alexander (2011, 20), the experience of African-Americans within the US correctional system reflects, in essence, a 'comprehensive and well-disguised system of racialized social control' which warehouses black people. It has been persuasively argued that

> slavery and mass imprisonment are genealogically linked and that one cannot understand the latter – its timing, composition, and smooth onset as well as the quiet ignorance or acceptance of its deleterious effects on those it affects – without returning to the former as historic starting point and functional analogue. (Wacquant 2002, 41–2)

Garland attests that there are two defining features of mass imprisonment. One is that a society imprisons more than the accepted norm for other comparable societies. The second is what Garland labels 'the social concentration of imprisonment's effects' (Garland 2001b, 6) by which he means the methodical and systematic incarceration of whole groups of the population rather than individual offenders. If we consider the case of African-Americans, there is a plethora of evidence to confirm that they are disproportionately imprisoned (for example, Miller 2010; Walker, Spohn and DeLone 2006). The United States neatly fits both categories of mass imprisonment. The scale of the US criminal justice system's disproportional impact upon African-Americans is summarised in the shocking observation that the United States incarcerates a greater proportion of its black population than South Africa did at the zenith of apartheid (Alexander 2010, 6).

Barack Obama's election as the forty-fourth president of the United States was envisioned by some commentators as a harbinger of the ending of deep-rooted conservatism in the American political system. As only the fourth Democratic president in the nation's history to win a majority of the popular vote, his remarkable popularity meant that his 2009 inauguration was accompanied by sustained optimism about a radical transformation of the nation's overloaded criminal and community justice system (Teague 2009).

Obama's 'Blueprint for Change' (Obama and Biden 2008), published prior to his election, comprehensively addressed a range of policies from the economy to healthcare, but omitted detailed discussion of penal policy (while also avoiding populist sloganeering on crime and punishment). President Obama inherited a series of enduring penal issues from his predecessor George W. Bush, including the bloated US mass incarceration project and overloaded community corrections system. It is worth noting, however, that the overriding imperative to incarcerate which pervades US political culture is hardly constrained by party politics. President-to-be George W. Bush's retributive mantra – 'Incarceration is rehabilitation' – during his 1994 Texas gubernatorial campaign reflected an archetypal neoliberal approach to imprisonment (Teague 2001). While this may be interpreted as the epitome of the traditional rightist 'tough on crime' approach favoured by Republicans, the Democratic Party has also endorsed the US carceral state's remorseless expansion. The doubling of the US inmate population – and the biggest leap in imprisonment during any presidency in history – occurred not under a Republican president, but rather during Bill Clinton's eight-year presidency (Teague 2008).

Whether history will record that Obama changed the course of US criminal and community justice and was able to check the progress of the juggernaut of penal expansionism remains to be seen. While there is scant evidence to date that significant change is imminent and much to suggest that other pressing economic and political issues have taken precedence, two changes are worth noting. The state prison population in the United States has recently fallen for the first time in almost forty years.[19] At the start of 2010 the first year-to-year drop (0.3 per cent) in the number of state prisoners since 1972 was recorded (Pew Center on the States 2010).[20] The drop may not be huge, but it does indicate a shift in the overall tide. In addition, the total of those supervised by community corrections fell by almost 1 per cent during 2009,[21] for the first time since annual recording began in 1980 (Glaze et al. 2010). The enduring impression remains, however, that these are changes wrought by fiscal austerity rather than the imperative to rehabilitate.

The Correctional System in England and Wales: The Futility of Penal Expansion

The correctional system in England and Wales has, like its US counterpart, experienced an overall trend of expansion during the past four decades. England and Wales, with a total population of 54.8 million,[22] now has almost a third of a million people either in prison or subject to probation and parole supervision (Ministry of Justice 2011a, 3).[23] One in every 138 adults is subject to some form of correctional supervision.[24] This degree of correctional intervention may not be on the United States' industrial scale, but it is substantial. Neoliberal UK governments have presided over an inexorable rise in the prison population over the last forty years. The average prison population in England and Wales was 39,028 in 1970 (Berman 2010, 18). From then until the early 1990s the population was relatively stable, experiencing gradual growth. In 1980 there were 42,264 offenders in prison. The inmate population reached 44,975 in 1990, then experienced a sustained growth spurt. The total of prisoners grew quickly between 1993 to 2008 (by an average of 4 per cent each year), though the pace of growth has begun to slacken since then to a 1 per cent average annual increase (Ministry of Justice 2011a, 4). The prison population remained at a historically high level of almost 85,000 in April 2011 (Ministry of Justice 2011b) representing a 90 per cent increase since 1993. In addition, the prison estate has been continually overcrowded since 1994 (Strickland 2010, 97). Given that overall crime rates have not been increasing since 1995 (Carter 2007, 5), this suggests a climate of increasing support for punitivism.

By New Labour's accession to power in 1997 the average incarcerated population in England and Wales was 61,110 (Barclay and Tavares 1999, 51) and the prison population rate was, at 120 per 100,000 population, the second-highest in the European Union (EU) (Berman 2010, 18).[25] This trajectory of growth was set to continue. The landmark figure of 80,000 prisoners was exceeded for the first time in December 2006. The speed and scale of the increasing prison population was evidenced by the fact that in February 2008 the total population of offenders behind bars surpassed the useable operational capacity of the prison estate for the first time.[26] The prison population went on to achieve a record high of 85,494 prisoners on 1 October 2010 (Berman 2010). This figure exceeded the prison estate's useable operational capacity by some 2,150 places. While the prison population in 2011 is estimated to be 154 prisoners per 100,000 population (ICPS 2011c) and is manifesting little evidence of a significant or sustained decrease,[27] the reality remains that incarceration is not especially effective in reducing reoffending; around half of adult prisoners reoffend within twelve months of release (Strickland 2010, 97).

Martin Narey, who joined the Prison Service in 1982 and rose to be its director general in 1998, was the National Offender Management Service's (NOMS) first chief executive in 2003 and subsequently the first commissioner for correctional services in England and Wales,[28] has delivered a damning indictment of correctional policy. While he saw it as his duty to serve the government loyally, he acknowledged the year after he left the Home Office that

...privately I was very troubled by the rise in the prison population... This country is in love with incarceration even when...everybody knows that it's futile. I led the Prison Service for 7 years and working in it for 23 years and I knew it was futile. (Jerrom 2006)

Perhaps unsurprisingly, the Ministry of Justice does not share Narey's perception of the futility of rising incarceration. It attributes the rise in imprisonment since the mid-1990s to:

- Courts sentencing more offenders to prison each year between 1995 and 2002.
- Offenders staying in prison for longer due to longer average sentences and a decline in parole rates.
- Tougher post-release enforcement, which means more recalls for longer periods (Strickland 2010, 97).

Other factors propelling the pace of growth in imprisonment over the past 20 years include a rise in the numbers of those sentenced to immediate custody between 1999 and 2002, greater use of indeterminate sentences and a boost in the total of those recalled to prison having breached the conditions of their licence (Ministry of Justice 2011a, 4). In 2008 England and Wales had the highest number of life-sentenced prisoners in Europe (PRT 2010, 12).[29] In addition, more people are serving indeterminate sentences. A new indeterminate sentence of Imprisonment for Public Protection (IPP) was available from 2005.[30] The IPP replaced the less-wide-ranging automatic life sentence and resembled a life sentence in that the court set the minimum tariff to be served before the parole board would agree to a release date. The proportion of the sentenced inmate population serving indeterminate sentences (life sentences and IPPs) grew from 9 per cent in 1995 to 18 per cent in 2010 (PRT 2010, 12). According to a scenario envisaged by the Ministry of Justice's own forecasting, the inmate population could reach 93,600 by June 2016 (Ministry of Justice 2010b, 13). This appears painfully self-evident to current justice secretary Ken Clarke. Reflecting upon the current inmate population, he noted that when he last had responsibility for incarceration as home secretary from 1992–3, the average prison population was 44,628 – just over half the current rate. The prison population in 2010, Clarke ruefully observed, had reached 'quite an astonishing number which I would have dismissed as an impossible and ridiculous prediction if it had been put to me as a forecast in 1992' (Clarke 2010a).

As the criminal justice system in England and Wales negotiates an era of fiscal pressures and shrinking resources, the system nevertheless has a greater per capita expenditure level than any of our European counterparts, or indeed the United States (PRT 2010, 3). The cost of the system has grown from 2 per cent of GDP to 2.5 per cent over the last decade. Additionally, prison expenditure over the five-year period ending in 2009 grew from £2.52 billon to almost £4 billion, a real-terms rise of almost 40 per cent (PRT 2010, 6). However, while England and Wales currently have Western Europe's second-highest imprisonment rate (Strickland 2010, 97), this inexorable growth in incarceration has not been prompted by a concomitant rise in crime. While the Conservative Party had asserted in opposition 'the simple, if uncomfortable, fact is that the United Kingdom is a high-crime country' (Conservative Party 2008, 22), this was contested. Lord Carter noted in his prisons review that there had been an overall reduction in total offending since 1995 (Carter 2007, 5). Far from increasing punitiveness as a response to escalating crime, sentencers had simply responded to 'legislative changes and to the prevailing punitive climate accordingly' (Carter 2007, 6). It may be that sentencers were toughening up their behaviour as a result of imbibing neoliberal culture. Though Carter had attested earlier that there was 'no convincing evidence that further increases in the use of custody would significantly reduce crime' (Carter 2004, 15), that demonstrable lack of evidence had evidently not impacted the growing recourse to incarceration. The shift to greater punitiveness is not always smooth. Current justice secretary Ken Clarke, far from endorsing previous Conservative home secretary Michael Howard's classic line that 'prison works' (Brown 1993), has rejected the view that incarceration is effective.

There is and never has been, in my opinion, any direct correlation between spiralling growth in the prison population and a fall in crime. Crime fell throughout most of the western world in the 1990's. Crime fell in countries that had and still have far lower rates of imprisonment than ours. (Clarke 2010b)

While this evidence of a ministerial conversion to cutting imprisonment may be prompted by unremitting economic pressures rather than the ethics of rehabilitation, Clarke's statement may be indicative of changes ahead.

Within the neoliberal penal cultures of the United Kingdom and the United States, offending behaviour is construed as a product of individual choice. Individuals can therefore be held to be culpable for choosing to offend. Cavadino and Dignan argue that a 'punitive counter-reformation…took off in 1993 [which] continues to maintain a stranglehold in the minds of penal policy markers' (Cavadino and Dignan 2007, 178). This punitive shift occurred within probation as well as the prison system. For much of the twentieth century, probation in the United Kingdom had functioned as a relatively benevolent justice agency focused on changing rather than containing its clients and facilitating their reintegration into society (Vanstone 2004; Whitehead and

Statham 2006). A flavour of earlier staff attitudes to probation work is offered by Walker and Beaumont's (1985) widely read textbook on probation practice, which approvingly quoted Attlee's view that 'Every social worker is almost certain to be also an agitator'. However, neoliberal culture was hardly likely to embrace agitation. Probation's professional ethos has undergone upheaval as the service has embarked on a process of radical transformation from what was, in essence, an organisation engaged in social work intervention to an agency unrelentingly driven by the key imperative of law enforcement. Contemporary probation, then, is a radically different institution from the model fashioned by those early rehabilitative pioneers, and this shift away from a social work value base has been paralleled by a substantial shift in the culture of probation in England and Wales. In less than three decades the role of probation staff has been transformed, under the aegis of neoliberal governments, from that of rehabilitative agents who prioritise therapeutic intervention to agents who function in a marketised environment. They are preoccupied by proving their 'effectiveness' (for example, see Chapman and Hough 1998) and prioritise performance management and meeting targets (Whitehead 2007). Those individuals with whom the probation service worked began to be labelled as 'offenders' rather than 'clients'.[31] As Whitehead (himself an ex-probation officer with some 26 years of practice experience) has observed, the framework for probation practice in what he labels 'the brave neo-Darwinian world created by neoliberalism' (2010, 94) does not prioritise rehabilitation; rather, the strongest survive while society's most vulnerable, including many probation service users, are subjected to punishment. The probation system was witnessing not just the crumbling of the rehabilitative ideal but the transformation of

> the professional probation officer with the potential for exercising therapeutic imagination into a functioning bureaucratic technician accompanied by the relentless pursuit of economy, efficiency and effectiveness; achieving value for money; chasing politically imposed objectives and targets; and the auditing of tasks in a more routinised environment. (Whitehead 2010, 88–9)

Privatising Justice in the United States: A 'More Efficient Gulag'?

Almost forty years of neoliberal governments have propelled the economic and social policies of the United States towards a stance which emphasises the centrality of markets and market processes. Private incarceration's expansion has been driven by the imperative to cut costs; shareholders demand profits and privatisation delivers them. The United States and England and Wales are not just leaders in incarceration in terms of prison numbers, they are also leaders in terms of the privatisation of imprisonment (Pozen 2003). While some private sector presence has long been evident in American juvenile justice, the full-scale privatisation of jails and prisons is a relatively recent phenomenon (Thomas 2003). Prior to the mid-1980s private prisons were relatively rare; though there was some private-sector incarceration in the nineteenth century in individual states (Pozen 2003, 257),[32] this had faded away by the start of the twentieth century. During the mid-1980s and 1990s annual growth in US private prisons ran at almost 20 per cent (Parenti 2003). Beginning with Hamilton County Jail in Tennessee in 1984, followed a year later by the first state contract between Kentucky and the United States Corrections Corporation, individual US states embarked upon a process of turning over entire penal institutions to private corporations (Bosworth 2010, 138–9). Privatisation's appeal under neoliberalism has been immense, reflecting the potential for profit in a 'free' economy, and its growth has been speedy. While in 1987 there were just over 3,000 inmates in private prisons, this had grown to 123,000 inmates within 15 years. By the end of 2004 the total US inmate population totalled 2,267,787 of whom 98,901 were behind bars in private facilities (Harrison and Beck 2005). Privately incarcerated prisoners in the United States constitute a relatively small fraction of the overall prison population (and, as we shall see, represent a smaller proportion of the overall national prison population than in England and Wales), but they are nevertheless a growing number.

The first serious United States venture into privatised incarceration came during the Reagan presidency (1981 89), but privatised prisons positively flourished during the centre-left Clinton presidency (1993–2001). The Corrections Corporation of America (CCA), founded as recently as 1983, now styles itself as the nation's leading provider of correctional solutions to federal, state and local government. This is hardly hyperbole – the company is the fifth-largest corrections system in the United States, surpassed in size only by the systems of the federal government and of four individual states. CCA extols its approach to correctional privatisation as combining 'the cost savings and innovation of business with the strict guidelines and consistent oversight of government' (CCA, 2011). The company's potential for growth is demonstrated by the scale of its operations; CCA designs, builds, manages and runs correctional facilities on behalf of the Federal Bureau of Prisons and almost of half of US states, as well a number of counties nationwide. It also provides facilities for the United States Marshals Service (USMS) and Immigration and Customs Enforcement (ICE), and runs inmate transportation services via its TransCor America subsidiary. The company joined the New York Stock Exchange in 1994 and has been nominated amongst 'America's Best Big Companies' by Forbes magazine.

While Marx had little to say specifically about crime,[33] a classical Marxist analysis would argue that the dynamic of capitalism, by its very nature, is propelled to search for new markets and new avenues of profit. This key concept of the *circuit of capital* permeates much of Marx's work (most notably, Marx 1956). What has happened in America and the United Kingdom with the growth of private sector participation in the prison and probation systems provides examples of this endless search for new markets. The reason behind the introduction of private imprisonment was simple:

> The pursuit of profit by alternative providers of correctional services… would bring competition into the marketplace which, in turn, would result in equivalent or superior correctional services being delivered at lower cost. (Thomas 2003, 59)

It did not always work out like that. An alternative view asserts that that some private prisons have become notorious for their 'deprivation, brutality, frequent escapes and inmate violence' (Parenti 2003, 32), questioning whether privatisation does in fact deliver 'a more efficient gulag' (Parenti 2008, 220). The Northeast Ohio Correctional Center, a CCA-run prison, came to prominence after six inmates escaped. Parenti characterised the prison as a

> chaotic gladiator's pit where nonviolent burglars and crack addicts were haphazardly thrust into cells with seasoned rapists, habitual killers and other high security predators. The fifteen months of operations preceding the escapes had seen forty-four assaults, sixteen stabbings (including one guard) and two murders. (2008, 222)

The political and social culture in America means that attitudes to contestability and privatised probation provision are unambiguously expressed.[34] Thomas (2003, 60), for example, acidly berated those academics who 'loudly bemoaned the arrival of corporate America in the nation's correctional system', then remarked on what he perceived as the irony that many of them 'were the same people who previously and equally loudly bemoaned the shortcomings of public correctional agencies'. Reynolds asserted that private sector involvement would render community supervision systems more effective and efficient. This was, he asserted, inherently non-problematic and straightforward, representing no more a transfer of 'the successful commercial principles of our bail system to the probation and parole systems' (Reynolds 2000, i). He envisaged that those on probation or on parole should be compelled to post a financial bond to guarantee their compliance with the terms of their supervision, or face return to prison.

To Reynolds, this made perfect sense, for 'If individual accountability is the answer to crime, then it must include the most powerful kind of accountability: financial responsibility' (2000, i). This represents a classic neoliberal cultural understanding of individual culpability for offending. Since bail bonds in Reynolds's view worked well, he saw no reason why a system of bonds could not achieve improved post-conviction behaviour and pointed to the support of organisations like the National Association of Bail Insurance Companies for the view that 'financially secured post-conviction release works far better than unsecured release' (2000, i). He has optimistically asserted that 'Bonding and the implied partial or complete privatisation of post-release supervision is a good idea whose time may be near' (2000, i). While the full privatisation of post-release has still to arrive, a number of states already utilise private companies to supervise offenders convicted in (less serious) misdemeanour cases. The state of Georgia legislated in the 1990s to utilise independent, privately owned services for community supervision after discontinuing some services run by the state's own Department of Corrections (Hanser 2010, 191–6). CSRA Probation Services Inc., who are part of the Georgia Corrections Corporation and whose services include supervision programmes, style themselves as 'uniquely qualified to provide a wide array of community supervision options to local courts, counties, and cities' CSRA Probation Services Inc., 2011). Part of what marketers might define as CSRA's unique selling proposition is that their services

> ...are generally offender funded which results in no cost to the courts or the taxpayers. We provide services that result in significant savings to the cities, counties, and courts that we serve. (CSRA Probation Services Inc., 2011)

The company was established in response to a need for local, privatised misdemeanour probation services. Since inception, the company has grown to serve over 60 courts and their overall focus has evolved from basic probation supervision to include a broad spectrum of community programmes. The Providence Service Corporation, founded in 1997, is also active in delivering community supervision. By 2006 they had over 100 contracts in community supervision in a number of states including Florida, Tennessee and Washington (Hanser 2010). They supply

> misdemeanant private probation supervision services, including monitoring and supervision of those sentenced to probation, rehabilitative services, and collection and disbursement of court-ordered fines, fees and restitution. (PSC 2010, 3)

The lucrative nature of the business is evidenced by their latest annual report which lauds the achievement of 'record results' (PSC 2010, 4). How this operates on the ground is instructive. In Athens-Clarke County, Georgia, for instance, they supervise over 2000 less-serious offenders (Hanser 2010, 192). In Murfreesboro, Tennessee, Providence Community Corrections collected over $6.3 million in fines and court costs from offenders convicted of less-serious crimes over a two-year period. Providence in Murfreesboro operates on the $45 per month offenders pay in probation fees (Marchesoni 2009). Hanser (2010) contends that such services bring a range of advantages including the provision of

> better collection rates of compensation for victims…substantially more pay for probation staff employed in the agency, and…caseloads that are relatively close to recommended levels for low-risk and administratively supervised probationers. (Hanser 2010, 194)

Those considering the inroads made by private companies in the rehabilitation revolution (Burke 2011; Ledger 2010) advanced in England and Wales may be interested to know that Hanser suggests privatised US probation companies can avail themselves of

> more latitude in hiring and firing decisions than do public service agencies, and therefore may make more expedient and effective decisions regarding personnel retention when qualification or professional service criteria are an issue. (Hanser 2010, 195)

In addition, private investigation agencies have been providing some sentencers with pre-sentence investigations (PSIs, approximately equivalent to our pre-sentence reports). These provide demographic, employment, educational and personal information on an offender and are influential in the final disposal. These reports frequently have the outcome of a less-serious sentence for the client, leading to concerns about whether private firms ought to play a role in the 'quasi-judicial function of recommending sentences' (Clear et al. 2009, 198). Since the defendant pays for the privately written PSI, this may advantage those clients who possess the financial resources to fund their own report.

The idea that individual offenders must pay the financial costs of their rehabilitation has gained ground in America. This is hardly unforeseen, given that neoliberalism prioritises individual responsibility for offending behaviour and accords a lesser degree of attention to the social context of crime. In a context of unrelenting pressure to save public money, correctional supervision fees (also known as 'user fees') have become an integral feature of the cultural landscape for American community corrections agencies. The logic which underpins charging clients a fee to fund their own supervision is clearly delineated by Hanser, who maintains that fees are especially appropriate for less-serious offenders.

> Given that companies have an obvious incentive to collect program fees, fines, and other monetary requirements from probationers, it is highly likely that private companies would provide appropriate follow-up and routine services… the level of accountability, at least in terms of economic accountability, is likely to be further improved since these companies' desire to generate profits from the fees and fines of the probationers under their supervision. (Hanser 2010, 193–94)

The number of US probation and parole agencies collecting correctional fees has increased exponentially. The American Probation and Parole Association (APPA) points out that charging individual offenders fees for correctional services is hardly ground-breaking; at least 28 American states were collecting probation supervision fees and 21 states were collecting parole supervision fees by 1991 (APPA 2011b). There has been vigorous debate about the appropriateness (or otherwise) of charging user fees, as well as discussion about whether fees increase the likelihood of completion of supervision. A number of agencies charge multiple fees to individual offenders. One author (Ring 1988) listed at least 26 separate types of fees. The title of his work, *Probation Supervision Fees, Shifting Costs to the Offender*, offers an authentic insight into the thinking underpinning the neoliberal agenda within probation. Though fees are generally not means tested, the reality may be that their imposition places a price upon probation intervention which many offenders may lack the capacity to pay. APPA distinguishes between 'programme fees' which are uniformly charged to all supervisees and 'service fees' which are only charged to those in receipt of specific (and expensive) services such as GPS tagging. Supervision fees can on occasion generate more than half of the agency's total operational budget. Two positive aspects of charging for community corrections services cited by APPA are that revenue raised has led directly to smaller caseloads and fees apparently may 'promote a greater sense of responsibility in offenders'. This is not to suggest that these advantages are the sole drivers for financial charges (APPA 2011b). As APPA cautiously asserts, 'Community corrections must not lose sight of the fact that fee collections are simply a means to help us achieve our mission, and not the mission itself' (APPA 2011b). However, offenders who may have chaotic lifestyles and are experiencing lives of pressured poverty may not find it easy to raise funds to pay for their supervision. Trying to raise money for fees may drive an offender to commit further crime. US probation agencies, which are fee-reliant, may exhibit professional cultures which are lacking in incentives to grant early termination of supervision. After all, the agency's financial solvency is inextricably linked to offenders who pay fees. As APPA maintains, 'Revocations for new crimes or for failure to report may simply mask fee overload' (APPA 2011b).

In a survey of 15 US states with the highest rates of imprisonment, most offenders on probation or parole were charged monthly supervision fees (Bannon et al. 2010). Fees were also charged to offenders for drug testing, mandatory treatment and therapy. In Texas and Illinois, supervisees convicted of sexual offences must pay the costs of their monitoring. In North Carolina, an offender who has driven under the influence of alcohol can be charged up to $1,000 to fund continuous alcohol monitoring, which is a condition of their probation (Bannon, Nagrecha and Diller 2010, 10). In Texas, up to a fifth of those on probation for a felony and up to a quarter of parolees are obliged to pay for child support. When people who are already poor incur further debt within the justice system, this may impede rehabilitation and inhibit their ability to meet their child support commitments. In a number of states, defence lawyers have observed that

> ...aggressive collection tactics by probation officers deter poor people from showing up to probation meetings if they lack the resources to make a required payment – leading these same probation officers to issue a probation violation for the failure to appear. (Bannon et al. 2010, 24)

The evidence suggests that punitive money collection practice for supervision fees in some states is engendering violations of both probation and parole, as well as promoting further offending aimed at addressing debt problems. This, in turn, may lead to further imprisonment. One in four US states have legislated to allow courts to prolong probation terms for failure to pay debt. Probation may be extended when the client has fulfilled all other requirements of the probation order, even if clear evidence exists that the probationer lacks the financial wherewithal to clear their supervision debts. The inevitable outcome is that

> individuals stay enmeshed in the criminal justice system for longer and face a risk of incarceration for longer – not for new crimes, but for technical violations of probation conditions, including payment conditions... In this way, extending probation for a failure to pay off criminal justice debt makes future interaction with the criminal justice system more likely, and creates a host of burdens unrelated to the debt payments themselves. (Bannon et al. 2010, 25)

When probation staffs have to focus their professional skills on revenue collection they compromise their capacity to concentrate on rehabilitation. If the parameters of the role of probation officers is blurred by demands that they act as revenue protection officers as well as neutral, professional rehabilitators focused on public protection, their ability to intervene to change behaviour may be diluted. Responding to an offender's failure to pay debt as a breach of their supervision conditions can also have other significant deleterious effects. Offenders who breach community supervision are disqualified by federal law from a range of social security benefits, including Temporary Assistance to Needy Families funds, Food Stamps, housing benefits, and Supplemental Security Income for the elderly and disabled (Bannon et al. 2010, 28). The uncompromising utilisation of community supervision for debt collection promotes further economic stress for offenders already experiencing poverty and multiple deprivations and impedes their reintegration into society. This was hardly what President George W. Bush meant when he told Congress in his annual State of the Union address that 'America is the land of the second chance, and when the gates of the prison open, the path ahead should lead to a better life' (Bush 2004).

Armed and Punitive: Probation Officers in the United States

One significant aspect of the shift towards punitivism in the United States has been the increasing number of armed probation staff. It is difficult to reconcile the reintegrative nature of probation with practitioners who carry firearms. As one Californian chief probation officer has observed,

> Our focus is on the rehabilitative side, rather than control and surveillance... If we go down the path of arming we're drifting from what our true function is. When you walk in with a gun on your hip, you have a different relationship with someone than when you don't. William Burke, Marin County, California. (Rogers 2008)

Many probation staff disagree. One northern Californian probation officer's unequivocal words neatly encapsulate the strength of feeling underpinning the argument for armed staff.

> Our entire department is armed, Glock 22.40s. I'm simply amazed that there is still a debate whether Probation Officers should be armed or not. Are you kidding me??... I'm not a gung-ho, cowboy officer either... I just think the arming of POs is a no-brainer. (Long 2005)

It hardly needs stating that armed probation personnel are not a feature of community justice in England and Wales. However, there is increasing pressure for American probation officers to carry firearms and the majority of US states now have some provision for armed probation and parole officers. While this may reflect clear cultural differentiation on gun control between the United States and the United Kingdom (Carter 2002), it also helps define the divergence in perspective between the probation systems of the two nations. The American Probation and Parole Association (APPA) observes that

> community corrections personnel work in a volatile and potentially dangerous environment which requires that individuals and their agencies take every precaution to provide and protect staff in the office and in the field. (APPA 2011a)

APPA further notes that probation's working environment embraces 'Increased societal violence, coupled with a changing profile of offenders served by community corrections agencies, influenced significantly by drug involvement and the associated violence' (APPA 2011c) which have combined to press probation staff to re-evaluate their stance on armed officers. While acknowledging this context of heightened threat to staff safety, APPA's current official position statement, first enacted in 1994, remains neutral on the arming of officers, but argues that any decision about arming staff 'must be made within the framework of actual need [and] officer safety demands' (APPA 2011c). Hanser, the author of a leading US community corrections academic textbook, sharply reminds critics of armed probation officers that carrying firearms is more about staff safety that about achieving compliance from supervisees. Armed probation staff, he contends, do not in any sense 'impair an integrative approach towards community supervision' (Hanser 2010, 142). A flavour of the nature of this endorsement of armed rehabilitation professionals is gained from his assertion that it is

> nearly a professional slight for agencies to prevent officers from carrying a firearm... even more so when one considers that they must come into contact with serious offenders during field visits. (Hanser 2010, 138)

The neoliberal shift away from rehabilitation in US probation is also reflected in official practitioner guidance for dealing with probation clients perceived as non-compliant. Probation officers are officially permitted to strike non-compliant clients if they feel threatened.

> When a probationer fails to comply with instructions, a probation officer may take action... The first option is to employ a command presence.

This can be accomplished by one or two officers standing face to face with the probationer. If this is unsuccessful, officers give vocal commands. If the situation warrants force, they must assess the level necessary. Officers may grab the probationer's shoulder or use take-down methods. They may strike a probationer with hands, feet, elbows or knees when threatened with bodily harm – Marin County probation guidelines for dealing with clients. (Marin County Civil Grand Jury 2008, 10)

Privatising Justice in England and Wales: A Rehabilitation Revolution?

In the United Kingdom, as in the United States, there was a degree of private sector intervention in correctional institutions in the eighteenth century. The public sector eventually ran prisons nationwide from the early nineteenth century, though prisons were operated by local authorities and their management was inconsistent and non-standardised. A significant milestone was the 1877 Prisons Act, which centralised prison administration in England and Wales. It was not until 1992 that Britain's first private prison was opened, and progress towards greater privatisation has been rapid since then; the United Kingdom currently possesses the most privatised prison system in Europe. There are now 11 prisons contractually managed by private companies such as Serco and G4S Justice Services, which defines itself as 'the world's leading international security solutions group' (G4S 2011). The Prison Reform Trust noted that in England and Wales 11.3 per cent of the prison population (almost 10,000 prisoners) are now incarcerated in privately managed prisons (PRT 2010, 56). This is, as we have noted, a significantly higher proportion of private prisoners than the United States. An additional number of prisons which are currently in the public sector will be competitively tendered upon the expiration of their current contracts. In 2008 the CBI, which defines itself as the 'Voice of Business', felt moved in support of its advocacy of a welfare-to-work model in criminal justice to advise the government to engender innovation in criminal justice. This required

> …taking steps to ensure a level playing field between all providers so that quality and value for money can be properly compared. A commitment to improving services also means not tolerating inadequate existing provision and introducing market testing. (CBI 2008, 21)

The coalition government supports the introduction of a 'rehabilitation revolution'. This arguably mirrors privatisation in the US criminal justice system and was presaged by the Conservative Party policy statement that

'The old monopolies in the prison and probation system need to be opened up to create a far more diverse range of suppliers of criminal justice services' (Conservative Party 2008, 49). This thinking has not met with universal approval from practitioners. When the under-secretary of state for justice with responsibility for probation and prisons, Crispin Blunt, addressed staff at the probation union Napo's conference in October 2010, he assured them that he was a pragmatist unconstrained by ideology. His audience was demonstrably unimpressed to learn that this meant outsourcing much of their work to private companies. Delivering the unpalatable news that the privatisation of some of their core tasks was imminent, he stated that the government was 'making a philosophical and practical shift to paying and measuring by results' (Blunt 2010). He clarified the government's position on probation: 'By linking payments to outcomes, providers of offender management services will be incentivized to provide improved services, while the public will only pay for what works' (Blunt 2010). While competition from the private sector for the provision of probation services has been relatively limited to date, the Offender Management Act (2007) enabled the private sector to participate in the market for such services. With the advent of probation trusts, which were created to deliver services on behalf of the Ministry of Justice, the government aims to expand the range of providers which, it is argued, will achieve greater efficiency and a higher level of practice innovation (Ministry of Justice 2009). Blunt's frank acknowledgment of the growth of the market in services for offenders came as the probation service experienced a decade of concentrated change, perhaps the most intense change that they have endured since its foundation over a century ago.

Jonathan Ledger, the general secretary of the National Association of Probation Officers (NAPO) has noted that justice secretary Ken Clarke's endorsement of private-sector intervention in community sentences and his robust support of 'payment by results' in the provision of community sentences raised apprehensions. Ledger professes bemusement by how the system of payment by results is defined. His understanding is that recidivism rates will be utilised to measure effectiveness and he cites the example of the social impact bond pilot scheme in Peterborough. This scheme offers post-release supervision to prisoners not subject to statutory supervision who have been sentenced to less than 12 months. Ledger has expressed unease that

> not only will it take some considerable time to measure the recidivism rates – two years is the most common timescale quoted – but also any experienced probation practitioner will tell you that recidivism is not in itself necessarily an accurate measure of change and improvement in an individual. (Ledger 2010, 418)

Just as privatised incarceration has prospered in America under regimes of both the right (Reagan, Bush) and the centre-left (Clinton, Obama), it has flourished under the administrations of the right (Thatcher, Major) and centre-left (Blair, Brown) in the United Kingdom. In the modern era, England was the first country in Europe to use private prisons. The parliamentary Home Affairs Committee visited private prisons in the United States in 1987 and returned to support the introduction of the private sector to the UK prison system (Pozen 2003, 259). This eventually led to what was then Group 4 Remand Services Limited opening HMP Wolds as the United Kingdom's first privately managed prison in 1992 (six years after US private incarceration had begun to grow in earnest with the establishment of Tennessee's Hamilton County Jail). Private prisons were rapidly established under the government's Private Finance Initiative (PFI),[35] which enabled public projects to be funded with private capital. Contracts were awarded for the entire design, construction, management and finance of a prison. The PFI, or variants of it, is now utilised in a range of countries and can be viewed in the context of the wider neoliberal project of privatisation. Prime minister Tony Blair, a classical neoliberal, did not favour private incarceration before he took office. Four years before his election he articulated his conviction that

> people who are sentenced by the state to imprisonment should be deprived of their liberty, kept under lock and key by those who are accountable primarily and solely to the state – then shadow Home Secretary Tony Blair in 1993. (Cavadino and Dignan 2007, 257)

For a brief period after Blair's landslide victory in 1997, it appeared that prison privatisation might be reversed. New Labour, in opposition, had vigorously insisted that they would return prisons to the public sector and the then shadow home secretary Jack Straw had unambiguously labelled private prisons as 'morally repugnant' (Cavadino and Dignan 2007, 257). However, Blair changed his view and private prisons continued to expand as Labour's 'modernising' agenda developed. In under a decade, there were eleven private prisons in England and Wales. A National Audit report on 'The Operational Performance of PFI Prisons' found that despite some evidence which suggested that a simple comparison of PFI prisons with public sector prisons would not be comparing like with like (National Audit Office 2003, 22); the best PFI prisons were superior to comparable public prisons. However, it also concluded that the worst PFI prison was worse than comparable public prisons across a range of indicators (National Audit Office 2003, 24). Private prisons were found to perform less well in safety and security and there were relatively high levels of assaults in PFI prisons. Prisoners expressed concerns about their personal safety due to the relative inexperience of private prison staff (National Audit Office 2003, 25). In addition, there was a very high staff turnover in private prisons, which may have contributed to lack of consistency and poor continuity of care for prisoners.

Sachdev (2004) found that UK private prison contractors reduced labour costs by slashing pay, extending hours, cutting holidays and downgrading pensions. Private incarceration's capacity to grow shareholder profits is bound to be particularly attractive in an era of fiscal tightening. In 2009 the Ministry of Justice announced that four existing public sector prisons and a new prison, Featherstone 2,[36] were to be market tested. The outcome of the competitive tendering for these five prisons was announced by justice secretary Ken Clarke in 2011. A decision was made to remove one of the prisons (HMP Wellingborough) from the competition process. Of the four remaining prisons, only one (HMP Buckley Hall) was to remain in the public sector. The contract for HMP Doncaster was awarded to Serco and included a trial of the Payment by Results (PBR) initiative,[37] which is seen as central to the government's rehabilitation reform plans. The other two prisons will be run by G4S. The new contracts will be operational by April 2012. Clarke frankly acknowledged what he saw as a fundamental benefit of competitive tendering and private incarceration.

[T]he new prison Featherstone 2 will be delivered at £31 million less than the costs originally approved by the previous government. Cumulative savings over the lifetime of the contracts for the three existing prisons are very impressive at £216 million. (Ministry of Justice 2011c)

Prison Officers' Association (POA) chair Colin Moses, in supporting members considering industrial action to challenge Clarke's initiative, noted that 'Prisons should not be run for profit... the POA remains of the view that it is the state's responsibility to imprison its citizens and not profiteers' (BBC News 2011). Questioned about the national ratio of prisoners to prison officers, Crispin Blunt told Parliament in 2010 that the ratio of prisoners to prison officers in public sector prisons in England and Wales was 1 officer to 3.03 prisoners.[38] However, the ratio of prisoners to prison officers in all private prisons in England and Wales on the same date was 1 officer to 3.78 prisoners,[39] which may suggest that more individualised personal intervention is available in public sector prisons (*Hansard* 2010, 1037W). While the Ministry of Justice later attested that privatisation was necessary to 'meet the specific needs of each individual offender' (Ministry of Justice 2011c), how these needs may be better met in privately managed prisons given these ratios is unclear. The Prison

Reform Trust estimates that no less than a quarter of the entire inmate population of England and Wales could be incarcerated by private sector jails by 2014 (PRT 2010, 56), assuming the private sector is successful in all tendering competitions and if currently planned private prisons are built as scheduled.

Neoliberal culture has permeated probation over the last decade. Whitehead (2010) noted that the NOMS management model in 2006 employed the language of 'brokerage' rather than social justice, and asserted that probation with a cultural history of embracing the rehabilitative ideal had witnessed the creation of a businesslike and market-driven environment (that) has transformed a people-orientated service into one of commodities and products that can be competed for in the marketplace by public, private and voluntary agencies according to the principles of contestability (Whitehead 2010, 89).

Support for private intervention in probation embraces neoliberal governments across the continuum of party affiliations. For example, Charles Clarke, the home secretary in Tony Blair's Labour government expressed his personal commitment 'to the creation of a vibrant mixed economy with NOMS' (Clarke 2005). HM Probation Inspectorate's (HMIP) annual report in the same year acknowledged that 'The drive to expose public services to competition emanates directly from the Cabinet Office...' (HM Inspectorate of Probation 2005, 5). This was not an initiative driven by grass roots practitioners. The Carter Report was also unambiguous in its endorsement of private profit as a key component of public-sector provision: 'Effectiveness and value for money can be further improved through greater use of competition from private and voluntary providers' (Carter 2004, 5). The changing cultural views around private probation provision and the managerial nervousness which accompanied these views are laid bare by a letter in which the then head of the National Probation Service formally forbade chief officers from lobbying against government policy. Writing to remind them of their responsibilities as 'statutory office holders, ministerial appointees and civil servants' on 7 November 2005, he reminded them:

> You should not engage in lobbying activity, you must not promulgate misinformation (e.g. contestability is privatisation) and you should avoid any action that might suggest that you are encouraging staff to lobby against government policy. (BBC News 2005)

This directive was poles apart from the collegial nature which had existed in probation. This was apparently no longer a difference of opinion or ideological perspective around the use of the term 'contestability', but a matter of 'promulgating disinformation', which could result in disciplinary action. This gives an unsettling sense of the prevailing atmosphere and does not suggest a cultural context permeated by glasnost.

Conclusion

Neoliberalism applies not just to the field of economics, but also to social and cultural spheres. Reiner has persuasively argued that neoliberalism has become the

> hegemonic discourse of our times, so deeply embedded in all corners of our culture that its nostrums...have become the common sense taken-for-granted orthodoxy underpinning most public policy debates. (Reiner 2007, 2)

This is particularly true of public policy debates on criminal justice. While this book explores the way in which neoliberalism has become institutionalised in different organisational formations, this chapter has focused on the specific ways in which this institutionalisation has occurred with the penal and probation systems of the United States and England and Wales. The punitive turn has been marked by significant moves in these countries to transform the criminal and community justice systems, via the pervasive influence of neoliberal culture and a process of marketisation, into a competitive marketplace where the attainment of financial return takes priority over the pursuit of criminal and social justice. Following decades of neoliberalism, we can no longer view the growing privatisation of correctional services in the United States or England and Wales as experimental. The predominance of neoliberal political economy and the pervasiveness of neoliberal culture have supported the punitive turn and have ensured that privatisation has put down firm roots, thus integrating criminal justice and penal policy into the circuits of capitalist production and accumulation.

One can understand the growing public concern about perceived crime levels. Under the hegemony of neoliberal culture, it is hardly surprising that there is a degree of public support for the idea that individual choices play a large part in determining criminal behaviour. The British Crime Survey indicates that drugs (cited by 69 per cent of respondents) and lack of discipline by parents (cited by 65 per cent) were the two factors most people commonly believe to be major causes of crime in England and Wales (Flatley et al. 2010, 110). Populist punitivism by vote-seeking politicians from a range of parties talking up the 'fear of crime' has also played its part. Yet institutionalising neoliberalism is not primarily about justice. Academic criminologists have long been aware that very few offences culminate in the outcome of the perpetrators actually being held to account. Reiner has sharply observed that 'the killer fact about criminal justice is that only a tiny proportion of crimes ever get cleared, let alone result in anyone being formally punished' (Reiner 2007, 10). The expansion of punitive responses to crime has not occurred as a result of increasing crime rates, but rather directly relates to decision-making processes within both the criminal justice system and the broader structures of government. The 'War on Drugs' in the United States is a case in point.[10] Neoliberal culture is also argued to reflect the existence of a 'depoliticized citizenry marked by apathy and cynicism' (McChesney 1998, 10). Certainly within the area of criminal justice there appears to be little public appetite for a decisive shift towards funding rehabilitation at the expense of incarceration – though economic pressures may play a part in changing that. In a society of atomised individuals, probation intervention has played its part in locating the primary locus for offending behaviour within the personality of the individual (Robinson and Raynor 2006) rather than within the wider context of his or her social and economic circumstances.

An example of the reality of falling crime in the United States is provided by the National Crime Victimisation Survey which confirms that property crime rates dropped by almost a third during the period 1999–2008 (Rand 2009, cited in Flatley et al. 2010, 3). In England and Wales, too, the risk of becoming a victim of crime is now lower than at any point since the mid-1990s, yet the British Crime Survey clearly demonstrates that crime reached a peak in 1995 and has subsequently gone into a decline with overall crime falling by 50 per cent since 1995. While there has been some variation from year to year, crime in England and Wales as measured by the BCS is now at the lowest level ever reported (Flatley et al. 2010, 20).

Attempts to reduce the prison population and support the burgeoning correctional population in the United Kingdom and America are now driven by the pressures of the deep fiscal crisis, rather than prompted by a profound reassessment of the futility of ever-rising incarceration, or the realities of life behind bars or subject to community supervision. Clients of the community justice system in the United States, many already experiencing racial discrimination and multiple social deprivation, must now fund their own supervision from inevitably limited personal resources or face incarceration. This context of economic crisis is laid bare by the latest UK Treasury Spending Review, which pronounced that the sentencing framework was to be reformed to ensure that it

> both punishes the guilty and rehabilitates offenders more effectively, stemming the unsustainable rise in the UK prison population. This

will include paying private and voluntary sector providers by results for delivering reductions in reoffending... (HM Treasury 2010, 8)

The spending review required the Ministry of Justice to achieve overall savings of some 23 per cent in real terms by 2014–15 by paying and tendering for criminal justice services, rather than automatically providing them. The US justice budget is also under extreme pressure. The economic crisis has provided a pressing incentive for individual states (for example California, Kentucky and Kansas) to slash their budgets by shutting prisons and by diverting offenders who might otherwise have been incarcerated to community supervision. In Kansas, the state government closed three prisons in 2009 and decreased the number of supervisees in breach of probation (who would previously have been imprisoned) to reduce detention costs. However, President Obama's government aims to increase the total Federal Bureau of Prisons budget to $6.8 billion and expand the capacity of the federal prison system up to 220,000 inmates.[41] Even in these straitened times, assistant attorney general Lee Lofthus states that the Bureau of Prisons 'needs the bed space' (Johnson 2010). Two new prisons will be opened, including a 'supermax' ultra-high-security institution in Illinois. The prison industrial complex continues its inexorable expansion.

McChesney (1998) argues that neoliberal democracy represents at its core 'trivial debate over minor issues by parties that basically pursue the same pro-business policies regardless of formal differences and campaign debate'. One could extend this argument to criminal and community justice by stating that neoliberalism within penality represents equally trivial debates over minor issues of crime, punishment and rehabilitation raised by the Conservative, Labour, Liberal Democratic or indeed, Democratic or Republican parties, that pursue what are essentially similar pro-punishment policies, formal ideological differences notwithstanding. After all, the prison and probation populations have continued their relentless expansion in the United States and the United Kingdom, regardless of who is in charge (be it Clinton or Bush; Blair or Thatcher; and now Obama and Cameron). For the past 40 years, neoliberalism – embraced by political parties across the political continuum – has exerted a global impact. The political climate and culture which neoliberalism has fostered have been manifested within the US and UK criminal and community justice systems, and the reach and breadth of that climate and culture have rendered it increasingly difficult to challenge. As long as private interests inspired by the overarching goal of profit are in a position to influence and even dictate policies and processes within the criminal and community justice, its impact will continue to be felt in criminal and community justice regardless of whether crime itself is actually rising. Under the auspices of neoliberal cultures, the juggernaut of penal expansionism continues to roll as the punitive turn maintains its relentless progress.

Notes

1 Some of the material on American probation contained in this chapter draws on research undertaken for the following article: M. Teague, 'Probation in America: Armed, private and unaffordable?' *Probation Journal* 58 (4) (2011): 317–22.

2 The total correctional population includes all individuals who are either imprisoned or supervised in the community, whether on probation or on parole

3 According to a Conservative policy, paper issued in 2008, 'Our rehabilitation revolution will first slow the growth of the prison population and then stabilise it. Whereas the prison population is currently expected to rise to 100,000 by the end of 2020, under our plans it will be at least 1,000 lower than this by 2015 and almost 6,000 lower by 2020'.

4 Along with Australia, New Zealand and South Africa; one could also argue that Britain is a residual social democracy with a neoliberal economic policy.

5 They also argue that murder rates are countries with social-democratic policies (which is to say most Western European countries).

6 Though murder rates did become lower, this may be explained to some extent by the huge increase in imprisonment for large numbers of violent offenders.

7 The US President's Commission on Law Enforcement and Administration of Justice was created in July 1965 to explore the causes of crime and the adequacy of the existing system of law enforcement and correctional intervention.

8 For example, Denmark incarcerates 71 in every 100,000 of its population. Canada imprisons 117 in every 100,000 (ICPS 2011b).

9 Community corrections (sometimes also known as 'community supervision' in the US), refers to the supervision of offenders in the wider community rather than in secure correctional facilities. The two main types of community corrections supervision are probation and parole.

10 According to the US Census Bureau the American population on 1 April 2010 numbers 308,745,538 (US Census Bureau 2010).

11 A range of data is used to estimate the US correctional population, including the National Prisoner Statistics Program, Annual Survey of Jails, Annual Probation Survey and Annual Parole Survey. The total correctional population is published annually in the Correctional Populations in the United States series. The latest available edition is L. E. Glaze (2010).

12 This total may also include a small number of offenders in halfway houses, boot camps, and other residential institutions which do not allow their residents free movement.

13 If we add the number of those on probation and parole to those who are incarcerated, we find that the US correctional authorities were responsible for an overall total of 7,225,800 offenders at the end of 2009.

14 If England and Wales attempted to emulate the US model of imprisonment, this would mean that 420,000 inmates would be incarcerated in at least 710 prisons, compared with around 85,000 inmates in 140 prisons.

15 To facilitate national comparisons for imprisonment both prison inmates and jail inmates are included in the US prison population figures in this chapter.

16 Between 1925 (when authoritative national prison statistics began to be compiled) and 1972, the number of state prisoners increased from 85,239 to 174,379 (Pew Centre on the States 2010).

17 However, even though the state prison population saw its first small decline since 1977 in 2009, the federal prison population continued its relentless rise (Glaze 2010).

18 But below the Russian rate in 1997 of 686 prisoners per 100,000 of population.

19 This applies only to the state prison population, not the federal prison population.

20 This figure is from data compiled by the Public Safety Performance Project of the
    Pew Center on the States, in partnership with the Association of State Correctional
    Administrators. It shows that on 1 January 2010 there were 1,404,053 prisoners under
    the jurisdiction of state prison authorities, 4,777 (0.3 per cent) fewer than there were on
    December 31, 2008 (Pew Centre on the States 2010).
21 By 0.9 per cent or 46,120 offenders.
22 54,809,100 in mid-2009, according to the Office for National Statistics (2010).
23 There were 323,141 people subject to correctional supervision in December 2010;
    84,548 in prison and 238,593 subject to the supervision of the probation service,
    according to Ministry of Justice. (2011a).
24 Adults refer to those aged 16 and over. According to the Office for National Statistics.
    (2010).
25 The highest rate of imprisonment in the European Union was Portugal at 142 prisoners
    per 100,000 of population.
26 The useable operational capacity of the prison estate is the sum of the total operational
    capacity of the prison estate less 1,700 places. This is known as the operating margin
    and reflects the constraints imposed by the need to provide separate accommodation for
    different classes of prisoner, i.e. by sex, age, security category and conviction status.
27 This International Centre for Prison Studies estimate is based on an estimated national
    population of 55.40 million at end of February 2011.
28 This post required Narey to lead the Probation Service, Prison Service and Youth
    Justice Board.
29 In 2008 England and Wales had the 6,922 of life-sentenced prisoners. This was more
    than the number of lifers in Turkey (2,571), Germany (1,985), Italy (1,396) and France
    (531) combined, according to the PRT (2010, 14).
30 This was created by the Criminal Justice Act of 2003. For a detailed account of the
    impact of indeterminate sentences see HM Chief Inspector of Prisons and HM Chief
    Inspector of Probation (2008).
31 I well remember then home secretary Jack Straw carefully corrected a probation officer
    who made the mistake of referring to 'clients' rather than 'offenders' at a probation
    conference in London in 1999.
32 In 1825 Kentucky was the first US state to employ the private sector to run its
    correctional system, and after the Civil War ended in 1865 some southern states also
    used private sector incarceration. But within 40 years private sector participation in
    corrections has begun to disappear.
33 Marx's occasional references to crime and criminal justice notwithstanding, Cowling
    (2008) offers an excellent account of Marxism's treatment of the study of crime.
34 For a detailed discussion of contestability and its application in the UK criminal and
    community justice system see Burke (2005).
35 The Private Finance Initiative (PFI) was originally announced by the chancellor of the
    exchequer in the then Conservative government, Norman Lamont, in his 1992 Autumn
    Statement. It aimed to increase the involvement of the private sector in the provision
    of public services by developing 'public–private partnerships'. It was subsequently
    supported by the New Labour government as part of the Blair/Brown 'Third Way'.
    With the PFI, the public sector does not own an asset such as a prison, but pays the PFI
    contractor for the use of the facilities over the contract period. Once the contract has
    expired, ownership of the asset may remain with the private sector or be returned to
    the public sector.

36 Her Majesty's Prisons (HMP) Birmingham, Buckley Hall, Doncaster and Wellingborough.

37 The PBR element means that 10 per cent of the contract price will only be payable if the operator reduces the one-year reconviction rates of offenders discharged from the prison by five percentage points.

38 This statement was made on 31 March 2010.

39 Prison officer include all officer grades. These data are based on a headcount basis (with part-timers counting as one).

40 The 'War on Drugs', initiated by President Nixon, has been presented as a campaign against the usage of and trade in illegal drugs with a clear focus on punishment rather than prevention. The imprisonment of drug users has played a very significant role in the expansion of the US prison population. By the second year of President Obama's administration, almost thirty-eight years after Nixon's original declaration of 'War', the 'War on Drugs' had been labelled counterproductive by Obama's 'drug czar' Gil Kerlikowske.

41 The federal prison system currently detains 213,000 inmates.

References

Alexander, M. 2010. *The New Jim Crow: Mass Incarceration in the Age of Colorblindness*. New York: The New Press.

———. 2011. 'The New Jim Crow'. *American Prospect* 22 (1): 19–21.

APPA. 2011a. *Staff Safety Standards*. Lexington, KY: American Probation and Parole Association.

———. 2011b. 'Supervision Fees'. Issue Paper. Lexington, KY: American Probation and Parole Association.

———. 2011c. 'Weapons'. Position Statement. Lexington, KY: American Probation and Parole Association.

Bannon, A., M. Nagrecha and R. Diller. 2010. *Criminal Justice Debt: A Barrier to Reentry*. New York: Brennan Center for Justice at New York University School of Law.

Barclay, G. C. and C. Taveres, 1999. *Digest 4: Information on the Criminal Justice System in England and Wales*. London: Home Office Research, Development and Statistics Directorate.

BBC News. 2005. 'Leaked letter reopens police row'. Available at http://news.bbc.co.uk/1/hi/uk_politics/4436238.stm (accessed 28 February 2008).

———. 2011. 'Prison officers to vote over privatisation row'. Available at http://www.bbc.co.uk/news/uk-13078277 (accessed 6 May 2011).

Bell, E. 2011. *Criminal Justice and Neoliberalism*. Basingstoke: Palgrave Macmillan.

Berman, G. 2010. 'Prison population statistics: Standard Note SN/SG/4334'. *Social and General Statistics*. London: House of Commons Library.

Blunt, C. 2010. Speech at Napo conference, 8 October 2010, Scarborough (recorded by the author).

Bosworth, M. 2010. *Explaining U.S. Imprisonment*. London: Sage.

Brown, C. 1993. 'Howard seeks to placate angry majority'. *Independent*, 7 October.

Burke, L. 2005. *From Probation to the National Offender Management Service: Issues of Contestability, Culture and Community Involvement*. London: Napo.

———. 2011. 'Revolution or evolution?' *Probation Journal* 58 (1): 3–8.

Bush, G. W. 2004. State of the Union Address. Washington, DC: United States Department of Justice Archive.

Carter, G. L. 2002. *Guns in American Society: An Encyclopedia of History, Politics, Culture, and the Law*. Santa Barbara, CA: ABC-CLIO.

Carter, P. 2004. *Managing Offenders, Reducing Crime*. London: Home Office.

————. 2007. *Lord Carter's Review of Prisons: Securing the Future: Proposals for the Efficient and Sustainable Use of Custody in England and Wales*. London: Home Office.

Cavadino, M., and J. Dignan. 2005. *Penal Systems: A Comparative Approach*. London: Sage.

————. 2007. *The Penal System: An Introduction*. London: Sage.

CBI. 2008. *Getting Back on the Straight and Narrow: A Better Criminal Justice System for All*. London: CBI.

CCA. 2011. *America's Leader in Partnership Corrections*. Nashville: Corrections Corporation of America.

Chapman, T. and M. Hough. 1998. *Evidence Based Practice: A Guide to Effective Practice*. London: HM Inspectorate of Probation.

Clarke, C. 2005. *Where Next For Penal Policy?* London: National Offender Management Service.

Clarke, K. 2010a. *The Government's Vision for Criminal Justice Reform: Speech to the Centre for Crime and Justice Studies*. London: Ministry of Justice.

————. 2010b. Speech at the Dinner for the Judges, Mansion House, 13 July. London: Ministry of Justice.

Clear, T. R., G. F. Cole and M. D. Reisig, 2009. *American Corrections*. Belmont: Thomson Wadsworth.

Conservative Party. 2008. 'Prisons with a Purpose: Our Sentencing and Rehabilitation Revolution to Break the Cycle of Crime'. Policy green paper. London: Conservative Party.

Cowling, M. 2008. *Marxism and Criminological Theory: A Critique and a Toolkit*. Basingstoke: Palgrave Macmillan.

CSRA Probation Services, Inc. 2011. 'About Us'. Evans, GA: CSRA/Georgia Corrections Corporation.

Flatley, J., C. Kershaw, K. Smith, R. Chaplin and D. Moon (eds). 2010. *Crime in England and Wales 2009/10, Issue 12/10*. London: Home Office.

G4S. 2011. *Securing Your World*. Crawley, West Sussex: G4S.

Garland, D. 2001a. *The Culture of Control: Crime and Social Order in Contemporary Society*. Oxford: Oxford University Press.

————. 2001b. 'Introduction: The Meaning of Mass Imprisonment'. *Punishment & Society* 3 (1): 5–7.

Glaze, L. E. 2010. 'Correctional Populations in the United States, 2009'. *Bulletins*. Washington: Bureau of Justice Statistics.

Glaze, L. E., T. P. Bonczar and F. Zhang. 2010. *Probation and Parole in the United States, 2009*. Washington, DC: Bureau of Justice Statistics.

Hall, S. and C. McLean. 2009. 'A tale of two capitalisms'. *Theoretical Criminology* 13 (3): 313–39.

Hall, S., S. Winlow and C. Ancrum. 2008. *Criminal Identities and Consumer Culture*. Cullompton: Willan.

Hansard. 2010. 15 Sep 2010, column 1037W. London: HM Government.

Hanser, R. D. 2010. *Community Corrections*. London: Sage.

Harrison, P. M. and A. J. Beck. 2005. 'Prisoners in 2004'. Washington, DC: Bureau of Justice Statistics.

Harvey, D. 2007. *Brief History of Neoliberalism*. Oxford: Oxford University Press.

HM Chief Inspector of Prisons and HM Chief Inspector of Probation. 2008. *The Indeterminate Sentence for Public Protection: A Thematic Review*. London: HM Inspectorate of Prisons and HM Inspectorate of Probation.

HM Inspectorate of Probation. 2005. *2004–2005 Annual Report*. London: Home Office.

HM Treasury. 2010. *Spending Review 2010*. London: The Stationery Office.

ICPS. 2011a. *World Prison Brief: American Imprisonment Figures*. London: International Centre for Prison Studies, King's College London.

————. 2011b. *World Prison Brief: Canadian Imprisonment Figures*. London: International Centre for Prison Studies, King's College London.

————. 2011c. *World Prison Brief: England and Wales Imprisonment Figures*. London: International Centre for Prison Studies, King's College London.

Jerrom, C. 2006. 'Interview with Martin Narey'. CommunityCare. Available at http://www.communitycare.co.uk/Articles/03/02/2006/52580/Int-with-Martin-Narey.htm (accessed 27 June 2012).

Johnson, K. 2010. '2011 budget gives federal prisons $528M'. *USA Today*, 4 February.

Jones, T. and T. Newburn. 2007. *Policy Transfer and Criminal Justice*. Maidehhead: Open University Press.

Ledger, J. 2010. 'Rehabilitation revolution: Will probation pay the price?' *Probation Journal* 57 (4): 415–22.

Long, J. D. 2005. 'Off-Duty Probation Officer Concealed Carry'. Police Forums and Law Enforcement Forums. Officer.com. Available at http://forums.officer.com/forums/archive/index.php/t-33797.html (accessed 5 May 2011).

Lynch, M. J. 2007. *Big Prisons, Big Dreams: Crime and the Failure of America's Penal System*. New Brunswick, NJ: Rutgers University Press.

Marchesoni, L. 2009. '$6.3M in fines, fees collected for county at no cost'. *Murfreesboro Post*, 15 February, 3

Mariani, P. 2001. 'Overview: Law, Order, and Neoliberalism'. *Social Justice* 28 (3): 2–4.

Marin County Civil Grand Jury. 2008. 'Probation Officers: Arming for Safety, Marin County: 2007–2008'. Report for 2007–8, issued on 9 June. Marin: Marin County.

Marx, K. 1956. *Capital: A Critique of Political Economy (Book Two)*. London: Lawrence and Wishart.

McChesney, R. W. 1998. 'Introduction'. In *Profit Over People: Neoliberalism and Global Order*, edited by N. Chomsky. London: Turnaround Publishing Service Ltd.

Miethe, T. D. and H. Lu. 2005. *Punishment: A Comparative Historical Perspective*. Cambridge: Cambridge University Press.

Miller, J. 2010. *Search and Destroy: African-American Males in the Criminal Justice System*. Cambridge: Cambridge University Press.

Ministry of Justice. 2009. *Capacity and Competition Policy for Prisons and Probation*. London: Ministry of Justice.

————. 2010a. *Draft Structural Reform Plan*. London: Ministry of Justice.

————. 2010b. 'Prison Population Projections 2010–2016 England and Wales'. *Ministry of Justice Statistics Bulletins*. London: Ministry of Justice.

————. 2011a. 'Offender Management Statistics Quarterly Bulletin July to September 2010, England and Wales'. *Offender Management Statistics Quarterly Bulletins*. London: Ministry of Justice.

————. 2011b. *Population and Capacity Briefing for 08 April 2011*. London: Ministry of Justice.

————. 2011c. 'Prisons competition outcome'. News release. London: Ministry of Justice.

National Audit Office. 2003. *The Operational Performance of PFI Prisons*. London: Stationery Office.

Newburn, T. 2002. 'Atlantic crossings'. *Punishment & Society* 4 (2): 165–94.

Obama, B. and J. Biden. 2008. *Blueprint for Change: Obama and Biden's Plan for America*. Chicago: Obama '08.

Office For National Statistics. 2010. Mid-year population estimates 2009. Available at http://www.statistics.gov.uk/statbase/Product.asp?vlnk=15106 (accessed 11 April 2011).

Parenti, C. 2003. 'Privatized Prisons: For Profit Incarceration In Trouble'. In *Capitalist Punishment: Prison Privatization and Human Rights*, edited by A. Coyle, A. Campbell and R. Neufeld. London: Zed Books.

Parenti, C. 2008. *Lockdown America: Police and Prisons in the Age of Crisis*. London: Verso.

Pew Center on the States. 2008. *One in 100: Behind Bars in America 2008*. Washington, DC: Pew Charitable Trusts.

———. 2009. *1 in 31: The Long Reach of American Corrections*. Washington, DC: Pew Charitable Trusts.

———. 2010. 'Prison Count 2010'. Washington, DC: Pew Center on the States.

Pozen, D. E. 2003. 'Managing a correctional marketplace: Prison privatization in the United States and the United Kingdom'. *Journal of Law and Politics* 19: 253–83.

Pratt, T. C. 2009. *Addicted to Incarceration: Corrections Policy and the Politics of Misinformation in the United States*. London: Sage.

PRT. 2010. 'Bromley Briefings Prison Factfile'. *Bromley Briefings*. London: Prison Reform Trust.

PSC. 2010. '2009 Annual Report'. Tucson, AZ: Providence Service Corporation.

Reiner, R. 2007. *Law and Order: An Honest Citizen's Guide to Crime Control*. Cambridge: Polity Press.

———. 2011. 'Foreword'. In E. Bell, *Criminal Justice and Neoliberalism*. Basingstoke: Palgrave Macmillan.

Reynolds, M. O. 2000. 'Privatizing Probation and Parole'. *NCPA Policy Report*. Dallas: National Center for Policy Analysis.

Ring, C. R. 1988. *Probation Supervision Fees, Shifting Costs to the Offender*. Boston: Legislative Research Bureau.

Robinson, G. and P. Raynor. 2006. 'The future of rehabilitation: What role for the probation service?' *Probation Journal* 53 (4): 334–46.

Rogers, R. 2008. 'Lack of guns puts probation officers at risk, report says'. *Marin Independent Journal* 19 (June).

Ruiz, R. 2011. 'Eyes on the Prize'. *American Prospect* 22 (1): 3.

Sachdev, S. 2004. *Paying the Cost? Public Private Partnerships and the Public Service Workforce*. London: Catalyst.

Strickland, P. 2010. 'Security and Liberty: Should We Build More Prisons?' *House of Commons Library Research*. London: House of Commons Library.

Teague, M. 2001. 'George W. Bush and the "Texas Solution"'. *Criminal Justice Matters* 44: 38–40.

———. 2008. 'America: The Great Prison Nation'. *Prison Service Journal* 176: 9–14.

———. 2009. 'Barack Obama: changing American criminal justice?' *Criminal Justice Matters* 78 (1): 4–5.

Teague, M. (2011) 'Probation in America: Armed, Private and Unaffordable?' *Probation Journal* 58 (4): 317–22.

Thomas, C. H. 2003. 'Correctional Privatization in America: An Assessment of its Historical Origins, Present Status and Future Prospects'. In *Changing the Guard: Private Prisons and the Control of Crime*, edited by A. Tabarrok and C. H. Logan. Oakland: The Independent Institute.

Tonry, M. 2009. 'Explanations of American punishment policies'. *Punishment & Society* 11 (3): 377–94.

US Census Bureau. 2010. '2010 Census and Apportionment'. Washington, DC. US Census Bureau.

Vanstone, M. 2004. *Supervising Offenders in the Community: A History of Probation Theory and Practice*. London: Ashgate.

Wacquant, L. 2001. 'The Penalisation of Poverty and the Rise of Neo-liberalism'. *European Journal on Criminal Policy and Research* 9: 401–12.

———. 2002. 'From Slavery to Mass Incarceration: Rethinking the 'race question' in the US'. *New Left Review* 13: 41–60.

———. 2009a. *Prisons of Poverty*. Minneapolis: University of Minnesota Press.

———. 2009b. *Punishing the Poor: The Neoliberal Government of Social Insecurity* Durham, NC: Duke University Press.

Walker, H. and B. Beaumont, 1985. *Working With Offenders*. Basingstoke: Macmillan.

Walker, S. 1978. 'Reexamining the President's Crime Commission'. *Crime & Delinquency* 24 (1): 1–12.

Walker, S., C. Spohn and M. DeLone. 2006. *The Color of Justice: Race, Ethnicity, and Crime in America*. Belmont, CA: Wadsworth Publishing Company.

Whitehead, P. 2007. 'Target practice in probation: Take aim for a reappraisal'. *British Journal of Community Justice* 5 (2): 83–95.

———. 2010. *Exploring Modern Probation: Social Theory and Organisational Complexity*. Bristol: The Policy Press.

Whitehead, P. and R. Statham. 2006. *The History of Probation: Politics, Power and Cultural Change 1876–2005*. Crayford: Shaw and Sons.

Chapter 4

THE NEOLIBERAL WINGS OF THE 'SMOKE-BREATHING DRAGON': THE CIGARETTE COUNTERFEITING BUSINESS AND ECONOMIC DEVELOPMENT IN THE PEOPLE'S REPUBLIC OF CHINA

Anqi Shen, Georgios A. Antonopoulos, Marin K. Kurti and Klaus von Lampe

Introduction[1]

The illegal trade in tobacco products is a phenomenon that only recently has gained some prominence despite the fact that it has a much longer history. There are three main schemes characterising this trade in the last two decades: (1) *bootlegging*: buying an amount of cigarettes that exceeds custom regulations, (2) *large-scale smuggling* of untaxed cigarettes diverted from licit international trade and (3) *counterfeiting* or manufacturing of fake brand cigarettes (Joossens 1999; von Lampe 2006). This chapter focuses on the third scheme and aims at providing an account of the social organisation of the counterfeiting business in the People's Republic of China (hereinafter, China), generally believed to be the main source for counterfeit cigarettes worldwide. According to recent estimates, up to 400 billion counterfeit cigarettes are produced in China per year (Chen 2009; Joossens, Merriman, Ross and Raw 2009), representing roughly the number of cigarettes (legal and contraband) consumed in the United Kingdom over a six-year period. China has criminalised cigarette counterfeiting through a net of general and specific laws and regulations. Section 140 (chapter 3) of the Chinese Criminal Law of 1997 has made the production and trade of counterfeit goods in general an 'Offence that

Undermines the Socialist Market Economy' punishable by a range of possible sentences from a financial penalty to life imprisonment. In addition, the Chinese Law of Tobacco Exclusive Sale stipulates that legal traders who sell counterfeit tobacco products must be fined at 50 per cent of the market value of the counterfeit products seized. There are also a number of regional and local legislations and administrative regulations governing cigarette counterfeiting such as the 2003 Jiangsu Provincial Council Resolution of Tobacco Exclusive Sale Management.

It is important to note that it was not cigarette counterfeiting which first put China on the map of the global illegal cigarette trade. Instead, as Figure 4.1 suggests, before China emerged as an exporter of illicit, mostly counterfeit cigarettes in the mid- to late-1990s, it had already attracted attention as a destination country for contraband, mostly genuine Western brand cigarettes. Figure 4.1 is the product of an analysis of more than 757 English-language media reports on cigarette smuggling into and out of mainland China from 1990 to 2010.

There is a wider perception that cigarette counterfeiting in China has been increasing and that no part of mainland China has remained immune from such activity. Governmental agencies, media and tobacco manufacturers portray cigarette counterfeiting – just as other illegal tobacco-related activities – as the business of serious 'organised criminals' and of threatening 'criminal organisations' (Chow 2003), and a gloomy picture has been painted by the

Figure 4.1. Media coverage on China and cigarette smuggling

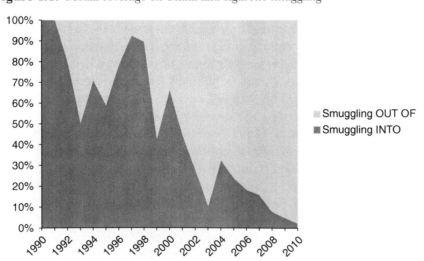

Source: English-language media reports (n=757) on cigarette smuggling into and out of mainland China 1990–2010, ratios per year (LexisNexis analysis).

authorities as far as measures against the cigarette counterfeiting business are concerned. At the National Anti-Cigarette Counterfeiting Conference held in 2008, Zhang, the deputy chief of the National Tobacco Exclusive Sale Bureau pointed out that

> ...the situation of cigarette counterfeiting in China is severe. In the hot spot areas cigarette counterfeiting has not been attacked effectively. Counterfeiting networks are operating. Materials are re-supplied after the law enforcement crackdowns, and there is smooth and frequent counterfeit cigarette distribution... Cigarette counterfeiting cannot be solved essentially within a short period of time so we cannot be over-optimistic...and should be prepared for the longer term battle against this illicit activity. (Zhang 2008)

China's leading role in cigarette counterfeiting cannot be understood without considering the broader social and economic importance of tobacco in this country. To begin with, China has the largest smoking population in the world, reaching approximately 300 million or one-third of the world's smokers (Tobacco Free Centre 2009). It has also been suggested that Chinese smokers spend 3 per cent of per capita GDP on tobacco (Wang 2006; Hu, Mao, Liu, de Beyer and Ong 2005), often at the expense of other, more vital commodities and services (Hu, Mao, Shi and Chen 2008). This huge market has traditionally been supplied almost exclusively by domestic sources. Until recently, foreign cigarettes accounted for only an extremely small share of the legal market (e.g. only 0.8 per cent from 1995 to 1999) as a result of high tariffs on cigarette imports (Hu and Mao 2002). It was not until the mid-2000s that these tariffs have been substantially lowered (Wang 2009). These barriers to imports, it seems, have encouraged the smuggling and counterfeiting of foreign brands. In fact, there is some evidence that the counterfeiting business has profited from expertise originally acquired from smuggling Western brand cigarettes into China during the 1990s (Chen 2009). Given the alleged corporate involvement (Lee and Collin 2006), one could argue that China's counterfeiting business of today is, in a way, the sorcerer's apprentice of the Western tobacco industry.

Given the size of its domestic market, it is not surprising that China is the biggest tobacco producer in the world, while its presence on the world market remains limited (Wang 2009). The tobacco industry is an extremely important economic sector in China. Organised as a state monopoly, it contributes significantly to the Chinese economy and provides substantial revenues for the central government and local governments, although at a declining rate (Hu et al. 2008; Wang 2006). In 2005, 7.6 per cent of the central government's total revenue came from a combination of tobacco taxes and monopoly profits, compared to 11.4 per cent in 1995 (Hu et al. 2008). Because local governments receive their share of revenues primarily from taxes on tobacco leaves rather than on cigarettes, they have an incentive to encourage farmers to increase the production of tobacco beyond set quotas, thus creating a source of raw tobacco for the manufacturing of counterfeit cigarettes (Hu, Mao, Jiang, Tao and Yurekli 2007).

Tobacco provides income for millions of Chinese people. According to Wang (2006), 4.1 million rural households are involved in the cultivation of tobacco, and 5 million (licensed) tobacco selling points create job opportunities in the private sector. The manufacturing industry, however, is less significant in this respect. Wang (2006) gives a recent figure of only 215,600 workers involved in the (legal) production of cigarettes, marking a continuous decline. Since 2001, when China joined the World Trade Organization (WTO), the administration has pursued an aggressive agenda to restructure the tobacco industry. The aim has been to establish a small number of large-scale tobacco enterprises with an ability to compete against major international brands. In the process, numerous small and inefficient factories have been closed down (Euromonitor International 2008; Hu et al. 2007). One apparent consequence of the restructuring of the legal tobacco industry is that a sizeable workforce of skilled labourers as well as production machinery has been made available for the illicit tobacco business.

A third historically developed characteristic of the Chinese tobacco industry may have contributed to the emergence of large-scale illegal cigarette trading: the high level of regulation. As indicated, despite China's shift to a market economy thirty years ago, the tobacco industry in the country is highly regulated by the central government and specifically, the State Tobacco Monopoly Administration (STMA). The state company, under the title China National Tobacco Corporation (CNTC), and a number of smaller companies (such as China Cigarette Sales & Marketing Corporation and China Tobacco Materials Corporation) are subject to this authority. The regulation provides numerous impediments to individual entrepreneurs wishing to be involved in the legal business. Specifically, a Permit of Exclusive Sale of Tobacco is required before a legal tobacco-selling business can be opened, a procedure which is lengthy and difficult because these legal requirements and processes are sometimes affected by corruption (see *Caijin* 2008). The formidable difficulties involved in obtaining a tobacco exclusive sale permit, it seems, in part account for the existence of the illicit cigarette business.

Of great relevance to this study is the cultural meaning of cigarettes (and other tobacco products) in Chinese society. Tobacco is a commodity that is often associated with success and affluence and has been used as a lubricant in social relationships and an 'instrument' of bribery (see Tomson and Coulter 1987). Particularly, international and Chinese expensive brands of cigarettes have been traditionally purchased as gifts, for example, on important occasions. In fact, counterfeit production and sales are said to peak around the New Year and spring festival celebrations (*China Daily* 2004). The relative income price (RIP) of cigarettes, namely, the percentage of per capita GDP required to buy 100 packs of cigarettes, has been on average approximately 22 per cent. In fact, China has had a *positive* RIP growth between 1990 and 2006, basically signifying that cigarettes have become less affordable during this period (Blecher and van Walbeek 2008 and 2009).

Another aspect, defining the broader environment under which the illegal cigarette business flourishes in China, is the global demand for cheap cigarettes. Since the late 1990s large quantities of counterfeit cigarettes from China have been introduced to illegal cigarette markets around the world, thus rendering China an important node in the global illegal tobacco trade. Although there are indications that the production of counterfeit cigarettes has increased in other Asian countries and Eastern Europe as well as Germany and the United Kingdom (see von Lampe 2006), China remains the major source for this particular commodity (Chen 2009; SOCA 2009). However, although there is a considerable amount of publications on tobacco and health issues, tobacco economics and the complicity of tobacco manufacturers in the illegal tobacco trade in China, there is comparatively little being published on the social organisation of the cigarette counterfeiting business in the country. This perhaps reflects the relatively slow development of criminology in China, and Asia in general, compared to the Western world (see Liu 2009 and 2008).

Our aim is to contribute to the research on the cigarette counterfeiting business in China. Specifically we aim to (1) describe the scale and nature of cigarette counterfeiting in mainland China, (2) discuss the practices and actors during the different phases of the trade and (3) examine the role of corruption and violence in cigarette counterfeiting. Our endeavour is based on open sources. Apart from a general literature and Internet search, we searched the news reports from the website of *Xinhua Ribao* – one of China's major official newspapers (http://www.news.cn) by using the keywords 'cigarette counterfeiting'. We obtained 381 cigarette counterfeiting-related news articles that were collected from a variety of online sources from 11 May 2001 to 22 September 2009. We also conducted a random online search by using the keywords 'cigarette counterfeiting in (name of province)'. The purpose of this was to obtain cigarette counterfeiting cases detected in the provinces that are not included in the *Xinhua* database. This search added another 106 news articles to our database.

The cases we have cited in this chapter are drawn from news articles carefully selected from our initial search. Through the initial search we also identified a handful of surveys conducted by journalists from newspapers such as *Caijun Ribao*, *Shichang Bao* and *Chengshi Wanbao*. Likewise, a large amount of data was collected from a tobacco-specialised website, namely, Tobacco China (http://www.tobaccochina.com). In addition, we searched all of China's tobacco authority official websites, including the website of the National Tobacco Exclusive Sale Bureau (NTESB), which has published annual reports from 2003 to 2008. These reports contain statistics on (1) the number of cases detected, (2) the number of counterfeiting sites, (3) the number of rolling machines seized, (4) tons of tobacco leaves seized, (5) the number of units of cigarettes seized and (6) the number of people arrested and sentenced for cigarette counterfeiting from 2002 to 2007. The sources were carefully selected in order to cover cigarette counterfeiting in *all* provinces of mainland China. The reason why the data we use for this study do not include Hong Kong, Macao and Taiwan is because they constitute special administrative and – primarily – economic zones that have adopted different policies and practices. Overall, these three areas are discernibly different from mainland China in terms of their historical, socio-political and economic features. We argue that cigarette counterfeiting is one of the side effects of China's reform and 'opening up' policy, and a feature of the country's economic development process.

The Scale of the Cigarette Counterfeiting Business in China

NTESB annual reports (NTESB 2003, 2004, 2005, 2006, 2007 and 2008) and *China Tobacco Market* (2009) provide some data on cigarette counterfeiting in China for the period 2002–8. Within this period, 1,492,814 cases became known to the Chinese authorities. The year with the largest number of cases detected was 2005 (347,000 cases). The number of counterfeit cigarette production sites that were found by the authorities for the particular period was 22,248, whereas 8,849 rolling machines used for the production of counterfeit cigarettes were seized along with more than 84 tons of tobacco leaves. Overall, 30,825 individuals were arrested for cigarette counterfeiting, 10,742 of whom were sentenced. (NTESB 2003, 2004, 2005, 2006, 2007 and 2008; *China Tobacco Market* 2009).

The aforementioned official statistics possess a number of limitations in addition to the ones relating to the lack of knowledge of or ambiguity about the data collection procedures. The superficial and at points, incomplete, figures presented above do not provide a picture of the actual extent of cigarette counterfeiting in China, but only those cases that the Chinese authorities have come across. The 'dark figure' may be considerable and the seized counterfeit cigarettes, as an official in one particular case is quoted as saying, may constitute 'only the tip of the iceberg' (*Shichang Bao* 2006). Data on 2007 and 2008 refer to cases involving merchandise of monetary value of more than 50,000 Yuan and 500,000 Yuan, respectively, which automatically excludes 'smaller' cases. In addition, as is obvious, there have been increases and decreases in the number of cases as well as in the number of seized cigarette packs that do not allow for a possible trend to be discerned, at least within these years. But even when trends could indeed be discerned, these could refer more to 'contextual variables' (von Lampe 2004), such as the level of intensity of law enforcement or resolution of the government.

The Production of Counterfeit Cigarettes

Counterfeit cigarette manufacturing and trading originated from the southern coastal provinces of mainland China, Fujian and Guangdong, which borders Hong Kong and Macao. Particularly, Yunxiao (Fujian province) and Chaoshan and Guangzhou (Guangdong province) are notorious for the production of counterfeit cigarettes. However, in recent years, due to the centrally coordinated operations persistently carried out to curb cigarette counterfeiting in these areas, a number of counterfeiting businesses have been displaced to inland China. The counterfeit cigarette production phase can be divided into three stages: (1) acquiring raw materials, (2) manufacturing counterfeit cigarettes and (3) packing counterfeit cigarettes.

Acquiring raw materials

In China, counterfeit cigarettes can be produced from tobacco of various levels of quality, second-hand tobacco or even waste. Some of the chemicals that are used to process low-quality tobacco, such as sulphur and carbamide, are poisonous and may cause health problems to cigarette consumers. Low-quality tobacco, directly and regularly bought from tobacco farmers, is usually used to make counterfeit cigarettes. Poor-quality tobacco includes the totally unprocessed raw tobacco and musty/rotten tobacco, which has to go through a process with sulphur and carbamide in order to look better (see *Chongqing Chenbao* 2002). Counterfeiters obtain their tobacco from 'irregular' channels as well. In a case that the authorities came across in Shenyang (Liaonin province), counterfeiters used dumped materials and *lajiyan* ('rubbish tobacco') to make cigarettes. In addition, the counterfeiters disguised themselves as professional recyclers and bought damaged packaging, 'unusable' wrapping paper and unsellable cigarettes from legitimate cigarette companies. Simultaneously, they employed 'workers' to collect cigarette butts from the rubbish bins (*Shidai Shangbao* 2002).

In some cases, counterfeit cigarettes are also made of non-tobacco waste such as sawdust, wood shavings and rotten vegetable leaves. In such cases, the cigarette wrapping paper, filters and other material are collected from waste sites (see, for example, *Hangzhou Ribao* 2007). In the municipality of Chongqing, rotten vegetable leaves were dried and processed with sulphur in order to be used instead of tobacco in counterfeit cigarettes (*Chongqing Wanbao* 2002). It is not unusual, however, for counterfeit cigarettes to be made of good quality tobacco. Mr Li Yang from the Central Inspection Team of the Beijing Tobacco Exclusive Sale Bureau commented that in some cases, 'the counterfeit cigarettes intercepted are of good quality. Consumers can hardly tell the difference between these counterfeit cigarettes and the genuine ones' (*China News Agent* 2002).

Manufacturing counterfeit cigarettes

The actual manufacturing of counterfeit cigarette requires rolling machines. In the past, purchasing cigarette rolling machines was extremely expensive. In order for costs to be cut down, counterfeiters bought used rolling machines from state-owned cigarette factories. The cost of these machines ranged from 600,000 to 1 million Yuan (approximately £53,000 to £89,000) per piece. In recent years, some machinery manufacturers have started to make copycat cigarette rolling machines and the price has dropped significantly to around 200,000 Yuan (approximately £18,000) per piece. Inevitably, the costs of cigarette manufacturing have been reduced accordingly. With the development and expansion of the cigarette counterfeiting businesses, counterfeiters, like their legitimate counterparts, have started to invest in more advanced equipment. Prior to 2004 only 30 per cent of the cigarette machines seized were automatic, while currently, the counterfeit cigarette production line is 90 per cent automatic (*Nanfang Ribao* 2009).

Packing of counterfeit cigarettes

Packing is an integral part of the counterfeit cigarette production process. There are legal and illegal enterprises which specialise in packing only. The district of Guangzhou (Guangdong province) is believed to be the largest counterfeit cigarette packing centre in China. The packing-only 'schemes' usually operate at a relatively small scale. In Beijing, a cigarette packing 'factory' operated in a warehouse with only ten to twenty workers who were manually packing loose cigarettes into the packaging of different popular brands (China News Agent 2002). Different methods are used for the packing of counterfeit cigarettes in order for consumers to be deceived and detection to be avoided:

- *'Pick 'n' mix'* – Genuine cigarettes are mixed with counterfeits in each pack. In a Changsha (Hunan province) case, Baisha cigarettes of this type were found. Inside the pack there were seven genuine and thirteen fake cigarettes (*Shangbao* 2002). However, this packing method appears to be rare in the cigarette counterfeiting business.
- *Genuine packs* – Counterfeit cigarettes are packed in used *genuine* packaging. This guarantees that health warnings are not misspelled, images are clear and other giveaways are not present.
- *Counterfeit packs* – Counterfeit cigarettes are placed in packaging resembling that of genuine brand cigarettes. The quality of counterfeit packs appears to have substantially improved from rather primitive beginnings in the 1990s, making it difficult nowadays to distinguish counterfeit from genuine cigarette packs (HM Treasury 2004).
- *Unique format of counterfeit packs* – In order to attract prospective customers' attention, some unique packaging is designed for counterfeit cigarettes of the most popular brands, which may even not exist for the genuine cigarettes. In Tianjin, gift boxes of Zhonghua cigarettes were sold in the market. Each box consisted of one sleeve of soft pack Zhonghua cigarettes, one hard-pack, one pack of 12 low-tar cigarettes and one pack of super-class Zhonghua cigarettes along with an ashtray and a lighter. The gift boxes looked elegant and delicately made and a lay person could not tell they were faked; however, the state-owned Zhonghua cigarette company had never offered this type of gift boxes (Xinhua Net 2008).

The Venues of Counterfeit Cigarette Production and Packing

There is a large and diverse set of venues used for the production of counterfeit cigarettes. These include legitimate factories producing other commodities, warehouses, farms in rural and semi-rural areas, martial arts training schools, temples and private homes. A number of illicit production facilities have also been discovered in underground chambers and in mountain caves. Investigative journalist Te-Ping Chen reports that in Yunxiao, factories are frequently hidden in dim, bricked-in facilities underground, accessible only via trapdoor and ladder, with turf masking the tobacco scent (Chen 2009; HM Treasury 2004).

The Sale of Counterfeit Cigarettes

Medium and large quantities of counterfeit cigarettes are sold in shopping centres, department stores, hotel-owned luxury shops and various legitimate small businesses such as groceries and kiosks. Most of these premises are licensed legitimate cigarette retailers that sell counterfeit cigarettes as well. For example, in a case in Fuzhou, a legitimate cigarette store displayed legal cigarettes on the shelves and counterfeit cigarettes (as well as smuggled foreign brands) were wholesaled (*Fuzhou Wanbao* 2002). There is also, as was mentioned earlier, a large (and increasing) number of floating street-sellers who trade counterfeit cigarettes outside nightclubs, discos, restaurants and other night-time-economy establishments or along the street and other public spaces. Although selling counterfeit cigarettes is a day-to-day routine business to sellers, and counterfeit cigarettes are sold at any time in virtually any public space to any interested customer, there are still preferable localities, venues, seasons and consumer groups that counterfeit cigarette sellers perceive to be ideal. Tourist spots are commonly chosen to sell counterfeit cigarettes, because local cigarette brands are part of the tourist-smokers' souvenir shopping in China. Tourists do not have knowledge of local brands and – with some exceptions – they cannot easily distinguish the counterfeit cigarettes from the genuine (Tobacco China Online 2006). Other places where a convergence of sellers and potential buyers is guaranteed, such as ports, coach and railway stations, or even on transportation means, are chosen by counterfeit cigarettes sellers. Counterfeit cigarettes are often sold in village marketplaces. These marketplaces meet the demand of villagers who have very little disposable income and cannot afford to buy quality, genuine cigarettes. Of great relevance here is the reluctance of legitimate cigarette sellers to trade in cheap legal cigarettes due to the small profit margin and the subsequent reduction or even cessation of production of cheap (or 'low class') cigarettes by authorised cigarette factories. Finally, counterfeit cigarettes are sold outside mainland China by mainland Chinese peddlers in Hong Kong, Macao and Taiwan (Lo 2009) and through global illicit distribution channels in North American, European, Australian, Asian and African markets (Chen 2009). According to an official from Yunxiao, 'the profit of selling counterfeit cigarettes abroad is 500 per cent whilst that of selling them in the internal market is only 200 per cent' (*Caijin* 2008). Interestingly, there seems to be an identification between countries that tend to be reported as receptive markets for counterfeit cigarettes and China's top trading partners – reluctance of customs to check merchandise and undermine commerce (Figure 4.2).

Counterfeiters have another incentive to export. Under China's Criminal Code, criminal liability is possible for sales of counterfeit goods in China, but it is debatable whether criminal liability exists for export of counterfeit goods. In addition, while counterfeiters do run the risk of law enforcement if they sell their illegal goods within China, there is much less risk if the counterfeiter ships the goods abroad. Where the goods have been shipped abroad, the

Figure 4.2. Export of counterfeit cigarettes

	Reports N=	1995	1996	1997	1998	1999	2000	2001	2002	2003	2004	2005	2006	2007	2008	2009
UK*	73					■	■	■	■	■	■	■	■	■	■	■
Canada	23									■	■	■	■	■		
Ireland	17				■						■	■		■	■	
USA*	17			■		■		■		■		■	■	■		
Hong Kong*	15			■	■					■		■	■			■
Philippines	14				■				■	■		■	■			
Australia*	13		■		■	■	■	■	■	■			■			■
Malaysia*	8						■			■			■	■		
Singapore*	8				■					■	■			■	■	

*Top trading partners.
Source: English-language media reports on counterfeiting and smuggling out of mainland China. Nine most mentioned countries (LexisNexis analysis).

boundaries of distance, different time zones and language make it difficult to trace the origin of the goods back to China or to discover the identity of the counterfeiter. Enforcement authorities within China usually have little interest in the harm or damage that is caused by counterfeit goods from China that are sold abroad.

Actors and Patterns of Cooperation in the Cigarette Counterfeiting Business in China

The cigarette counterfeiting business requires a degree of sophistication and management of resources and labour. Towards this end, counterfeiting networks tend to have a naturally defined horizontal 'structure'. In fact, there appear to be independent, autonomous 'entities' involved in production of counterfeit cigarettes and sale of the merchandise and a constellation of actors who are subcontracted, in a way, around those two particular stages of the counterfeit cigarette business. In many cases, and in contrast to other contexts, the structures involved in the *production* of counterfeit cigarettes are hierarchical and this is most probably a result of the fact that the production of counterfeit cigarettes involves someone who owns the (unauthorised) factory or workshop and workers who are employed *by* him. In essence, a counterfeit cigarette factory is almost identical to a legal cigarette factory. A number of individuals act as intermediaries who assist in the introduction of the merchandise into the market or who identify persons that can be subcontracted by the counterfeit cigarette producers and offer specialised services (e.g. packers, transporters, etc.). The presence of the intermediaries was evidenced in many of the sources consulted. Thus, once observers of the business move from one stage to the other, they realise that clearly defined structures and management systems along the *overall* counterfeit cigarette business do not exist. What merely exist are individuals or small groups forming temporary collaborations in order for their shared objective – making a profit – to materialise. Unfortunately, the available data cannot offer additional information as to how these collaborations emerge in the first instance.

What is also extremely important to note is that in many cases the production phase of the business is 'demand based'; counterfeit cigarette production is based upon an order. The persons who order the counterfeit cigarettes, however, should be viewed as the 'initiators' or the initial customers of the business rather than the 'organisers' of the process. There is a range of individuals from various socio-economic and geographic backgrounds who directly or indirectly engage in the cigarette counterfeiting business in various ways and play different roles in the counterfeiting process according to competencies and skills. Similar to other contexts (see, for instance, Antonopoulos 2008), not all actors are present in all counterfeiting schemes and one actor may assume more than one role. The different roles are as follows:

- *Tobacco farmers* – They provide the primary raw material for the business. They have an incentive to sell their product irrespective of whether the buyer is an illegal entrepreneur since, as was indicated earlier, there is a surplus of tobacco in China.
- *Unauthorised manufacturers* – They have the capital to invest, consider the counterfeiting of cigarettes a lucrative business and engage in running illegal cigarette manufacturing sites. Some of the unauthorised manufacturers are individuals from families with a tradition in small-scale cigarette making. For example, in Yunxiao, 'home cigarette making' has a tradition since the Qing Dynasty (1644–1912). It was virtually absent from 1949, when the People's Republic of China (PRC) was established, until the late 1970s when it re-emerged as a normal entrepreneurial activity. In terms of the quantities of counterfeit cigarette introduced to the market, unauthorised manufacturers are the equivalent of the wholesalers in the non-counterfeit illegal cigarette markets.
- *Intermediaries* – In those cases in which the production of counterfeit cigarettes is based upon demand, it is the intermediaries who link manufacturers and prospective customers, by collecting orders through their social networks and then placing the order with the manufacturer. Intermediaries also link

other participants in the business, such as manufacturer and transporters. Intermediaries may not be involved in the actual manufacture or sale of counterfeit cigarette, but are what Morselli and Giguere (2006) call 'critical actors'.

- *Specialised workers. Former workers of state-owned cigarette factories* – Many workers have been made redundant from the state-owned factories and have been employed by cigarette counterfeiting entrepreneurs, particularly in the southern regions of China such as Fujian, Guangdong and Guangxi provinces (*Caijin* 2008). In one of the cases we came across, all 30 workers in a counterfeit cigarette manufacturing site were former workers of state-owned cigarette factories in Hunan and Anhui provinces (*Guizhou Dushibao* 2002). These specialised workers, who are basically tobacco experts or 'recipe specialists', enjoy more benefits than simple workers because of their technical expertise, which is functional for the counterfeiting business. To seek long-term commitment to the illegal enterprise, cigarette manufacturers pay relatively high salaries to specialised workers (*Caijin* 2008).
- *Packaging producers* – Packing materials, such as boxes, cigarette packs, wrapping foil, plastic wrapping and other packing accessories are produced by individuals and small, legal businesses specialising in this part of the process. In some cases, authorised and unauthorised cigarette manufacturers are also the customers of the same packaging producers.
- *Trademark and barcode printers* – They make packaging trademarks, barcodes and even counter-counterfeiting fiscal marks available to counterfeiters. In September 2007 a printing workshop was found in Shantou city of Guangdong province, and several printing machines as well as 414,000 empty cigarette packs with printed trademarks were seized (*Shantou Ribao* 2007). These services are not necessarily provided only by professional printers; they can also be offered by individuals in their own houses. *Liaoshen Wanbao* (2002), for instance, reports the case of a 60-year-old woman specialising in spraying barcodes on Zhonghua and Xiaoxiongmao packs.
- *Non-specialised workers* – These are usually internal migrants – including children – from the countryside who are used as cheap labour for primarily menial tasks, such as cleaning the tobacco, carrying the merchandise from the factory to trucks or other means of transportation or even collecting cigarette butts and packs from rubbish bins and the street to be used for the manufacturing of counterfeit cigarettes. In many cases, these non-specialised workers are introduced to a 'short migration' system of work that has been adopted in the cigarette counterfeiting business. This basically entails the workers not being allowed to leave the workshop until the end of their 'contract', working double shifts in operations that run 24 hours a day and not being allowed to use mobile phones (e.g. *Changjiang Yancaobao* 2002).

Caijin (2008) reports that a large-scale Yunxiao counterfeit cigarette site was built underground. All workers were taken from the train station to the site in a closed container so that they would not be aware of the exact location of the site. A person was assigned to shop for necessities for the workers, who would be transported to the train station in the closed container after the termination of their 'contract'.

- *Warehousemen/storage providers* – Warehouses and other legitimate storage services are used by counterfeiters for storing the merchandise. Some unusual premises have been reported. For example, in one of the cases we came across, a pigsty was used to store counterfeit cigarettes. The front of the pigsty was occupied by pigs and at the back, underneath the pile of pig food, the counterfeit cigarettes were hidden, while two watchdogs guarded the premises (*Sichuan Ribao* 2002).
- *Security guards* – To avoid detection of the manufacturing sites, individuals are employed to carry out physical surveillance. In a case in Yunxiao, security guards were hired to be present at each junction of the country road leading to the manufacturing site. These security guards were equipped with walkie-talkies to report any suspicious activities (*Caijin* 2008). In another case in Inner Mongolia, cameras were installed above an underground cigarette factory and individuals were hired for the control room (Xinhua Net 2005).
- *Transporters* – Transporters play a crucial role in the cigarette counterfeiting business from the moment the merchandise leaves the manufacturing site. The ways of transportation for counterfeit cigarettes vary. Locally, counterfeit cigarettes are transported by vans, cars and motorbikes. In Nannin (Guangxi province), a man transported 50 sleeves of Santa cigarettes on his motorbike (*Nanguo Zaobao* 2002). Nationally, legitimate transport companies, logistic centres and individual (professional or non-professional) lorry drivers are hired by counterfeiters, although sometimes the transporters are not aware of the illegal merchandise. In some cases, transportation companies are set up specifically for the purpose of delivering counterfeit cigarettes. Merchandise is often concealed among other commodities. In Wenzhou (Zhejiang province), for instance, 298 units of counterfeit cigarettes were disguised as boxes of insoles (*Wenzhou Dushibao* 2002). Counterfeit cigarettes are also delivered by air through air-cargo companies. In Guangzhou, there were more than ten air-cargo agencies around the airport, of which eight answered that they would have no problem delivering counterfeit cigarettes when a fake request was made by a journalist (*Nanfang Ribao* 2009). Quantities of counterfeit cigarettes are also transported to markets abroad, usually by ship, from important commercial hubs in the east and south of the country, such as Shenzhen and Shanghai (*Caijin* 2008).

- *Sellers* – There are two types of counterfeit cigarette sellers. The first type is the *street-seller*. In most cases, street-sellers, particularly in urban centres, are internal migrants from the countryside and unemployed city residents. Some of them work as sellers of counterfeit cigarettes parallel to their legitimate (or in some cases, illegitimate) job. In one of the cases we came across, a seller used to work simultaneously as a street shoe repairer. It is also very common for females to be involved in the street sale of counterfeit cigarettes. Increasingly, large numbers of street-sellers act as 'entrepreneurs' by depositing a small amount to purchase a number of counterfeit cigarette packs or sleeves. The second type is the *seller operating in legitimate enterprises* and with larger quantities. For example, in Fuzhou (Fujian province), a grocery had a permit to trade in tobacco products. However, along with trading in legitimate cigarettes, the owners of the business were also distributing counterfeit cigarettes (*Fuzhou Wanbao* 2002).
- *Lookouts* – The role of lookouts has been identified in the cigarette black markets of other countries (Antonopoulos 2008; von Lampe 2003). Lookouts 'patrol' the area of street selling and warn the sellers about the presence of uniformed law enforcement agents as well as journalists and TV crews.
- *Corrupt public officials* – Having power, information and powerful social networks, public officials can be actively or passively involved in the cigarette counterfeiting business.

Counterfeit Cigarettes Business and Corruption

There are basically three forms of corruption of Chinese public officials which relate to the cigarette counterfeiting business:

Active engagement – This is the extreme form of corruption in cigarette counterfeiting in which public officials take advantage of their power due to their position, specialised knowledge and social networks to establish cigarette counterfeiting manufacturing sites. In an Inner Mongolia (Neimenggu) case, the four owners of a counterfeit cigarette manufacturing site were officials of the local Bureau of Industry and Commerce. One of them was also the former head of the Market Unit in the Fengyuan Bureau of Industry and Commerce (Xinhua Net 2005).

Protective umbrella – Public officials may play a role of a 'protective umbrella' (*baohusan*) for cigarette counterfeiters. For various reasons, corrupt officials protect cigarette counterfeiters and intervene in case cigarette counterfeiters are arrested. This protective umbrella allows for the termination of the illegal business to be extremely short-term and the business is virtually uninterrupted, irrespective of the number of detections. As an officer employed in the Shanxi tobacco management authority confessed to a *Shichang Bao* newspaper journalist:

> There are several illegal cigarette traders in every city of our province, and they all have close relationship with the officials… The dealers and officials have an alliance and they share the illicit profits. Counterfeit cigarette dealers control the counterfeit cigarette markets in Taiyuan and the peripheral cities. When things go wrong, someone would come out and exculpate the illicit dealers from trouble. (*Shichang Bao* 2006)

In another case involving the large-scale production of counterfeit cigarettes, an individual reported the details of a manufacturing site to the local law enforcement agency and obtained his reward. After months, the counterfeit cigarette manufacturer was still in business (*Caijin* 2008).

Turning a blind eye – Public officials may not be directly engaged in cigarette counterfeiting or in providing a protective umbrella to participants in the counterfeit cigarette business; however, some of them may ignore the activities of cigarette counterfeiters in exchange for financial rewards. In some cases, a financial reward may not even need to be available, and this appears to be the case in relatively small, primarily rural and semi-rural localities in which there are pre-existing social relationships between counterfeiters and public officials.

In this context, it should be noted that provincial governments in China are being treated as enterprises by the central government in terms of economic performance and success (see Chen 2002). Since cigarette counterfeiting through the use of locally grown raw tobacco is a source of revenue for the provincial government and provides employment for many individuals, *local* governments seem to be reluctant to crack down on counterfeiting businesses, especially when the unauthorised production relates to international brands (e.g. Marlboro, Benson & Hedges) or brands that are not produced in the particular province and therefore does not cause conflict of interests with local authorised manufacturers (Yao 2006; White 1996). In French's (2007) words 'it is the froth in the economy that [counterfeiting] creates that counts most, not niceties like intellectual property or fussy product safety details'. It should be noted, however, that corruption was not present in all cigarette counterfeiting cases we came across and thus, similar to other contexts, it is *not* necessarily to be considered as an essential feature of the counterfeiting business. It is also important to acknowledge that the Chinese government, partly to protect its own brands, partly in compliance with international obligations and aided by tobacco corporations, has undertaken increasing efforts to crack down on cigarette counterfeiting, thereby creating a more hostile environment for cigarette counterfeiters and their facilitators (Hu et al. 2008; Levin 2003).

Discussion and Conclusion

The counterfeit cigarette business highlights 'the enormous symbolic presence that images of organised crime have in popular discourse' (Sheptycki 2008, 23). Our study suggests that unlike popular representations, cigarette counterfeiting in China, just as with illegal tobacco-related activities in other contexts, is characterised by a high degree of heterogeneity and a range of organising the business (see van Duyne 2003; von Lampe 2003 and 2005; Antonopoulos 2008). There appear to be independent 'entities' involved in different parts of the business and actors who are subcontracted to provide commodities and services about the process in the context of what is essentially an open market with a very low threshold for market entry. At the same time, it is a market with intensifying competition that prompts retailers to improve competitiveness through selling counterfeit and contraband cigarettes. The fragmented nature of the counterfeit business is also facilitated by the Chinese cultural characteristic that permeates entrepreneurship – the desire to be one's own boss (see Liao and Sohmen 2001, 29). There is a relatively high level of sophistication in the business which does not, however, refer to the links between actors or stages of the business, but to the technical sophistication necessary for the production of counterfeit cigarettes. Relationships between actors in the business are very often based on a customer–supplier relationship or a 'business-to-business market', which is a very common characteristic of the Chinese (legal and illegal) economy (see Simons 2009). A large number of individuals are involved in illegal tobacco-related activities simply because this offers them an entrepreneurial opportunity in a relatively low-risk environment and in the absence of state welfare provisions that address the income inequalities and economic exclusion facing, particularly, internal migrants (see Wing Lo and Jiang 2006).

The role of corruption and violence in the cigarette counterfeiting business is not to be underestimated. Corruption, although not mentioned in all counterfeiting cases we encountered, seems to be at least a facilitating factor of a large part of the business. In addition, although violence could attract the unnecessary attention of law enforcement, it is nevertheless more prevalent in the counterfeit cigarette market in China than in other contexts. This perhaps highlights the fact that the American and European experience of illegal markets may not be entirely compatible with the extremely diverse

Chinese context. It also highlights the dynamism of illegal markets in this particular country and calls for additional, preferably empirical, research in this 'exemplary society' (Bakken 2000).

We mentioned earlier that the illegal cigarette business in general and counterfeiting in particular emerged as a problem in China in the late 1970s and early 1980s when the 'open door' policy and economic reforms made profit and economic development a national movement (*quanming jingshang*) (Liu 2005, 619). The economic reforms facilitated the emergence of cigarette counterfeiting in a variety of ways. Firstly, it introduced a new ethos of entrepreneurship. Deng Xiaoping's saying, 'Be the cat white or be the cat black, it is the clever cat that will catch the mouse', is indicative of the mentality emphasising success regardless of the approach. The increasing political emphasis on market forces has promoted a blurring of the legal and the illegal sectors. Secondly, there was the paradox of the private sector becoming increasingly dynamic while at the same time, the tobacco industry continued to remain a state monopoly. It proved extremely difficult for private entrepreneurs to become involved in the huge and highly lucrative Chinese market, and the smuggling and counterfeiting of cigarettes provided the only alternative avenues to market entry. Thirdly, the transition to a market economy and the subsequent restructuring of the tobacco industry led to the *technical* facilitation of the cigarette counterfeiting business by setting free two important types of resources: skilled workers and production machinery. Simultaneously, the reluctance of licensed cigarette sellers to trade in cheap legal cigarettes due to the small profit margin and the subsequent reduction or even cessation of production of cheap cigarettes by local authorised factories, despite the demand for cheap cigarettes, created a niche in the market that was filled by counterfeiters. It seems that in the case of counterfeit cigarettes, authorised manufacturers and the state have been 'victims' of their profit-oriented mentality. Fourthly, the trade liberalisation that has been an important pillar of the economic reforms not only allowed for an increased volume of legitimate trade, but also created a façade for illegitimate trade (Andreas 1999), of which counterfeit cigarettes are an important aspect.

However, it is not only the opening of the Chinese market and economy to the rest of the world that has facilitated the booming of the cigarette counterfeiting business; it is also the other way around. The most populated country of the world has an annual development rate of approximately 10 per cent, which is four times higher than the average development rate of developed world economies. This development is 'fed' to a great extent by the country's cheap labour, which along with the governmentally maintained low exchange rate for the Chinese currency, directly or indirectly supports the export of Chinese products. Counterfeit cigarettes, like other licit and illicit commodities, fall within the category of cheap exported goods. However, counterfeit cigarettes are also an indication of the importance of tobacco for China and of the commodity's surplus. The counterfeit cigarette business has informalised the process of manufacturing cigarettes to an extent that a comparative advantage has been created for unauthorised manufacturers over authorised Chinese and international manufacturers (see Castells and Portes 1989).

The way in which the *legal* and the *illegal* intersect is also evident in the Chinese counterfeit cigarette business. Cigarette counterfeiters benefit from the legal sector and some legal businesses also benefit from cigarette counterfeiters in various ways. The case of the air-cargo companies mentioned earlier is just one striking example of this symbiosis. When it comes to the links between China as the counterfeit cigarette *source* country and (primarily) Western markets, the role of the Western states as the ultimate 'market determiners' (van Duyne 2007) by imposing prohibitive taxes on cigarettes – a socially and culturally embedded commodity – has to be highlighted. High taxation imposed by governments has contributed to an environment of demand for cheap cigarettes, which has been exploited by entrepreneurs capitalising on huge price differentials and 'global market ambiguities' (Hornsby and Hobbs 2007, 565). Thus, in both a Mertonian and Schumpeterian sense, cigarette counterfeiting emerged, developed and consolidated through the exploitation of new commercial networks and economic opportunities and the rearrangement of productive processes and organisation. Overall cigarette counterfeiting in China and by extension, the rest of the world, appears to be an integral part of the neoliberal marketplace jigsaw in the country (and beyond), and a result of an uneasy symbiosis between state planning, local government competition emphasising profit, personal greed, aspirations and needs, as well as market dynamics that are exacerbated by the forces of globalisation.

Note

1 This chapter is an updated and revised version of an article that was published in the *British Journal of Criminology* 50 (2).

References

Andreas, P. 1999. 'When Policies Collide: Market Reform, Market Prohibition, and the Narcotisation of the Mexican Economy'. In *The Illicit Global Economy & State Power*, edited by H. R. Friman and P. Andreas, 125–41. Lanham, MD: Rowman and Littlefield.

Antonopoulos, G. A. 2008. 'The Greek Connection(s): The Social Organisation of the Cigarette Smuggling Business in Greece'. *European Journal of Criminology* 5 (3): 263–88.

Bakken, B. 2000. *The Exemplary Society: Human Improvement, Social Control and the Dangers of Modernity in China*. Oxford: Oxford University Press.

————. 2005. *Crime, Punishment and Policing in China*. Lanham, MD: Rowman and Littlefield.

Blecher, E. and C. van Walbeek. 2008. 'An Analysis of Cigarette Affordability'. Paris: International Union Against Tuberculosis and Lung Disease.

————. 2009. 'Cigarette Affordability Trends'. *Tobacco Control* 18: 167–75.

Brewer, J. D., A. Guelke, I. Hume, E. Moxon-Browne and R. Wilford. 1996. *The Police, Public Order and the State*, 2nd ed. London: Macmillan.

Caijin. 2008. 'Report'. *Caijin*, 18 December. Available at http://news.fznews.com.cn/sdbd/2008-12-18/2008121871L-0N6bXW171443.shtml (accessed 22 June 2009).

Castells, M. and A. Portes. 1989. 'World Underneath: The Origins, Dynamics and the Effect of the Informal Economy'. In *The Informal Economy: Studies in Advanced and Less Developed Countries*, edited by A. Portes, M. Castells and L. A. Benton, 11–37. London: Johns Hopkins University Press.

Changjiang Yancaobao. 2002. 'Chongqing Attacked a Blockhouse Cigarette Counterfeiting Factory'. *Changjiang Yancaobao*, 6 June. Available at http://news.tobaccochina.com/news/data/20026/606102214.htm (accessed 1 June 2009).

Chen, T.-P. 2009. 'China's Marlboro Country'. *Slate*. Available at http://www.slate.com (accessed 17 July 2009).

Chen, Y. 2002. 'From Monopoly to Consolidation'. *China International Business*, 26–8 October.

Chen, Z. 2008. 'Gansu Detected an Extremely Large-Scale Cigarette Counterfeiting Case'. Ministry of Public Security of the People's Republic of China. Available at http://www.mps.gov.cn/n16/n1252/n1642/n1987/899791.html (accessed 22 June 2009).

China Daily. 2004. 'Fake cigarette makers closed: 20 detained'. *China Daily*, 24 December. Available at http://www.chinadaily.com.cn/english/doc/2004-12/24/content_402846.htm (accessed 25 July 2008).

China Newsagent. 2002. 'Beijing Detected a Large Scale Zhonghua Cigarette Counterfeiting Site'. *China Newsagent*, 10 September. Available at http://news.tobaccochina.com/news/data/20027/702100416.htm (accessed 1 June 2009).

China Tobacco Market. 2009. 'Reviewing 2008 National High Profile Cigarette Counterfeiting Cases'. *China Tobacco Market*, 17 March. Available at http://www.etmoc.com/look/looklist.asp?id=18153 (accessed 22 July 2009).

Chongqing Chenbao. 2002. 'A Large-Scale Counterfeiting Case Detected in Chongqing Involving Counterfeit Cigarettes Worth 1.8 Million Yuan'. *Chongqing Chenbao*, 2 July. Available at http://news.tobaccochina.com/news/data/20029/910095812.htm (accessed 1 June 2009).

Chongqing Wanbao. 2002. 'Rotten Vegetable Leaves Disguised as Zhonghua Cigarettes in Chongqing'. *Chongqing Wanbao*, 10 July. Available at http://www.tobaccochina.com/news/data/20027/710101735.htm (accessed 23 June 2009).

Chow, D. C. K. 2003. 'Organized Crime, Local Protectionism, and the Trade in Counterfeit Goods in China'. *China Economic Review* 14: 473–84.

Davies, M. and A. Shen. 2009. 'Questioning Suspected Offenders: The Investigative Interviewing Process in the People's Republic of China'. Unpublished document.

Dongya Jinmao News. 2008. 'A Cigarette Counterfeiting Case Involving More Than 1 Billion Was Detected in Siping'. *Dongya Jinmao News*, 29 December. Available at http://news.sohu.com/20081229/n261467092.shtml (accessed 2 June 2009).

Euromonitor International. 2008. *Tobacco in China*. Available at http://www.euromonitor.com/Tobacco_in_China (accessed 15 May 2009).

French, H. W. 2007. 'China's Economic Revival is Minted in Counterfeit'. *New York Times*, 3 August. Available at http://www.nytimes.com/2007/08/03/world/asia/03iht-letter.1.6970880.html (accessed 16 July 2009).

Fuzhou News Net. 2005. 'They Are Living in the Dark'. Fuzhou News Net, 10 October. Available at http://dsb.gd.gov.cn/ruizheng/Article/ShowArticle.asp?ArticleID=3190 (accessed 4 July 2009).

Fuzhou Wanbao. 2002. 'Fuzhou Detected a Large-Scale Illicit Cigarette Trading Case'. *Fuzhou Wanbao*, 26 September. Available at http://news.tobaccochina.com/news/data/20029/926103830 (accessed 1 June 2009).

Guizhou Dushibao. 2002. 'Nayong, Guizhou, Cracked Down an Illegitimate Cigarette Factory Involving the Daily Production of 5,000 Sleeves'. *Guizhou Dushibao*, 4 February. Available at http://news.tobaccochina.com/data/20022/204092818.htm (accessed 1 June 2009).

Heimer, M. and S. Thogersen (eds). 2006. *Doing Field Work in China*. Copenhagen: NIAS Press.

HM Treasury. 2004. *Counterfeit Cigarettes*. London: HM Treasury.

Hornsby, R. and D. Hobbs. 2007. 'Zones of Ambiguity: The Political Economy of Cigarette Bootlegging'. *British Journal of Criminology* 47: 551–71.

Hu, T.-W. and Z. Mao. 2002. *Economic Analysis of Tobacco and Options for Tobacco Control: China Case Study*. Washington, DC: The World Bank.

Hu, T.-W., Z. Mao, H. Jiang, M. Tao and A. Yurekli. 2007. 'The Role of Government in Tobacco Leaf Production in China: National and Local Interventions'. *International Journal of Public Policy* 2 (3–4): 235–48.

Hu, T.-W., Z. Mao, J. Shi and W. Chen. 2008. 'Tobacco Taxation and Its Potential Impact in China'. Available at http://www.worldlungfoundation.org/downloads/Taxation_English.pdf (accessed 4 September 2009).

Hu, T.-W., Z. Mao, Y. Liu, J. de Beyer and M. Ong. 2005. 'Smoking, Standard of Living, and Poverty in China'. *Tobacco Control* 14: 247–50.

Jiang, Chengkang. 2009. *The China Tobacco Exclusive Sale Bureau Annual Report 2009*. Available at http://www.eastobacco.com/ReadNews.asp?NewsID=73408 (accessed 22 June 2009).

Jianghuai Chenbao. 2002. 'Hefei Found More Than 300 Sleeves of Smuggled and Counterfeit Cigarettes in a Small Private-Owned Shop'. *Jianghuai Chenbao*, 17 May. Available at http://news.tobaccochina.com/data/20025/517102137.htm (accessed 1 June 2009).

Joossens, L. 1999. *Smuggling and Cross-Border Shopping of Tobacco Products in the European Union: A Report for the Health Education Authority*. London: Health Education Authority.

Joossens, L., D. Merriman, H. Ross and M. Raw. 2009. 'How Eliminating the Global Illicit Cigarette Trade Would Increase Tax Revenue and Save Lives'. Available at http://www.fctc.org/dmdocuments/INB3_report_illicit_trade_save_revenue_lives.pdf (accessed 30 August 2009).

Klein, M. W. and M. Gatz. 1989. 'Professing the Uncertain: Problems of Lecturing on Chinese Social Control'. In *Social Control in the People's Republic of China*, edited by R. J. Troyer, J. P. Clark and D. G. Rojek, 169–87. New York: Praeger.

Lee, K. and J. Collin. 2006. '"Key to the Future": British American Tobacco and Cigarette Smuggling in China'. *PLoS Medicine* 3: 1080–89.

Levin, M. 2003. 'Counterfeit Cigarettes Force Tobacco Firms to Fight Back'. *Los Angeles Times*, 24 November.

Liao, A. 1999. 'China: Why the Crackdown on Smuggling is Working this Time'. *Tobacco Asia*. Available at http://www.tobaccoasia.com/archive/9902/current/features/fe1.htm (accessed 31 May 2009).

Liao, D. and P. Sohmen (2001), 'The development of modern entrepreneurship in China'. *Stanford Journal of East Asian Affairs* 1: 27–33.

Liaoshen Wanbao. 2002. 'Lady in Her Sixties Arrested for Illegally Printing More Than 4,000 Cigarette Barcodes'. *Liaoshen Wanbao*, 1 November. Available at http://news.tobaccochina.com/news/data/200211/01091230.htm (accessed 1 June 2009).

Liu, J. 2005. 'Crime Patterns during the Market Transition in China'. *British Journal of Criminology* 45: 613–33.

————. 2008. 'Data Sources in Chinese Crime and Criminal Justice Research'. *Crime, Law and Social Change* 50: 131–47.

————. 2009. 'Asian Criminology – Challenges, Opportunities and Directions'. *Asian Journal of Criminology* 4: 1–9.

Lo, S. S.-H. 2009. *The Politics of Cross-Border Crime in Greater China: Case Studies of Mainland China, Hong Kong, and Macao.* Armonk, NY: M. E. Sharpe.

McKay, J. 1992. 'China's Tobacco Wars'. Available at http://multinationalmonitor.org/hyper/issues/1992/01/mm0192_06.html (accessed 15 May 2009).

Morselli, C. and C. Giguere. 2006. 'Legitimate Strengths in Criminal Networks'. *Crime, Law and Social Change* 46: 185–200.

Nanfang Ribao. 2009. 'Wuxianqiao, Guangdong Cigarette Counterfeiting Making More Profits than Drug Trafficking'. *Nanfang Ribao*, 26 April. Available at http://news.dayoo.com/guangzhou/200904/27/53872_5785011_4.htm (accessed 1 June 2009).

Nanguo Zaobao. 2002. '50 Sleeves of Illegal Cigarettes Found on a Motorbike'. *Nanguo Zaobao*, 2 September. Available at http://news.tobaccochina.com/data/20029/902101206.htm (accessed 1 June 2009).

NTESB. 2003. 'Annual report 2002'. Available at http://www.eastobacco.com/ReadNews.asp?NewsID=15827 (accessed 21 June 2009).

————. 2004. 'Annual report 2003'. Available at http://www.eastobacco.com/ReadNews.asp?NewsID=24908 (accessed 21 June 2009).

————. 2005. 'Annual report 2004'. Available at http://www.eastobacco.com/ReadNews.asp?NewsID=34840 (accessed 21 June 2009).

————. 2006. 'Annual report 2005'. Available at http://www.eastobacco.com/ReadNews.asp?NewsID=43439 (accessed 21 June 2009).

————. 2007. 'Annual report 2006'. Available at http://www.eastobacco.com/ReadNews.asp?NewsID=52352 (accessed 21 June 2009).

————. 2008. 'Annual report 2007'. Available at http://www.eastobacco.com/ReadNews.asp?NewsID=62437 (accessed 21 June 2009).

Onder, Z. 2002. *The Economics of Tobacco in Turkey: New Evidence and Demand Estimates.* Washington, DC: The International Bank for Reconstruction and Development/The World Bank.

Pappas, R. S., G. M. Polzin, C. H. Watson and D. L. Ashley. 2007. 'Cadmium, Lead, and Thallium in Smoke Particulate from Counterfeit Cigarettes Compared to Authentic US Brands'. *Food and Chemical Toxicology* 45: 202–9.

Pearson, G. and D. Hobbs. 2001. *Middle-Market Drug Distribution.* HORS 227. London: Home Office.

Philip Morris. 2004. *The Illicit Trade in Cigarettes: The PM International Perspective – February 2004.* Available at http://www.philipmorrisinternational.com/pmintl/pages/eng/stories/f002_i_trade.asp (accessed 28 May 2009).

Shantou Ribao. 2007. 'Shantou Carrying Out Specialised Operations against the Printing of Counterfeit Cigarette Trademarks'. *Shantou Ribao,* 3 September. Available at http://news.pack.net.cn (accessed 1 June 2009).

Sheptycki, J. 2008. 'Transnationalisation, Orientalism and Crime'. *Asian Journal of Criminology* 3: 13–35.

Shichang Bao. 2006. 'Sanxi Market is Full of Counterfeiting Cigarettes'. *Shichang Bao,* 17 April. Available at http://news.xinhuanet.com/fortune/2006-04/17/content_4432350_1.htm (accessed 13 May 2009).

Sichuan Ribao. 2002. 'Illicit Cigarettes Were Hidden in the Pigsty'. *Sichuan Ribao,* 7 November. Available at http://news.tobaccochina.com/data/200211/07092715.htm (accessed 1 June 2009).

Shangbao. 2002. 'Changsha Detected an Extremely Large Scale Cigarette Counterfeiting Case'. *Shangbao,* 21 August. Available at http://news.tobaccochina.com/data/20028/821100118.htm (accessed 1 June 2009).

Shidai Shangbao. 2002. 'Shenyang Detected a Counterfeiting Cigarette Manufacturing Case Involving the Use of Waste Materials'. *Shidai Shangbao,* 29 September. Available at http://news.tobaccochina.com/data/20029/929102531.htm (accessed 1 June 2009).

Simons, C. 2009. 'Generic Giants'. *Newsweek,* 27 July, 32–5.

SOCA. 2009. *The UK Threat Assessment of Organised Crime, 2009/1010.* London: SOCA.

Tobacco China Online. 2006. 'Helongjiang Detected the Largest Cigarette Counterfeiting Case Since the Establishment of the PRC'. Tobacco China Online, 6 February. Available at http://so.16888.com.cn/snapshot/20060206162146120.html (accessed 3 July 2009).

———. 2008. 'Shangqiu, Henan Detected an Extremely Large-Scale Cigarette Counterfeit Network'. Tobacco China Online, 6 March. Available at http://www.tobaccochina.com/news/China/monopoly/20083/2009163111_340139.shtml (accessed 2 July 2009).

Tobacco Free Centre. 2009. 'Tobacco Burden Facts-China'. Available at http://tobaccofreecentre.org (accessed 15 May 2009).

Tomson, D. and A. Coulter. 1987. 'The Bamboo Smoke Screen: Tobacco Smoking in China'. *Health Promotion* 2 (2): 95–108.

van Duyne, P. C. 2003. 'Organising Cigarette Smuggling and Policy Making, Ending Up in Smoke'. *Crime, Law and Social Change* 39: 285–317.

———. 2007. 'The Upperworld Side of Illicit Trafficking'. *Crime & Justice International,* November/December, 46–47.

von Lampe, K. 2003. 'Organising the Nicotine Racket: Patterns of Cooperation in the Cigarette Black Market in Germany'. In *Criminal Finances and Organising Crime in Europe,* edited by P. C. van Duyne, K. von Lampe and J. L. Newell, 41–66. Nijmegen: Wolf Legal Publishers.

———. 2004. 'Making the Second Step Before the Step: Assessing Organised Crime – The Case of Germany'. *Crime, Law and Social Change* 42: 227–59.

———. 2006. 'The cigarette black market in Germany and in the United Kingdom'. *Journal of Financial Crime* 13 : 235–54.

Wang, H. 2006. 'Tobacco Control of China: The Dilemma Between Economic Development and Health Improvement'. *Salud Publica De Mexico* 48 (1): S140–S147.

Wang, J. 2009. 'Global-market building as state building: China's entry into the WTO and market reforms of China's tobacco industry'. *Theory and Society* 38 (2): 165–94.

Wenzhou Dushibao. 2002. 'Wenzhou Intercepted 60,000 Sleeves Contraband Cigarettes Within Three Days'. *Wenzhou Dushibao,* 1 August. Available at http://news.tobaccochina.com/news/data/20028/801103638/htm (accessed 1 June 2009).

White, G. 1996. 'Corruption and Market Reform in China'. *IDS Bulletin* 27 (2): 40–47.

Wing Lo. T. and G. Jiang. 2006. 'Inequality, Crime and the Floating Population in China'. *Asian Journal of Criminology* 1: 103–18.

World Bank. n.d. 'China – The Economics of Tobacco in Brief'. Available at http://www1. worldbank.org/tobacco/pdf/country%20briefs/China.pdf (accessed 25 May 2009).

Xingxi Shibao. 2009. 'Security Guards of a Cigarette Trader Beat to Death a Consumer Who Wanted to Return the Counterfeit Cigarettes'. *Xingxi Shibao*, 26 April. Available at http://news.xinmin.cn/rollnews/2009/04/26/1874431.html (accessed 23 June 2009).

Xinhua Net. 2005. 'Inner Mongolia Detected a Cigarette Counterfeiting Case Involving Industry and Commerce Bureau Officials'. Xinhua Net, 30 August. Available at http:// news.xinhuanet.com/legal/2005-08/30/content_3421650/htm (accessed 1 June 2009).

————. 2008. 'Tianjin Detected an Extremely Large Cigarette Counterfeiting Network'. Xinhua Net, 21 November. Available at http://chinacourt.org/html/ article/200811/21/331812.shtml (accessed 11 June 2009).

Yao, V. W. 2006. 'An Economic Analysis of Counterfeit Goods: The Case of China'. *Journal of the Washington Institute of China Studies* 1 (1): 116–24.

Zhang, H. 2008. Speech at the National Tobacco Exclusive Sale Bureau Counter Cigarette Counterfeiting Conference 2008. Available at http://www.tobacco.gov.cn/ html/54/779364_n.html (accessed 22 June 2009).

Zhong, L. Y. 2009. *Communities, Crime and Social Capital in Contemporary China*. Cullompton: Devon.

Chapter 5

A NEOLIBERAL SECURITY COMPLEX?

Georgios Papanicolaou

Introduction

The global onslaught since the late 1970s of policies obsessed with levelling
obstacles to free markets, the privatisation of public services and entire sectors
of the economy, the marketisation of public goods and the deregulation
particularly of the labour market, in short, neoliberalism as economic dogma
and policy recipe is today regularly associated with developments in criminal
justice, particularly with what many critical scholars today identify as a decisive
punitive turn in penal policy (e.g. Garland 2001; Simon 2007; Wacquant
2001, 2009b; Young 1999). It is less certain whether the study of policing
makes this association with the same intensity. It is true that the dominance
of neoliberalism and the social and political restructuring it brings about is
present in considerations of changes in the role, organisation and operations
of the police. However, the particular paths that the sociology of the police has
taken seem to be preventing a systematic unravelling of the relation between
neoliberalism and change in policing. On one hand, there is a clear trend to
take a wider approach to the questions of policing and security (Johnston and
Shearing 2003; Loader and Walker 2007), one that draws its ancestry from
an earlier bold change of focus away from the workings of the public police
to a wider institutional assemblage of public and private actors involved in
the provision of security (Shearing and Stenning 1981, 1983). On the other,
investigations of the public police, when they do not fall squarely into an
administrative sociology of the police concerned with strictly operational and
organisational questions (for a critique see Manning 2005), often pose the
question of change in policing in light of the more volatile social and political
environment in which the public police must operate (Bayley and Shearing
1996; Leishman, Loveday and Savage 2000; McLaughlin 2007; Reiner 1992;
Smith and Henry 2007).

There is no doubt that the question of neoliberalism is implicit in analyses of either type. A new division of labour between public and private actors in the provision of security is consonant with the new modalities of social discipline instilled by neoliberalism. This is, after all, one of the reasons why public policing must respond to the exigencies of the new social landscape forged by the unbridled rule of markets, and accounts for the more prescriptive political environment that neoliberalism enforces within the state. Something important, however, is left out. Neoliberalism has not been an inescapable development which occurred in history according to the dictates of a natural law, as it were. Rather, it has a specific content – indeed, class content – as it constitutes a strategy aiming to attack and remove particular economic and social conditions adverse to capital accumulation. Equally, particular people, ideas, power centres and even particular powerful states have been involved in developing it into a recognisable social and political programme. Its ascendancy has been secured not by abstract social forces, but rather through established and specific means, not least, state actions and policies. What the sociology of policing fails seriously to take into account is that if neoliberalism has been 'a political project to re-establish the conditions for capital accumulation and to restore the power of economic elites' (Harvey 2007, 19; see also Duménil and Lévy 2004), then its blatant success has inextricably involved the state and its apparatuses, including the police. At the same time, the successful implementation itself has created a need to adjust and develop these initial tools into a form which can contribute to further success. The increasing involvement and intervention of the government in police management and policy direction, the growth of managerialism, the formulation of priorities and goals by centres external to the police organisation, the adoption of new methods, technologies and tactics, and even the hollowing out of its remit in favour of private providers of security are but instances of this process. More often than not, contemporary police sociology sets itself to the task of examining this partial aspect of the transformation of policing, whereas in reality, the problem is more widely the neoliberal form of the capitalist state itself (Wacquant 2009a).

The purpose of this chapter is to draw some broad analytical lines by which developments in policing can be related to the neoliberal state from within a more consciously historical materialist approach. The general idea advanced here is that seeking more boldly the connections between ideas in Marxist state theory and the conceptual armoury which radical criminology crafted in the early days of capitalist crisis and restructuring (Platt and Cooper 1974; Quinney 1977; CRCJ 1977), and which to a certain extent still uses today (e.g. Mariani 2011; Parenti 2008; Weiss 2007), is a rewarding enterprise, potentially offering a better elucidation of contemporary policing. A brief discussion in the first section is due on how the question of the state appears in mainstream police sociology before moving on to the second section, a discussion of the relevance of the concept of authoritarian statism (Poulantzas 2000) as a framework for understanding the wider trajectory of policing under neoliberalism. The third section stops to take a look on four major incidents that have shaped the public image of policing in Britain. This discussion is then taken forward to make a case for a renewed radical research agenda on policing reflecting more directly the wider structural role of the neoliberal state.

A Few Remarks on the Question of the State in Police Sociology

The reasons why police sociology shuns the question of the state can be traced quite clearly to its theoretical coordinates. Firstly, the vibrant stream of literature which situates public policing within the wider institutional assemblage of social control and is particularly credited with the interrogation of private policing (Jones and Newburn 2002; Kempa, Carrier, Wood and Shearing 1999; Rigakos 2002; Shearing and Stenning 1981, 1983), builds on a theoretical framework and an imagery within which the state, as an instrument of control, regulation and surveillance, itself occupies a significantly less prominent position. Theorists in this vein mobilise a vocabulary and conceptual apparatus derived from the work of Foucault (Burchell, Gordon and Miller 1991; Rose and Miller 1992) and reinforced by conceptions of a postmodern social world in which modern institutional forms, including the (nation-) state and its (public) police, are essentially disaggregated; neoliberalism itself is seen as a constitutive force of such developments (O'Malley 1997). But beyond the powerful imagery that drives this mode of inquiry into strategies and mechanisms of rule in advanced liberalism, it is questionable whether the unbridled rise of private authority, the 'hollowing out' of the state and 'governance' as an institutional form of political rule have not been developments sanctioned by a state which has been fully co-opted to neoliberal strategies. It is one thing to speak of a growth of private policing at the expense of public policing building on a juridical concept of the state and of the public/private distinction. It is quite another to speak of a weakening of state power when in fact, the promulgation, implementation and enforcement of neoliberal policies has, since the late 1970s, been the key job of the state in advanced capitalist countries and, progressively, across the globe.

The situation is different within analyses of a second type, where a conceptual relative separation of the police organisation from its social and political environment gives rise to an analytical strategy seeing the police as a recipient of challenges to be addressed in the interest of 'law and order'. Thus, an analysis of the modes and implications of organisational and operational adjustments in policing is made possible without ever genuinely needing to question the coordinates of this change within the wider institutional arrangements, that is, the form of state that neoliberalism has been forging with its ascendance. This approach, when it does not simply accept environmental change as a fact of life to be managed somehow, often conveys the sense that it instead constitutes an aberration from a desirable state of separation of the police not only from the political arena, but also from the circuits of economic activity as well as the wider ideological struggles in society. Such an understanding rests firmly on a liberal approach towards the question of the state and its role, according to which the latter stands outside civil society and politics, acting as a fair and neutral arbiter, bound by the law and serving the benefit of society as a whole (Bunyan 1976).

One particular problem with this understanding, which explicitly or implicitly informs all varieties of sociological liberalism in the study of policing (see Grimshaw and Jefferson 1987), is the tendency to pathologise organisational dysfunction and asynchrony, operational biases and abuses of power despite the fact they constitute persistent and recurrent characteristics of police work. Such phenomena are never seen as inherently related to the (class) nature of state power, and therefore intrinsic to the social purpose of police work, through which particular class strategies and interests are materialised. From this conceptualisation follows the literature's insistence on such topics as (professional) malpractice, corruption, lack of representation, lack of transparency and accountability, and so on. A further corollary of this approach is the tendency to isolate and treat as special cases areas of police activity such as political policing or public order policing where a perceived threat to the established political order posed by particular social groups constitutes the very raison d'être of the activity (Brodeur 1983). But if mainstream police studies follow such patterns and continuously revolve around these particular issues for more than a half century, one wonders whether the problem is not the object of their research, but, in fact, the very conceptual apparatus underpinning this intellectual enterprise. What if these pathologies constitute in reality a normal state of police organisation and action? In reality, both the 'ugly' faces of policing and its special forms (and this idea of special is today becoming increasingly untenable) are as normal as is the effort to suppress or ameliorate them: it is exactly this unstable equilibrium between these normal states that reveals that the police, as a specifically capitalist state apparatus, condense and relay rather than oversee a wider ensemble of economic, political and ideological processes. Not only must the liberal assumption of separation be abandoned, but an understanding of what is involved in this unstable equilibrium necessarily depends on questioning the role of the capitalist state.

The State and Authoritarian Statism

What liberal police scholars tend to perceive as pathologies hopefully amenable to cure, and the continuous conflict between those and the effort to maintain police legitimacy through reform, Marxist thinkers have understood as core characteristics of the police role in capitalist society. Essentially, the police unambiguously perform a decidedly repressive function which is indispensable in capitalist society, as class society: 'the police have primarily served to enforce the class, racial, sexual and cultural oppression that has been an integral part of the development of capitalism' (CRCJ 1977, 11). Nevertheless, the performance of this role and function does not 'hang in mid-air', as it were. Policing is not naked physical violence, but rather, its material and symbolic aspects are inscribed in the role of the state in capitalist society more generally; while it is historically organised around the particular specialisation of the police apparatus in the division of labour within the state, its social purpose and the forms it assumes in the exercise of organised violence or the provision of security are shaped by the general political role of the state as regulator and organiser of the totality of economic, political and ideological relations in a given society.

Elements of the above conceptualisation of the role of the state and its apparatuses are clearly found in the work of the founders of Marxist thought, and they all point to the idea that the state, being an indispensable instrument of class rule in a society divided in classes, is, in capitalist society, a special institutional field where the particular interests and strategies of the capitalist class are aggregated and articulated as policy. Through the state, the interests of the capitalist class acquire a specifically political form through which that class is able to materialise its objective interests in the perpetuation of conditions of capital accumulation and exploitation. According to Engels' formulation, which echoes the positions taken in various texts including, most notably, the Communist Manifesto (Marx and Engels 1976), the role of the state is to 'maintain the general external conditions of the capitalist mode of production against encroachments either by workers or by individual capitalists'. Engels goes on to observe that 'the modern state, whatever its form, is essentially a capitalist machine, the state of the capitalists, the ideal aggregate capitalist' (Engels 1975, 91).

Crucial to the understanding of the idea that the state is a 'machine' is the distinction between state apparatus and state power, which can be traced back to the political texts of Marx, Engels and Lenin. State apparatus refers to the diverse organisational forms and functions carried out by the state and its personnel. It is a concept which is defined broadly to include not only the public core of the state such as the administration, army, police courts, and so on, but also a wider institutional ensemble which while extending into what is juridically defined as private, it nevertheless performs political and ideological functions crucial to the reproduction of relations of (class) domination and subordination in society (Althusser 1971). State power, on the other hand, is the power of the dominant class in a historically given social formation. Class powers have their roots in the specific economic form which defines the fundamental class divisions and thus, the relations of production in which exploitation is taking place and the social division of labour under capitalism (Marx 1991, 927). They are also a product of the organisation and strategies of the different classes in political and ideological struggle, since relations of domination and subordination are not of merely economic nature, but cover the entire gamut of economic, political and ideological relations in society. The existence of the state is a necessity in a class society, as it constitutes a specifically political institutional field functioning as a 'regulating factor of society's equilibrium as a system' (Poulantzas 1978, 44).

We owe to Nicos Poulantzas two decisive advances in the above general conceptualisation of the state which clarify to a significant extent the specificity of the state machine as an apparatus of political rule in capitalist society and also provide invaluable methodological guidelines for understanding the connection between class struggles and the variable form and geometry of the capitalist state. Breaking an economism unable to explain why the dominant capitalist class takes recourse to a popular-democratic state, a form which is far from being perfectly suitable for the materialisation of that class's objective interests, Poulantzas built on the Gramscian idea of hegemony to develop the concept of the power bloc as a coalition of social forces in struggle which hold state power under the hegemony of a class or particular class fraction. While the Gramscian idea of hegemony expressed in more ideological (or 'cultural') terms the capacity of a social class to provide leadership and elicit consent in a society divided in classes (Anderson 1976; Gramsci 1971), Poulantzas specifically saw the state as a vehicle of political rule embodying the realisation of an equilibrium between politically dominant social forces under the hegemony of the one class or one of its fractions. The realisation of this coalition of social forces, the power bloc, does not cancel out the contradictions between them or suspend class struggle: on the one hand it reflects the capacity of the hegemonic class to represent its particular interests as 'general' interest; on the other hand, the presence of more classes or fractions of classes in the power bloc shapes the very form of the state insofar as the latter constitutes a specifically political institutional field, where contradictory interests are articulated and ultimately transformed into state policies (again, this is a contradictory process) capable of serving the long-term interests of the ruling capitalist class as a whole. Furthermore, a particular form of state also reflects the contradictions and struggles of the classes present in the power bloc with the subordinate classes, insofar as it must incarnate a series of material concessions to the latter while still serving as a machine of political rule and social order (Poulantzas 2008 and 1978). The state therefore possesses an institutional specificity reflected in variable concrete organisational forms which enables it on the one hand to organise the general interest of dominant classes and on the other, to intervene as a factor of disorganisation against the subordinate classes. Thus, Poulantzas is able to speak firstly of a relative autonomy of the state vis-à-vis the particular factions of the power bloc, capable of ensuring the long-term interest of the dominant (capitalist) class and to define, more generally, the state as 'a relationship of forces, or more precisely the material condensation of such a relationship among classes and class fractions such as this is expressed within the State in a necessarily specific form' (Poulantzas 2000, 128–9). Insofar as the form of the state reflects materially the state of class struggle, Poulantzas's analyses are a forceful assertion of the primacy of class struggle over institutions. It is in the above sense that we must understand neoliberalism as a successful *political* project, reflecting both a victorious ruling class and the state's organic complicity in that victory.

Indeed, in the later phases of his work, Poulantzas engaged actively in the analysis of the emerging form of state shaped by the capitalist restructuring and nascent neoliberalism of the 1970s. His analysis of the form of state which he called 'authoritarian statism' remains relevant exactly because it engages with the fundamental contradiction between the state's 'economic role and its role in maintaining order and organizing consent' (Poulantzas 2000), which is exacerbated under conditions of crisis. We now recognise that neoliberalism has been a radical political solution to an overaccumulation crisis which could not be dealt with effectively for capital's interests without abandoning redistributive politics, public expenditures and the expansion of welfare state that complemented the post–World War Two economic boom. The overcoming of capitalist crises entails an effort to intensify forces running counter to falling profitability and thus, the difficulties in sustaining capital reproduction. From an economic perspective, this entails the destruction (devaluation) of less-profitable capitals, the reorganisation of production through technological innovations and the reshuffling of the power balance between capital and labour, on the one hand by means of laying off part of the workforce, and on the other by restricting or curtailing the power of labour in the workplace and also politically and ideologically (Duménil and Lévy 2004; Harvey 2006b). The ascendancy of neoliberalism, ensured by the coming to power of political forces in Britain and particularly in the state that exercises hegemony over global capitalism, the United States, meant that the restructuring of capital in the capitalist metropolises was not merely complemented but actively reinforced by force if needed, by state policies of privatisation and deregulation, the adoption of suitable monetary policies, new public management, the 'flexibilisation' of the labour market and the dismantling of the welfare state (Harvey 2006a; Saad-Fihlo and Johnston 2005). In turn, a nexus of international organisations, particularly (US-controlled) International Financial Institutions, have orchestrated the promulgation of these policies internationally (Gowan 1999; Peet 2009), actively shaping what even during the present economic crisis appears as the politically unquestioned dominance of neoliberalism.

Poulantzas clearly saw that an exit from a structural crisis of capitalism compelled an intensification and deepening of the characteristics of a form of state appropriate to an advanced stage of monopoly capitalism and imperialism, those which more recent discussions now associate directly with the neoliberal state (e.g., Panitch 2000). It is a state that actively and intensively assumes the economic role of supporting capitalism in crisis by realigning the totality of its operations, political and ideological, around this role (Poulantzas 2000). The political implications in particular involve an increasing tension between the state's role in maintaining the conditions of the political domination of the ruling classes, the power bloc of the dominant class and its allies, and its capacity to retain a popular–democratic form. As Poulantzas saw it, this form of state authoritarian statism entails

greater exclusion of the masses from the centres of political decision making; widening of the distance between citizens and the state apparatus, just when the state is invading the life of society as a whole; an unprecedented degree of state centralism; increased attempts to regiment the masses through participation schemes. (Poulantzas 2000, 238)

The implications of the state's thickening of economic functions through increasing intervention in the fine-tuning of the production and circulation cycles do not only involve a wholesale decline of democratic institutions, but also a corresponding readjustment of the internal workings of the state. A new architecture of order thus emerges, characterised by the strengthening of the state's executive functions and the development of parallel policy networks linking parts of the state with special interests outside it at the expense of parliamentary control, democratic representation and even the rule of law. Importantly, the significance of the ideological apparatuses, particularly of the mass media, is increased as they operate as transmission belts of the state (neoliberal) ideology to the people and as means of eliciting consent, particularly of the middle class, through plebiscitary (and pseudo-coinvolvement) tactics.

Returning to policing, what can we make of these analyses? They certainly fully situate important factors underpinning not merely the authoritarian turn, but also the deeper enmeshing of the police with other apparatuses within aggressive ruling-class strategies, as witnessed in the major social conflicts of the late 1970s and 1980s (see, e.g. Milne 2004). We must see, however, how this process extends well beyond the exercise of coercion and the reinforcement of powers at the juridical level. Rather, the irresistible rise of police powers is further boosted by a deeper meshing of the police apparatus with particular circuits of capital accumulation. At a material level, a new field for capital valorisation is opened up with the acquisition of technologically advanced equipment, including Information Technology, surveillance and investigative equipment and not least, weapons. On the other hand, the greater capacity of the police apparatus to define areas of activity as 'technical matters' and thus insulate itself from political scrutiny from elected bodies or officials is receiving a further decisive boost by the mass media by means of the transformation of crime, law and order into an intensively exploitable spectacle for the masses.

A Normal Year in Policing?

It is instructive to turn to the sequence of events and stories that in 2010–11 have occupied the forefront of publicity in the country where these lines are being written. The use of the account that follows is not to offer a record of events to which research, analysis and discussion will undoubtedly return repeatedly in the future. But it is worth taking the risk an early chronicle involves because, arguably, these events may offer a conspectus of the nature of change that policing has undergone in close conjunction with the form of the neoliberal state.

Containment

Public order policing is not only the chronological beginning for this brief overview, but also an appropriate beginning. The control of mass protest is regarded as a special case (Waddington 1991; della Porta and Reiter 1998); it is excluded from modal accounts of police work, which have typically focused on the experience of the individual officer, and also from analyses of the use of force by the police, which again consider incidents at the level of individuals (see Alpert and Dunham 2004). Yet, it is in this domain that a noticeably aggressive change in police tactics and equipment, as well as the nature and levels of violence deployed, has taken place, featuring the generalisation of 'kettling' and other highly disruptive tactics in the handling by the police of large, and largely peaceful, mass demonstrations.

The use of containment tactics with the aim of restricting the movement of demonstrating crowds and controlling them is not by any means new, but the kettling or corralling tactic as such was first used in the United Kingdom in the late 1990s and most notably, in the Oxford Circus May Day protest in 2001. What is novel in kettling is the planned effort of the police to completely immobilise crowds within a limited area and for a prolonged period of time (in practice, several hours), the metaphors conveyed by the term being the complete surrounding of the enemy (Joyce 2010) or the herding of cattle in a pen (Hayman 2009). The hemming in of the marching crowd is achieved through appropriate deployment of police along the route followed by the demonstrators. The same method also prevents smaller groups from leaving the main body of the march. The police cordon is then tightened once the crowd has arrived in an area that has been deemed suitable according to police plans, and then the members of the entrapped public are completely prevented from exiting that area (Campbell 2009a). Use of additional force may be involved to suppress the reactions from within the kettle or further restrict the area occupied by the enclosed crowd.

From a police viewpoint, kettling aims to restrict violent or potentially violent crowds, thus to prevent serious disorder and to protect bystanders and non-participating members of the public from personal injury or the damage of property. Ultimately, kettling facilitates the identification and ultimately the arrest of individuals committing any offences. According to an Association of Chief Police Officers (ACPO) manual published in the aftermath of the G20 protest in London, containment is a 'contingency' tactic to be used when alternative methods have failed or are expected to fail. The manual requires that the tactic be proportionate to the threat and linked to police intelligence providing 'reasonable grounds to believe that there is actual violence or a threat of imminent violence' (ACPO 2010, 110). These requirements reflect the judgement in *Austin v Commissioner of Police of the Metropolis*, which found kettling lawful insofar as the actions of the police were proportionate and reasonable, confinement was restricted to a reasonable minimum as to discomfort and as to time and was necessary for the prevention of serious public disorder and violence.

Whether these conditions were present in the 2009 G20 protest and the student demonstration against the introduction of higher fees in higher education in December 2010 is doubtful, if only because the unfolding of events suggests that the police do not, in fact, regard kettling as a 'contingency' tactic, but rather adopt this tactic for the control of mass demonstrations as a matter of course. In the case of the G20 protest police response, a former high-ranking Metropolitan Police officer offered, in a *Times* article published just a day before the events, an overview of police preparations, and a preview of what was going to happen was offered in full detail (Hayman 2009). Police planning appears to have involved extensive surveillance (including the monitoring of social media) and undercover operations aiming to produce intelligence about the participants and their intentions, and the use of kettling appears to have been decided in advance of the actual event.

> Police spotters will be stationed at key vantage points while undercover officers mingle among the protesters... Disorder has to be nipped in the bud... If needed 'snatch squads' will be used to remove troublemakers. A protest on the move is harder to police than a stationary rally... Tactics to herd the crowd into a pen, known as 'the kettle', have been criticized heavily before, yet the police will not want groups splintering away from the main crowd... We can expect mounted police officers to guide the crowd along the routes. Reinforcements able to deal with any eventuality will be on standby in side streets. The control room at Lambeth will be receiving pictures from across the city and from cameras in the air. (Hayman 2009)

Despite the fact that serious issues with the implementation of the tactic were found in an official review of public-order policing in 2009 (HMIC 2009), and despite the serious doubts expressed by media commentators about the effectiveness of the approach and the outcry about its blatant cruelty, the police again implemented it as a matter of course during student marches against university tuition fees in late 2010 (Bowcott 2011; Campbell 2009b; Gabbat, Lewis, Taylor and Williams 2010). On these occasions, the entrapped young crowd also included schoolchildren who proved particularly vulnerable to the physical and psychological conditions forced by the police inside the kettle, namely, freezing weather conditions, lack of food and water, near complete lack of mobility (within the kettle), lack of access to medical help, the psychological distress and shock and the occasional use of force by the police (Townsend 2010).

The police insist that 'containment' is necessary to prevent serious disorder and violence, and it is true that violence can be a real possibility in situations of mass protest. One must of course take into account the fact that at the core of the police action are the officers who are specially trained to operate in public order situations, are specially equipped with a variety of weapons and sophisticated protective gear and are organised to act within units subject to special command and coordination (Jefferson 1990). The contrast between the police side and that of the protesters could not be more stark. Whether mass detention in public spaces is a proportionate response and whether it can reasonably constitute action aiming at containing incidents of violence by isolated individuals or small groups of protesters is doubtful. This is more so because the assessment of what constitutes a threat is left entirely for the police to judge. This was the very real implication of *Austin*, and subsequent court rulings now confirm this was indeed the case. Moreover, the police are able to justify the recourse to kettling more easily, not only because political support of their action is readily available (the British prime minister spoke of a 'feral mob' while the December incidents were developing), but also because they are better prepared to manage the flow of information directed to the media and thus, the general public. A significant part of the ACPO manual deals specifically and in detail with the question of managing the media coverage of such events (ACPO 2010, 79), and of course, it is no coincidence that on these occasions the key message to the public was about uncontrolled violence, not justified protest (Addley 2010).

Deceit

Second in the sequence of events, we again find a category of police activity that is typically excluded from accounts of 'everyday' policing. In the light of what has become public knowledge this year, however, one wonders whether undercover political policing is in fact in need of more urgent and intensive academic scrutiny. In January 2011 the print media took up and began to investigate further the case of undercover Metropolitan Police officer Mark Kennedy, who, using the alias Mark Stone, had infiltrated, between 2003 and 2009, a number of activist groups, primarily environmentalist, but also antiracist, antifascist, anarchist and animal rights groups (Evans and Lewis 2011). In autumn 2010 Kennedy had been exposed by members of protest groups close to him (UK Indymedia 2010). What the media investigation of the story revealed was the extent not only of his undercover activities in Britain and other European countries (Hill and Harding 2011), but also of undercover police activity more generally, as the presence of more undercover officers began to be reported (Lewis, Evans and Wainwright 2011b).

Having joined the Metropolitan Police in the mid-1990s, Kennedy presented himself as a professional freelance climber who shared in the culture of protest groups and began to create ties with environmental activists as early as 2003. He gradually established himself as a member of various protest groups taking part in 'almost every major environmental protest in the United Kingdom', including actions such as breaking into or disrupting the operation of power stations or invading airports, and so on. According to the media investigation, Kennedy's 'perfect activist' profile began to raise suspicions, particularly after a police pre-emptive raid in Nottingham which resulted in mass arrests of environmentalist planning protest at a nearby power station. While police were reported to have extensive surveillance operations in that instance (Jowitt and Taylor 2009), it was believed at the time that the raid specifically followed a tip-off from an informer. Kennedy was among the 27 individuals who were prosecuted and he was known to have been actively involved for four months in the planning of the demonstration and of the action at the power station, but as he distanced himself from the other defendants and charges against him were later dropped, suspicions against him grew. Following the discovery of his passport, Kennedy was confronted by activist friends in October 2010 and confessed his true identity (Lewis and Evans 2011).

Revelations about Kennedy's activity immediately took on an international dimension, as he had developed contacts with groups in several other European countries. In a secret hearing in Germany following public accusations from a German parliamentary member of the left-wing party Die Linke, it was revealed that Kennedy spent long periods in Germany and maintained long-term relationships with German activists. He was present in a number of protest events and had been arrested for committing various offences including arson during these events, but charges were dropped, as his presence was known to the German police authorities and he was considered a 'trusted agent and safe pair of hands'. The German government successfully stalled further inquiries into Kennedy's activities for 'operational reasons' (Hill and Harding 2011; Pidd and Lewis 2011). Whether Kennedy also acted as an agent provocateur remains uncertain. The investigation of the story made clear that the police operated a network of undercover agents within protest groups. A second (female) officer whose presence was known to Kennedy had reportedly spent four years in Leeds and had played a role in activist plans to shut down a coal-fired power station in North Yorkshire (Lewis, Evans and Dodd 2011a). The extent and depth of the information made available to the police by undercover agents appears to be significant since the intelligence produced not only was used for overt police operations, such as the Nottingham raid, but was also shared with security officers of the energy companies involved with a view to the planning of counterprotest measures (Taylor and Lewis 2009).

The Kennedy incident brought to light the extent and terms under which undercover policing has become more politically aggressive and more impenetrable to mechanisms for accountability. The undercover activities of Kennedy and apparently of other officers active within the various environmentalist groups were part of a counterterrorism operation managed by the National Public Order Intelligence Unit. NPOIU, which is (evidently) an operational unit and maintains a database which is reportedly comfortably couched within the structure of ACPO, essentially a senior police officials club, which had, however, assumed the form of a private limited company

(Jenkins 2011). Thus, despite the fact that it has an operational role pertaining to the murky domain of domestic extremism, it lies completely outside the structures of police accountability. In the wake of the Kennedy affair, a review of covert operations was launched by Her Majesty's Inspector of Constabulary and plans were announced to transfer domestic extremism operations under a new Metropolitan Police command (Travis, Lewis and Wainwright 2011). It nevertheless remains true that for more than ten years a domain of police activity which poses known and tangible threats to civil liberties had been defined and managed by a structure which enjoyed complete insulation from public view and control.

Collusion

Later in 2011 the police were again found at the centre stage of publicity in the *News of the World* phone-hacking scandal, as it has become known. This a story which has only now begun to unravel, but has already resulted in the resignations of the commissioner and another high-ranking officer of the Metropolitan Police amid allegations of serious negligence and corruption in the Metropolitan Police, and possibly in other UK police forces. The scandal, which in the summer of 2011 exploded to transatlantic dimensions, as it essentially involved a global media corporation, now appears to involve to a considerable extent and preoccupy almost in its entirety, the British political–media elite in the sense that News International–owned media maintained ties and held a highly influential role over political and other power centres in Britain (Harris 2011).

The epicentre of the crisis had been the News International–owned newspaper the *News of the World*, whose royal family correspondent was arrested in 2006 on suspicion of intercepting phone messages of Prince William and members of the royal staff. He was collaborating with a private investigator who was also prosecuted at the same time. At the time of the arrests, the police seized a large volume of computer records, notes and audio tapes. As it turned out, these contained information on royal family members, politicians, footballers and others. This material was obtained by phone message interceptions and other unlawful methods and was fed routinely into the *News of the World* newsroom and appeared in published stories (Daoust 2011). The actions of the *News of the World* reporter and his accomplice were at the time denounced by its management even though the two were on contract and paid for their services and the incident was presented as unfortunate and isolated. 'Phone hacking', however, exploited, in a relatively simple way, a security hole in mobile phone services which allowed the hacker to gain access to the targeted individual's voicemail messages, and it was thus believed that such practices were widespread for years among a larger number of media and involved a larger number of investigators (Tryhorn 2007). Nevertheless, a Press Complaints Commission investigation in 2007 failed to reveal a wider illegal conspiracy beyond the royal phone-hacking scandal. For its part, the Metropolitan Police, having initially decided to narrow the focus of the investigation of the prosecution of the correspondent and his associate, and on the national security risks the case involved, never proceeded to a full analysis of the material (which ran up to 11,000 pages of documents) and apparently failed to allocate a sufficient number of officers for this purpose (Home Affairs Committee 2011).

In July 2009 the *Guardian* returned to the story, revealing that News Group (the News International subsidiary that published the *News of the World*) had paid significant amounts of money to settle out-of-court legal cases involving interceptions of communications and other confidential and sensitive information records (such as criminal and social security records, itemised phone bills, and so on) of a number of public figures by private investigators (Davies 2009a, 2009b). The newspaper's investigation also revealed that senior editors of the *News of the World* and executive staff of News Corporation were implicated, as they were fully aware of and even encouraged hacking. This new development prompted an internal review of the evidence by the Metropolitan Police that was conducted informally by Assistant Commissioner for Specialist Operations Yates at the request of Commissioner Sir Paul Stephenson. No further investigation was deemed necessary. Yet, the unfolding of revelations gained pace in 2010: more cases, out-of-court settlements and new evidence emerged, including indications of extensive phone hacking made available by the telephone companies themselves; pressure began to mount for a reopening of the investigation which eventually materialised in January 2011 under the direction of Deputy Assistant Commissioner Akers. The extent of phone hacking activity became apparent, as it emerged from the review that the material possessed by the police contained information on 3,870 individuals, about 5,000 landline numbers and 4,000 mobile numbers (Home Affairs Committee 2011).

As phone hacking developed into a major scandal in the first half of 2011, a more complex image began to emerge. Several individuals were arrested, including the former assistant editor and the chief reporter of the *News of the World*, a development which indicated clearly the extent to which News International senior and other staff knew about or were involved in unlawful interceptions. Ultimately, under the weight of the scandal and the negative publicity for its parent company News Corporation, which was involved in an £8 billion takeover bid for satellite broadcaster BSkyB, a decision was made to shut down the *News of the World*. Furthermore, questions arose about the conduct of the police amid revelations regarding the relations of News International with the Metropolitan Police while the investigation of phone hacking was underway. Firstly, it was revealed that a senior Metropolitan Police officer who oversaw the initial investigation had a number of meals with senior News International figures, and shortly after his resignation in 2008 became a columnist for a News International–owned newspaper; secondly a former employee of News International had been appointed in 2009 as assistant to the Met's director of public affairs, but in light of the escalation of the scandal, the relationship was deemed inappropriate and the contract was terminated in autumn 2010 (Home Affairs Committee 2011); finally, in March 2011 it became known that a private investigator employed by the *News of the World* was able to obtain confidential records from a network of police officers for a payment (Davies and Dodd 2011), a development which led to the launch of a parallel investigation into payments made to police by News International. In July 2011 both Metropolitan Police commissioner Sir Paul Stephenson and assistant commissioner John Yates resigned.

Exclusion

The fourth major – and most recent, relative to the time these lines are being written – incident for UK policing was what is now being referred to as 'the 2011 riots'. There is more involved in the story of these riots than a mere return to the question of public-order policing. The riots did reveal, in a most emphatic manner, chronic and severe tensions between the police and the people, particularly young people and those belonging to ethnic minorities in some of Britain's most deprived areas (Dorling and Thomas 2011). But it is the police response to the riots as well as the overall, and mostly united, reaction of the political, criminal justice and media apparatuses that invites a number of observations and raises a number of significant issues.

The incident that ignited the four-day-long period of rioting in several areas of London and several other English cities, including Birmingham, Bristol, Liverpool, Manchester and Nottingham, was the shooting of 29-year-old Mark Duggan, who was a member of the black Caribbean community in Tottenham. Duggan was under police surveillance on suspicion of drug dealing and gun crime, and during an attempt to arrest him in a location close to Tottenham Hale tube station on the 4 August 2011, he was fatally wounded by gunshots fired by the police. Duggan died at the scene of the incident. The initial impression created by media reports was that Duggan opened fire on the police and was subsequently killed after an exchange of shots. As a police officer was taken to hospital, early media reports conveyed an unambiguous portrait of Duggan as a well-known gangster who was armed at the scene of the incident (*Telegraph* 2011b; Camber 2011b). The Independent Police Complaints Committee (IPCC) later acknowledged that verbal communications to the press might have supported the impression that an exchange of shots had taken place (IPCC 2011a). As the official statements of the IPCC did not support the initial account, and given the constraints on the flow of information and communication inevitably posed by the launch of a formal inquiry (IPCC 2011b), a more complex picture of both the incident and of Duggan himself began to emerge, featuring a background of deeply ingrained tensions between the local black minority community and the police. On 6 August a peaceful protest march to Tottenham police station was organised by friends and relatives of Duggan. They demanded to speak to a senior police officer, but apparently were not met with a satisfactory response (Lewis 2011). The riot in Tottenham erupted later in the evening of that day when two police cars and a bus were set afire, windows were smashed and buildings were also set on fire (Laville, Lewis, Dodd and Davies 2011).

While it has been possible to quickly establish an accurate timeline of the riots as they spread from Tottenham to other areas in London and then to a number of other cities in England, an analysis of the conditions that made possible this mass violent eruption will require a much more concentrated and prolonged research effort, not least because of a number of novel elements that differentiate them from older ones, even within the very same communities (Hernon 2006). All these areas are not only among the hardest hit by the ongoing economic crisis, but they possess a long record of economic hardship, poverty and unemployment (Dorling and Thomas 2011). They all feature large ethnic minority communities whose experience of economic disadvantage and severe tensions with the police and the criminal justice system is a well-established fact (see, e.g. Home Office 1999; Ministry of Justice 2010). These may be necessary conditions for a riot to erupt, but it could be a more complicated task to determine more precisely the forces that shaped the timing and the mode of the modern precariat's explosion of protest (Žižek 2011; Bauman 2011). The media reports, apart from the obligatory focus on violence and destruction, did pay a rather disproportionate amount of attention to these novel characteristics such as the looting of consumer goods and gadgets or the use of social media and mobile phone messaging in the mobilisation of rioters (Douglas 2011; Halliday 2011).

It nevertheless appears that on several occasions, the rioters did not merely clash with police forces posing an obstruction to their supposedly primary 'targets', but that the police themselves have been the targets. The riots started as a protest against the police and throughout those four days, it appears that police personnel, vehicles and buildings did not, in fact, fail to specifically attract the rioters' attention and anti-police sentiment (Rogers, Sedghi and

Evans 2011). This alone invites questions about the nature and levels of regular presence in these areas and about the response of the police to the riots as they occurred, which was met with criticisms for weak presence and inaction (Camber 2011a; *Daily Mail* 2011). The timing of the events in the month of August 2011 may, of course, have posed a number of logistical problems in the mobilisation of personnel and equipment. On the evening of 6 August, from a total of 3,000 uniformed officers on duty across London, the Metropolitan Police had deployed in the Tottenham area a force of about 500, including specialist riot police, and another hundred officers were added overnight. But these numbers increased dramatically over the following two days, reaching a total of 6,000 uniformed officers on duty on Monday and a total of 13,000 and 16,000 uniformed officers on duty on the morning and evening respectively of 9 August, following the return of David Cameron from holiday and an emergency meeting of ministers (Goodwin 2011). We may also recall that the force not only possessed fresh guidelines for public-order policing (ACPO 2010), but was by no means unfamiliar with emergency public-order situations. Furthermore, in the early stages of the riots, the number of arrests reached 215 on 6–7 August and 153 on 7–8 August, respectively (Rogers 2011a). While criticisms of the police response are, of course, possible from a *police* tactical viewpoint (Travis 2011), it is difficult to suggest that it has been lukewarm – considering that the 'worst day' was Monday, 8 August, at which point the Metropolitan Police numbers on duty had been already doubled.

It may be more instructive to consider not the police response as such, but rather, the overall institutional mobilisation that took place during the riots and more importantly, the overall unfolding of what can be seen as a strategy in the period following the riots up to date. The media, building on the abundance and power of the images of destruction, looting and buildings on fire,[1] had successfully established an overwhelming sense of crisis and by effectively labelling the rioters as a 'mob', 'burglars, thugs and bullies' (Camber 2011a), it was also possible to drown out any critical voices – recall the crude dismissal of Darcus Howe from a live interview on the BBC news programme on 9 August (*Telegraph* 2011a). Home secretary Theresa May immediately spoke of 'sheer criminality' and the need 'to make sure that people are brought to justice so that people see there are consequences to these actions' (Watt and Sparrow 2011), thus offering a preview of David Cameron's return the following week to the 'Broken Britain' agenda and the denunciation of the rioters as 'people showing indifference to right and wrong; people with a twisted moral code; people with a complete absence of self-restraint' (Stratton 2011). The police campaign to apprehend the perpetrators of violence and looting relied on the same images, reaping the benefits from the extensive network of CCTV cameras and from the distribution of images of individual offenders on social media and Internet sites such as flickr.com (Laville 2011). Unsurprisingly, this campaign required fast-track processing of cases by the courts in industrial proportions (Ministry of Justice 2011), and the process then continued unabated: in late September, as the police released on flickr. com more images of people wanted in connection with the riots, the number of arrests had exceeded 2,500 with more than 1,500 charged (Metropolitan Police 2011). An early analysis of court data made available by the Ministry of Justice in September showed that those convicted in connection with the riots were more likely to be given a custodial sentence and that the sentence was likely to be longer than the average for offences such as theft or burglary (Rogers 2011b). The unison of criminal justice, media and government could not have been more harmonious.

Towards a Research Agenda

One wonders whether some of the processes and the changes involved in policing under authoritarian statism are not visible to the naked eye. That some of them nowadays must surface in the public domain through a great deal of good investigative journalism is, of course, a testimony to the very reality of the neoliberal state; most, however, shape beyond the dramatic events of a suppressed mass protest or a riot, the everyday experience of policing, from the increasing volume of hardware attached to the patrolling constable's uniform, to the ever-present deafening sound of police car sirens, to the accumulation of the machinery of surveillance in the streets (see, e.g. Coleman 2009) and perhaps not too far in the future, in the skies (Lewis 2010). The yield from a casual, incomplete and partial look in this last year is, in itself, unsettling:

- The capacity of the police to justify on technical – therefore, largely exempt from substantive scrutiny – grounds, derived from their own operational logic and objectives, a tactic of crowd containment which comes very near to torture; and of course, the capacity to execute it fully by means of superior technical coordination of communications, advance equipment and, not least, full command of the field.
- The capacity of power centres within the police but outside the reach of mechanisms for democratic scrutiny and control not merely to organise key areas of police activity, but also to bypass legal-judicial procedural guarantees that is the very code by which the state itself declares to abide.
- The intermeshing and, to some extent, interlocking of the police with private interests, whether these involved energy companies, private investigators or a powerful media corporation; the essential point is that police activity

appears in all these cases to be functional to, if not underpinned by, these private interests.

• The synergy of police, media and the political apparatus in translating and representing a situation which raises uncomfortable questions about the role and levels of police presence among marginalised groups and territories (this applies both to the rioting youth and the self-defending residents and shopkeepers) as a situation of emergency and as a criminal threat devoid of any significance for social cohesion and inclusion; and not least, the common mobilisation of both police resources and an already omnipresent infrastructure of surveillance in order to identify and persecute the individual perpetrators of criminal acts.

In the early days of neoliberalism's ascent in Britain, the characteristics of an emerging British state articulating an authoritarian solution to the disintegration of the social democratic state and the problem of working-class militancy was insightfully diagnosed by the work of Stuart Hall and his colleagues.

> [T]he extension, over the period, of police power and surveillance of political groups and individuals; the use of the police and legal apparatuses in a wide area of social conflicts; the role of the judicial forces in containing the economic and industrial class struggle; the employment of new judicial instruments – the Industrial Relations Act, constraints on picketing and strikes; the extension of the conspiracy charge and political trials; the abuse of habeas corpus under a loose definition of emergency. (Hall 1980, 171)

In *Policing the Crisis* (Hall, Critcher, Jefferson, Clarke and Roberts 1978) and other subsequent texts reflecting this strand of analysis, the reworking of Gramscian themes similar to those informing Poulantzas's work gave birth to the concept of 'authoritarian populism' as a ruling class strategy capable of effecting a recomposition of the power bloc and a renewal of the state's capacity to elicit popular consent. Because of its theoretical roots, authoritarian populism was particularly sensitive to the ideological aspect of class struggle waged in the political scene at the time, naturally and usefully invoking the idea of 'moral panics' (Cohen 2002) – a staple of critical criminological analysis of law and order politics. For all the indisputable value of these analyses, one must, however, go beyond the emphasis on ideological processes and the construction of consensus around the neoliberal law and order agenda as a response to a carefully promulgated and intensively exploited acute and pervasive sense of social crisis in that earlier period. The theoretical stakes do not simply involve the form of state of crisis, or of state in crisis. This is exactly what the idea of authoritarian populism captures as a concept applying to a particular conjuncture (Hall 1985).

Authoritarian statism, insofar as it captures the key characteristics of a form of state corresponding to the advanced stage of monopoly capitalism – or perhaps more precisely, imperialism in Lenin's (1970) terms – characterising today's Western societies, that is, of the neoliberal state, is more suitable to guide investigation into the normal state of policing today. A long period of time has passed since the sense of emergency has subsided and popular militancy (against *capitalism*) has given way to a reign of law and order politics easily representing and targeting as a threat to the quasi-permanently disconnected and unrepresented or the excluded and vilified social categories, such as the modern precariat, inner-city youth or the long-term unemployed segments of a defeated industrial working class. It is thus possible to create an inventory of concepts pertaining to aspects of neoliberal state recomposition (see, e.g. Fairbrother 2006; Rainnie and Fairbrother 2006), which can directly apply to changes in police organisation, internal management, infrastructure and operations (Leishman et al. 2000; Smith and Henry 2007). But to the extent to which such concepts exclude from their vista the organic role of the state in organising and shoring up an increasingly precarious capitalism, they are unlikely to capture fully how this relation is irremediably embedded in the very institutional fabric and the practice of the police.

Yet, particular concepts suitable for integration into the above overarching theoretical framework did reside in that early, highly productive period of radical criminology. Take, for example, the idea of the 'criminal justice–industrial complex': radical theory borrowed the idea from the vocabulary of intra-ruling-class struggle. It was US president Dwight Eisenhower himself who spoke in 1961 of a 'military–industrial complex' at a time when it was becoming apparent that patterns of defence spending in the United States could be influenced by emerging policy networks, a 'delta of power' linking the legislature, the army bureaucracy and the arms industry, thus engendering inefficiency, waste, corruption and mismanagement (Roland 2007). But the idea of a 'criminal justice–industrial complex' makes a forceful appearance within an explicitly Marxist political economy framework in the work of Richard Quinney (see also Teague, this volume). Beginning with an analysis of increasing criminal justice budgets and the formation of a federal administrative apparatus to coordinate the spending and activity in the policy area of criminal justice, Quinney spoke of an alliance between state and the monopoly sector of the economy, a 'symbiotic relationship' which, while opening up a 'multimillion-dollar market in domestic control' for private enterprise, mobilised state resources for administration and research in a process which ultimately augments capacities of control (Quinney 1977, 117, 120). More can and should be made theoretically of Quinney's cursory observations of how the intermeshing of state and particular capitals engaging in the production of hardware as well as 'systems analysis, managerial improvement, computerized intelligence and administrative reorganization' (1977, 122) and the simultaneous growth of the private security industry effect a transformation in the very material practices constituting the police apparatus and thus its form and geometry.

Despite its obvious relevance and its potential for integration into a more general framework problematising changes in the state, Quinney's formulation of the concept, while still being used today, particularly in the context of the penal system and prisons (the 'prison–industrial complex'), is not consciously informing a programme of critical research, but is, rather, found in a practical form highlighting what is to be resisted (Davis 2003, 1995; Goldberg and Evans 2009). It may also be the case that the particular context of the prison system may not yet be mature enough empirically to reveal the formation of a prison industrial complex (see, e.g. Parenti 2008), as this is a gradual process (Papageorgiou and Papanicolaou 2011). Yet, what we may be witnessing today in the field of security is a robust and mature form of a security industrial complex which, firmly embedded in an insulated nexus between policy making, the police organisation and the circuits of capital accumulation, provides the rationale and drive for further augmentation of control capacities and perhaps paves the ground for decidedly authoritarian solutions for an increasingly crisis-ridden capitalism. The existence of such a field is suggested by insightful studies, which, however, do not adopt an explicit political economy perspective, nor do they sufficiently draw links with state theory (Bigo 2008; Hayes 2009).

Thus, the urgency of reviving a political economy research agenda, taking a theoretically informed and thorough look into not merely the processes through which policing is ideologically co-opted into ruling class strategies, but also the very material processes, including strictly economic ones, through which it contributes to the sustenance of capital accumulation, cannot be stressed enough. In present times of renewed and genuinely structural economic crisis, the neoliberal solution installed by the Thatcher governments, unchallenged by New Labour and restored by the present coalition government, may be exhausting its vital force; even though the circumstances of today's increased mass protest and militancy differ profoundly from those of the earliest stages of neoliberalism's emergence, it may be the case that we are again reaching a critical historical bifurcation where profound changes are again a possibility. We know all too well one of the possible outcomes.

Note

1 This is not to deny or dismiss the real extent or the seriousness of harm, destruction and distress caused by the riots. But the very same circumstances can also serve as resources to be exploited within a strategy of containment and control – in this context, the real plight of the victims becomes irrelevant for power. The emphasis here is exactly on this aspect. The sequence of events beginning from the Duggan incident suggests that a different approach by the authorities involved could have prevented the outburst of violence.

References

ACPO. 2010. *Manual of Guidance on Keeping the Peace*. London: National Policing Improvement Agency.

Addley, E. 2010. 'Student fees protests: Who started the violence?' *Guardian*, 10 December. Available at http://www.guardian.co.uk/education/2010/dec/10/student-protests-tuition-fees-violence?INTCMP=ILCNETTXT3487 (accessed 30 September 2011).

Alpert, G. P. and R. G. Dunham. 2004. *Understanding Police Use of Force: Officers, Suspects, and Reciprocity*. Cambridge: Cambridge University Press.

Althusser, L. 1971. 'Ideology and ideological state apparatuses (notes towards an investigation)'. In *Lenin and Philosophy and Other Essays*. New York: Monthly Review Press.

Anderson, P. 1976. 'The antinomies of Antonio Gramsci'. *New Left Review* 100: 5–78.

Bauman, Z. 2011. 'The London riots – on consumerism coming home to roost'. *Social Europe Journal*. Available at http://www.social-europe.eu/2011/08/the-london-riots-on-consumerism-coming-home-to-roost/ (accessed 1 October 2011).

Bayley, D. H. and C. D. Shearing. 1996. 'The future of policing'. *Law and Society Review* 30: 585–606.

Bigo, D. 2008. 'Globalized (in)security. The field and the banopticon'. In *Terror, Insecurity and Liberty: Illiberal Practices of Liberal Regimes after 9/11*, edited by D. Bigo and A. Tsoukala. London: Routledge.

Bowcott, O. 2011. 'Met police kettled pupils aged 11 during fee protests, court told'. *Guardian*, 5 July. Available at http://www.guardian.co.uk/uk/2011/jul/05/met-police-kettling-children-high-court/print (accessed 5 July 2011).

Brodeur, J.-P. 1983. 'High policing and low policing: Remarks about the policing of political activities'. *Social Problems* 30: 507–20.

Bunyan, T. 1976. *The History and Practice of the Political Police in Britain*. London: Julian Friedmann Publishers.

Burchell, G., C. Gordon and P. Miller (eds). 1991. *The Foucault Effect: Studies in Governmentality with Two Lectures and an Interview with Michel Foucault*. Chicago: University of Chicago Press.

Camber, R. 2011a. '"We don't do water cannon, we rely on consent": May rules out tough action as vigilantes are forced to defend shops'. MailOnline. Available at http://www.dailymail.co.uk/news/article-2023932/London-riots-2011-Theresa-May-rules-tough-action-vigilantes-defend-shops.html (accessed 5 October 2011).

———. 2011b. 'Pictured: The "gangsta" gunman whose death sparked riots'. MailOnline Available at http://www.dailymail.co.uk/news/article-2022670/The-gangsta-gunman-death-sparked-riots.html# (accessed 5 October 2011).

Campbell, D. 2009a. 'Did the handling of the G20 protests reveal the future of policing?' *Guardian*, 3 April. Available at http://www.guardian.co.uk/world/2009/apr/03/g20-protests-police-kettling (accessed 28 September 2011).

———. 2009b. 'G20: Did police containment cause more trouble than it prevented?' *Guardian*, 2 April. Available at http://www.guardian.co.uk/world/2009/apr/02/g20-protests-police-kettling (accessed 11 October 2011).

Cohen, S. 2002. *Folk Devils and Moral Panics: The Creation of Mods and Rockers*. Abington: Routledge.

Coleman, R. 2009. 'CCTV surveillance, power and social order'. In *Unmasking the Crimes of the Powerful: Scrutinizing States and Corporations*, edited by S. Tombs and D. Whyte. New York: Peter Lang.

CRCJ. 1977. *The Iron Fist and the Velvet Glove: An Analysis of the US Police*. Berkeley, CA: Centre for Research on Criminal Justice.

Daily Mail. 2011. 'So where were the police? Shopkeepers mystified at tactics that left them defenceless'. MailOnline. Available at http://www.dailymail.co.uk/news/article-2023984/London-riots-2011-Where-police-Shopkeepers-mystified-theyre-left-defenceless.html (accessed 3 October 2011).

Daoust, P. 2011. *Phone Hacking: How the Guardian Broke the Story*. Guardian eBook.

Davies, N. 2009a. 'Murdoch papers paid £1m to gag phone-hacking victims'. *Guardian*, 8 July. Available at http://www.guardian.co.uk/media/2009/jul/08/murdoch-papers-phone-hacking (accessed 20 September 2011).

———. 2009b. 'Trail of hacking and deceit under nose of Tory PR chief'. *Guardian*, 8 July. Available at http://www.guardian.co.uk/media/2009/jul/08/murdoch-newspapers-phone-hacking (accessed 21 September 2011).

Davies, N. and V. Dodd. 2011. 'Murder trial collapse exposes News of the World links to police corruption'. *Guardian*, 11 March. Available at http://guardian.co.uk/media/2011/mar/11/news-of-the-world-police-corruption (accessed 2 October 2011).

Davis, A. Y. 2003. *Are Prisons Obsolete?* New York: Seven Stories Press.

Davis, M. 1995. 'Hell factories in the field'. *The Nation*, 20 February, 229–34.

della Porta, D. and H. Reiter (eds). 1998. *Policing Protest: The Control of Mass Demonstrations in Western Democracies*. Minneapolis: University of Minnesota Press.

Dorling, D. and B. Thomas. 2011. *Bankrupt Britain: A Post-recession Atlas*. Bristol: Policy Press.

Douglas, T. 2011. 'Social media's role in the riots'. BBC News. Available at http://www.bbc.co.uk/news/entertainment-arts-14457809 (accessed 1 October 2011).

Duménil, G. and D. Lévy. 2004. *Capital Resurgent: Roots of the Neoliberal Revolution*. Cambridge, MA: Harvard University Press.

Engels, F. 1975. *Socialism: Utopian and Scientific*. Peking: Foreign Languages Press.

Evans, R. and P. Lewis. 2011. 'Undercover officer spied on green activists'. *Guardian*, 9 January. Available at http://www.guardian.co.uk/uk/2011/jan/09/undercover-office-green-activists/print (accessed 10 January 2011).

Fairbrother, P. 2006. 'The emergence of the 'de-centred' British state'. In *Globalization, State and Labour*, edited by P. Fairbrother and A. Rainnie. London: Routledge.

Gabbat, A., P. Lewis, M. Taylor and R. Williams 2010. 'Student protests: Met under fire for charging at demonstrators'. *Guardian*, 26 November. Available at http://www.guardian.co.uk/uk/2010/nov/26/student-protests-police-under-fire/print (accessed 9 December 2010).

Garland, D. 2001. *The Culture of Control: Crime and Social Order in Contemporary Society.* Oxford: Oxford University Press.

Goldberg, E. and L. Evans. 2009. *The Prison-Industrial Complex and the Global Economy.* PM Press Pamphlet Series No. 0004. Oakland, CA: PM Press.

Goodwin, T. 2011. 'A letter from Tim Goodwin, Metropolitan Police to the Home Affairs Committee, 23 August'. Available at http://www.parliament.uk/documents/commons-committees/home-affairs/PLD02 Tim Godwin without details.pdf (accessed 5 October 2011).

Gowan, P. 1999. *The Global Gamble: Washington's Faustian Bid for World Dominance.* London: Verso.

Gramsci, A. 1971. *Selections from the Prison Notebooks.* New York: International Publishers.

Grimshaw, R. and T. Jefferson. 1987. *Interpreting Policework: Policy and Practice in Forms of Beat Policing.* London: Allen and Unwin.

Hall, S. 1980. 'Popular-democratic vs. authoritarian populism'. In *Marxism and Democracy,* edited by A. Hunt. London: Lawrence and Wishart.

———. 1985. 'Authoritarian populism: A reply to Jessop et al.' *New Left Review* 151: 115–24.

Hall, S., C. Critcher, T. Jefferson, J. Clarke and B. Roberts. 1978. *Policing the Crisis: Mugging, the State, and Law and Order.* Basingstoke: Palgrave Macmillan.

Halliday, J. 2011. 'London riots: How Blackberry Messenger played a key role'. *Guardian,* 8 August. Available at http://www.guardian.co.uk/media/2011/aug/08/london-riots-facebook-twitter-blackberry (accessed 1 October 2011).

Harris, J. 2011. 'How the phone-hacking scandal unmasked the British power elite'. *Guardian,* 18 July. Available at http://www.guardian.co.uk/media/2011/jul/18/phone-hacking-british-power-elite (accessed 26 September 2011).

Harvey, D. 2006a. *Spaces of Global Capitalism: Towards a Theory of Uneven Geographical Development.* London: Verso.

———. 2006b. *The Limits to Capital.* London: Verso.

———. 2007. *A Brief History of Neoliberalism.* Oxford: Oxford University Press.

Hayes, B. 2009. *Neoconopticon: The EU Security-Industrial Complex.* London: Transnational Institute and Statewatch.

Hayman, A. 2009. 'Police at G20 will be tense, despite months of planning'. *Times,* 31 March. Available at http://www.timesonline.co.uk/tol/news/politics/G20/article6005080.ece (accessed 30 September 2011).

Hernon, I. 2006. *Riot! Civil Insurrection from Peterloo to the Present Day.* London: Pluto Press.

Hill, A. and L. Harding. 2011. 'Mark Kennedy infiltrated German anti-fascists, Bundestag told'. *Guardian,* 26 January. Available at http://www.guardian.co.uk/environment/2011/jan/26/mark-kennedy-german-bundestag/print (accessed 27 January 2011).

HMIC. 2009. *Adapting to Protest.* London: Her Majesty's Chief Inspector of Constabulary.

Home Affairs Committee. 2011. 'Unauthorized tapping into or hacking of mobile communications'. Thirteenth Report of Session 2010–12 HC907. London: House of Commons.

Home Office. 1999. *Statistics on Race and the Criminal Justice System. A Home Office Publication under Section 95 of the Criminal Justice Act 1991, 1999.* London: Home Office.

IPCC. 2011a. 'Release of information in early stages of Mark Duggan investigation'. Independent Police Complaints Commission, 12 August. Available at http://www.ipcc.gov.uk/news/Pages/pr_120811_Release-of-information-in-early-stages-of-Mark-Duggan.aspx (accessed 1 October 2011).

————. 2011b. 'Update on Mark Duggan investigation including details of ballistic tests'. Independent Police Complaints Commission, 9 August. Available at http://www.ipcc.gov.uk/news/Pages/pr_090811_dugganupdate.aspx (accessed 1 October 2011).

Jefferson, T. 1990. *The Case Against Paramilitary Policing*. Buckingham: Open University Press.

Jenkins, S. 2011. 'The state's pedlar's of fear must be brought to account'. *Guardian*, 11 January. Available at http://www.guardian.co.uk/commentisfree/2011/jan/11/police-reformmark-stone-terrorism (accessed 5 October 2011).

Johnston, L. and C. D. Shearing. 2003. *Governing Security: Explorations in Policing and Justice*. London: Routledge.

Jones, T. and T. Newburn. 2002. 'The transformation of policing? Understanding current trends in policing systems'. *British Journal of Criminology* 42: 129–46.

Jowitt, J. and M. Taylor. 2009. 'Mass arrests over power station protest raise civil liberties concerns'. *Guardian*, 14 April. Available at http://www.guardian.co.uk/environment/2009/apr/14/police-arrests-environment-campaigners (accessed 30 September 2011).

Joyce, J. 2010. 'Police "kettle" tactic feels the heat'. BBC news, 9 December. Available at http://www.bbc.co.uk/news/uk-11963274 (accessed 25 September 2011).

Kempa, M., R. Carrier, J. Wood and C. D. Shearing. 1999. 'Reflections on the evolving concept of "private policing"'. *European Journal of Criminal Policy and Research* 7: 197–223.

Laville, S. 2011. 'London riots: 450 detectives in hunt for looters'. *Guardian*, 9 August. Available at http://www.guardian.co.uk/uk/2011/aug/09/london-riots-detectives-police (accessed 2 October 2011).

Laville, S., P. Lewis, V. Dodd and C. Davies. 2011. 'Doubts emerge over Duggan shooting as London burns'. *Guardian*, 8 August. Available at http://www.guardian.co.uk/uk/2011/aug/07/police-attack-london-burns (accessed 1 October 2011).

Leishman, F., B. Loveday and S. P. Savage (eds). 2000. *Core Issues in Policing*, 2nd ed. Harlow: Longman.

Lenin, V. I. 1970. *Imperialism, the Highest Stage of Capitalism: A Popular Outline*. Peking: Foreign Languages Press.

Lewis, P. 2010. 'CCTV in the sky: Police plan to use military-style spy drones'. *Guardian*, 23 January. Available at http://www.guardian.co.uk/uk/2010/jan/23/cctv-sky-police-plan-drones/print (accessed 23 January 2010).

————. 2011. 'Tottenham riots: A peaceful protest, then suddenly all hell broke loose'. *Guardian*, 7 August. Available at http://www.guardian.co.uk/uk/2011/aug/tottenham-riots-peaceful-protest (accessed 1 October 2011).

Lewis, P. and R. Evans. 2011. 'Mark Kennedy: A journey from undercover cop to "bona fide" activist'. *Guardian*, 10 January. Available at http://www.guardian.co.uk/environment/2011/jan/10/mark-kennedy-undecover-cop-activist/print (accessed 25 January 2011).

Lewis, P., R. Evans and V. Dodd. 2011a. 'Revealed: Second undercover police officer who posed as activist'. *Guardian*, 13 January. Available at http://www.guardian.co.uk/uk/2011/jan/12/second-undercover-police-officer (accessed 15 September 2011).

Lewis, P., R. Evans and M. Wainwright. 2011b. 'Mark Kennedy knew of second undercover eco-activist'. *Guardian*, 10 January. Available at http://www.guardian.co.uk/environment/2011/jan/10/mark-kennedy-second-undercover-ecoactivist (accessed 15 September 2011).

Loader, I. and N. Walker 2007. *Civilising Security*. Cambridge: Cambridge University Press.

Manning, P. K. 2005. 'The study of policing'. *Police Quarterly* 8: 23–43.

Mariani, P. (ed.) 2011. 'Law, order and neoliberalism'. *Social Justice* 28 (3).

Marx, K. 1991. *Capital: A Critique of Political Economy*, vol. 3. London: Penguin Books in association with New Left Review.

Marx, K. and F. Engels. 1976. 'Manifesto of the Communist Party'. In *Karl Marx, Frederick Engels, Collected Works*, vol. 6. London: Lawrence and Wishart.

McLaughlin, E. 2007. *The New Policing*. London: Sage.

Metropolitan Police. 2011. 'London disorder – Photos'. Available at http://www.met.police.uk/disordersuspects/ (accessed 10 October 2011).

Milne, S. 2004. *The Enemy Within: The Secret War against the Miners*. London: Verso.

Ministry of Justice. 2011. 'Riots: Minister praises work to fast track court cases'. Available at http://www.justice.gov.uk/news/features/features-110811.htm (accessed 7 October 2011).

———. 2010. *Statistics on Race and the Criminal Justice System: A Ministry of Justice Publication under Section 95 of the Criminal Justice Act 1991*. London: Ministry of Justice.

O'Malley, P. 1997. 'Policing, politics and postmodernity'. *Social and Legal Studies* 6: 363–81.

Panitch, L. 2000. 'The new imperial state'. *New Left Review* 2: 5–20.

Papageorgiou, I. and G. Papanicolaou. 2011. 'Theorizing the prison industrial complex'. Paper presented at the York Deviancy Conference, York, 29 June–1 July.

Parenti, C. 2008. *Lockdown America: Police and Prison in the Age of Crisis*. London: Verso.

Peet, R. 2009. *Unholy Trinity: The IMF, World Bank and WTO*. London: Zed Books.

Pidd, H. and P. Lewis. 2011. 'MP in Germany says Mark Kennedy "trespassed" in Berlin activists' lives'. *Guardian*, 10 January. Available at http://www.guardian.co.uk/world/2011/jan/10/mp-germany-mark-kennedy-activists?intcmp=239 (accessed 15 September 2011).

Platt, A. M. and L. Cooper (eds). 1974. *Policing America*. Englewood Cliffs: Prentice-Hall.

Poulantzas, N. 1978. *Political Power and Social Classes*. London: Verso.

———. 2000. *State, Power, Socialism*. London: Verso.

———. 2008. 'The political crisis and the crisis of the state'. In *The Poulantzas Reader: Marxism, Law and the State*, edited by J. Martin. London: Verso.

Quinney, R. 1977. *Class, State, and Crime: On the Theory and Practice of Criminal Justice*. New York: Longman.

Rainnie, A. and P. Fairbrother. 2006. 'The state we are in (and against)'. In *Globalisation, State and Labour*, edited by P. Fairbrother and A. Rainnie. London: Routledge.

Reiner, R. 1992. 'Policing a postmodern society'. *Modern Law Review* 55: 761–81.

Rigakos, G. S. 2002. *The New Parapolice: Risk Markets and Commodified Social Control*. Toronto: University of Toronto Press.

Rogers, S. 2011a. 'Metropolitan police arrests for the London riots, the key data'. *Guardian*, 8 August. Available at http://www.guardian.co.uk/uk/2009/apr/20/police-intelligence-e-on-berr (accessed 1 October 2011).

———. 2011b. 'Riots broken down: Who was in court and what's happened to them?' *Guardian*, 15 September. Available at http://www.guardian.co.uk/news/datablog/2011/sep/15/riot-defendants-court-sentencing#data (accessed 10 October 2011).

Rogers, S., A. Sedghi and L. Evans 2011. 'UK riots: Every verified incident – interactive map'. *Guardian*, 11 August. Available at http://www.guardian.co.uk/news/datablog/interactive/2011/aug/09/uk-riots-incident-map (accessed 1 October 2011).

Roland, A. 2007. 'The military-industrial complex: Lobby and trope'. In *The Long War: A New History of US National Security Policy Since World War II*, edited by A. J. Bacevich. New York: Columbia University Press.

Rose, N. and P. Miller. 1992. 'Political power beyond the state: Problematics of government'. *British Journal of Sociology* 43: 173–205.

Saad-Fihlo, A. and D. Johnston (eds). 2005. *Neoliberalism: A Critical Reader.* London: Pluto Press.

Shearing, C. D. and P. C. Stenning 1981. 'Modern private security: Its growth and implications'. In *Crime and Justice: An Annual Review of Research*, vol. 3, edited by M. Tonry and N. Morris. Chicago: University of Chicago Press.

———. 1983. 'Private security: Implications for social control', *Social Problems* 30: 493–506.

Simon, J. 2007. *Governing through Crime: How the War on Crime Transformed American Democracy and Created a Culture of Fear.* New York: Oxford University Press.

Smith, D. J. and A. Henry (eds). 2007. *Transformations of Policing.* Aldershot: Ashgate.

Stratton, A. 2011. 'David Cameron on riots: Broken society is top of my political agenda'. *Guardian*, 15 August. Available at http://www.guardian.co.uk/uk/2011/aug/15/david-cameron-riots-broken-society?INTCMP=SRCH (accessed 2 October 2011).

Taylor, M. and P. Lewis 2009. 'Secret police intelligence was given to E.ON before planned demo'. *Guardian*, 20 April. Available at http://www.guardian.co.uk/uk/2009/apr/20/police-intelligence-e-on-berr (accessed 1 October 2011).

Telegraph. 2011a. 'London riots: BBC apologizes for accusing Darcus Howe'. *Telegraph*, 10 August. Available at http://www.telegraph.co.uk/news/uknews/crime/8693842/London-riots-BBC-apologises-for-accusing-Darcus-Howe.html (accessed 10 October 2011).

———. 2011b. 'Man killed in shooting incident involving police officer'. *Telegraph*, 4 August. Available at http://www.telegraph.co.uk/news/uknews/crime/8682655/Mark-Duggan-killed-in-shooting-incident-involving-police-officer.html (accessed 30 September 2011).

Townsend, M. 2010. 'Metropolitan Police face legal action for kettling children during tuition fees protest'. *Guardian*, 26 December. Available at http://www.guardian.co.uk/uk/2010/dec/26/metropolitan-police-lawsuit-student-protest?INTCMP=ILCNETTXT3487 (accessed 30 September 2011).

Travis, A. 2011. 'Metropolitan police got riot tactics wrong, says new commissioner'. *Guardian*, 11 October. Available at http://www.guardian.co.uk/uk/2011/oct/11/metropolitan-police-riot-commissioner (accessed 11 October 2011).

Travis, A., P. Lewis and M. Wainwright 2011. 'Clean-up of covert policing ordered after Mark Kennedy revelations'. *Guardian*, 18 January. Available at http://www.guardian.co.uk/uk/2011/jan/18/covert-policing-cleanup-acpo/print (accessed 19 January 2011).

Tryhorn, C. 2007. 'Murdoch defends NoW journalists'. *Guardian*, 7 February. Available at http://www.guardian.co.uk/media/2007/feb/07/newsoftheworld.pressandpublishing (accessed 20 September 2011).

UK Indymedia. 2010. 'Mark "Stone/Kennedy" exposed as undercover police officer'. www.indymedia.org.uk, 21 October. Available at http://www.indymedia.org.uk/en/2010/10/466477.html?c=on#c257998 (accessed 15 September 2011).

Wacquant, L. 2001. 'Deadly symbiosis: When ghetto and prison meet and mesh'. *Punishment and Society* 3: 95–134.

————. 2009a. *Prisons of Poverty.* Minneapolis: University of Minnesota Press.

————. 2009b. *Punishing the Poor: The Neoliberal Government of Social Insecurity.* Durham, NC: Duke University Press.

Waddington, P. A. J. 1991. *The Strong Arm of the Law: Armed and Public Order Policing.* Oxford: Clarendon Press.

Watt, N. and Sparrow, A. 2011. 'David Cameron chairs emergency Cobra meeting after third night of riots'. *Guardian*, 9 August. Available at http://www.guardian.co.uk/uk/2011/aug/09/david-cameron-emergency-cobra-meeting-riots (accessed 1 October 2011).

Weiss, B. (ed.) 2007. *Social Justice* 34 (3–4): *Securing the Imperium: Criminal Justice Privatization and Neoliberal Globalization.*

Young, J. 1999. *The Exclusive Society.* London: Sage.

Žižek, S. 2011. 'Shoplifters of the world unite'. *London Review of Books*, 19 August. Available at http://www.lrb.co.uk/2011/08/19/slavoj-zizek/shoplifters-of-the-world-unite (accessed 20 August 2011).

Chapter 6

THE INFLUENCE OF NEOLIBERALISM ON THE DEVELOPMENT OF THE ENGLISH YOUTH JUSTICE SYSTEM UNDER NEW LABOUR

Raymond Arthur

Introduction

This chapter will examine the way in which the ideology of neoliberalism has impacted upon and consequently reshaped the youth justice system in England and Wales in the period 1997–2010 (for policy developments during 2010–15, see Ministry of Justice 2010). Neoliberal conceptions of the role of the state have encouraged the formulation of policies based on principles of social inequality, penal expansionism and on the diminution of welfare concerns. In the neoliberal context, less attention is paid to the social contexts and social analytics of crime and more on prescriptions of individual/family/community responsibility and accountability. Neoliberal discourse emphasises eliminating the concept of the community and replacing it with individual responsibility (Gray 2001). Social problems consequently become defined in terms of the individual rather than state responsibility. The best outcomes for society will be realised when governments retreat from involvement in social programs that breed welfare dependency. This chapter will show some of the relationships between the violations of law in youth and the neoliberal model as a factor of increasing marginalisation of concern for the welfare needs of young people. It will critically examine whether the influence of neoliberalism has led to a renewed criminalisation of young people and their families and argue that society must acknowledge that it, as well as the offender, has some responsibility for youth offending.

Neoliberalism and the Youth Justice System

Neoliberalism represents an ideological commitment to rolling back the state and reducing welfare intervention. Neoliberal conceptions of the market and international capital promote the view that unfettered markets lead to maximal efficiency and prosperity and encourage the formulation of policies based less on principles of social inclusion and more on social inequality, deregulation, privatisation, penal expansionism and welfare residualism (Muncie 2005). As Brown (2005) argues,

> Neoliberal rationality, while foregrounding the market, is not only or even primarily focused on the economy; it involves extending and disseminating market values to all institutions and social action, even as the market itself remains a distinctive player. (2005, 39–40)

Nikolas Rose (1999, 74) suggests that neoliberalism involves a 'technology of the self' which in turn entails an ongoing process of 'responsibilisation'. This means that, in a neoliberal era, the 'good citizens' are increasingly those who are capable of appropriate degrees of self-regulation such that they ultimately reduce their demands on the state and take responsibility for themselves. Neoliberal penal policies encourage the dissemination of punitive and exclusionary practices (Newburn 2002). For neoliberals, there has to be a turn away from the welfare approach towards retributive punishment and just desserts. Neoliberalism relies upon the construction of self-governing individuals who accept that the responsibility for improving the conditions of their existence lies in their own hands. This individualisation involves more than just the devolution of responsibility; neoliberal discourses locate the sources of these problems in the attributes and supposed deficiencies of people themselves (see Rose 1999; Higgins 2002; Cheshire and Lawrence 2005).

The advent of the 'New' Labour government in 1997 signalled the development of a youth justice system subject to a neoliberal responsibilising mentality in which the position historically afforded to children is dissolving (Muncie 2008). Since 1997 the welfare needs of young people who engage in antisocial and offending behaviour have become marginalised within the youth justice system. The marginalisation of the young persons' welfare needs was reflected in the white paper *No More Excuses*, which stated that

> punishment is necessary to signal society's disapproval when any person including a young person breaks the law... Young people...should be in no doubt about the tough penalties they will face. (Home Office 1997a, 5.1)

Subsequently, Section 37 of the Crime and Disorder Act 1998 places all those carrying out functions in relation to the youth justice system under a statutory duty to have regard to the principal aim of preventing offending by children and young people. The Crime and Disorder Act 1998 gives no direction to the courts or anyone else working in the youth justice system that the child's welfare should also be of primary consideration. Consequently, the primary duty of those involved in the youth justice system, including the police, is to prevent offending and not necessarily to promote the child's best interests (Hollingsworth 2007). Section 9 of the Criminal Justice and Immigration Act 2008 has elevated the aim of preventing offending and reoffending to the principal consideration when sentencing young offenders. While the courts are required to have regard to the welfare of the young person who has engaged in offending behaviour when sentencing, in accordance with Section 44 of the Children and Young Persons Act 1933, the 2008 Act makes clear that welfare needs will not have equal status, nor will they override the primary aim of preventing offending (Arthur 2010). Section 44 of the Children and Young Persons Act 1933 imposes an important welfare principle which requires every court to have regard to the welfare of a child or young person who is brought before it, either as an offender or otherwise. The welfare principle's main virtue is that it requires that a decision made with respect to a child be justified from the point of view of a judgment about the child's interests. It would be inconsistent with the welfare principle to make a decision that is overtly justified by reference to the way the outcome benefited some other interests (Eekelaar 2002). Welfarism reflects a prevailing assumption that the role of the state is to try to realise a more just, equitable and inclusive society (Stenson 2001, 20). It is characterised by the pursuit of social justice and the promotion of solidarity through the provision of universal services. Welfarism is accompanied by a belief that social workers and other professional agencies can rehabilitate those involved in deviant lifestyles and who are suffering from personal and social pathologies (Stenson 2001). The recommendations of the 1927 Moloney Committee formed the basis of the Children and Young Persons Act 1933. The Moloney Committee recognised the importance of the welfare of young offenders, most of whom were victims of social and psychological conditions and in need of individualised treatment, and recommended that welfare principles should dominate the youth justice system (Home Office 1927). The Moloney Committee recommended the development of a juvenile court whose duty was not to punish the young person, but to readjust and rehabilitate the young person.

The Children and Young Persons Act 1969 was similarly underpinned by a philosophy of treatment which promoted welfarism. The 1969 Act advocated a rise in the age of criminal responsibility and sought alternatives to detention by way of treatment, noncriminal care proceedings and care orders. The 1969 Act also advocated a range of interventions intended to deal with young offenders through systems of supervision, treatment and social welfare in the community rather than punishment in custodial institutions. It was quite explicitly based on a social welfare approach to young offenders. Authority and discretion were shifted out of the hands of the police, magistrates and prisons and into the hands of the local authorities, social workers and the Department of Health. The 1969 Act gave primacy to the family and the social circumstances of the deprived and underprivileged; it aimed to reduce the criminalisation of young people and to increase the support and care available to them. The 1969 Act effectively legislated to abolish prosecuting any child under 14 years of age for any criminal offence except homicide. Although the Children and Young Persons Act 1969 aimed to reduce the criminalisation of young people and to increase the support and care available to them, it did not have an easy passage through Parliament. Conservative politicians argued that it was unjust, that it gave insufficient recognition to the constructive role of the juvenile court, and that it interfered with police work with young people, especially in regard to more serious offences (Bottoms 1974). The Magistrates' Association was also opposed to the Children and Young Persons Act 1969, blaming it for the vast increases in youth crime (Berlins and Wansell 1974), thus precipitating a moral panic about the powerlessness of the juvenile court. Following the defeat of the Wilson government in the 1970 general election (see Cowling this volume), large sections of the 1969 Act were never implemented and the social welfare ideology underlying the Act never came to fruition. The new Conservative government elected in 1970 declared that it would not implement those sections of the Act that were intended to raise the age of criminal responsibility from 10 to 14 and to replace criminal proceedings with care proceedings. Essentially, the Conservative Party government objected to state intervention in criminal matters through welfare rather than judicial bodies. Similarly, magistrates and the police responded to the undermining of their key positions in the justice system by becoming more punitively minded and declining the opportunity to use community sentences on a large scale. Consequently, since the 1970s the youth justice system in England and Wales has seen the decline of penal welfarism in place of the development of forms of neoliberal governance. When Margaret Thatcher came to power, her government was able to take advantage of growing public dissatisfaction with the costs of maintaining the welfare state to challenge ideas of social citizenship, 'notions of community and collective welfare were cast aside before the altar of individualism, enterprise and consumerism' (Lister 1998, 312).

For the conservatives, the role of the government was to protect the interests of the individual. This protection of the individual also extended to young people accused of committing crimes. In the 1980s the view emerged that if children's liberty was going to be interfered with, it should be done in a legal arena and children's rights should be protected in the same way as adults' rights are. This was fuelled by the report of the US President's Commission on Law Enforcement and Administration of Justice and the landmark US Supreme Court decision *In re Gault* (387 US 1 [1967]). The report of the President's Commission on Law Enforcement and Administration of Justice stated that 'the juvenile court is a court of law, charged like other agencies of criminal justice with protecting the community against threatening conduct' (United States Government 1967). In *In re Gault*, the US Supreme Court ruled that where a young person faced incarceration, the young person should be entitled to the protection of due process of law in the same way as adults. Any period spent in an institution should be proportionate to the offence. This position is contrary to the welfare model where you look to the child's needs and keep the child in care for as long as needs be, despite the potential for disproportionate incarceration. The US Supreme Court condemned a system whereby young people could be subjected to long periods of detention in various forms of institutions without rights of due process, such as the right to counsel, rights against self-incrimination and other procedural protections automatically accorded to adult defendants in criminal trials. The Supreme Court held that due process of law is the primary and indispensable foundation of individual freedom. *In re Gault* also highlighted a second failing of the welfare approach, namely, the lack of proportionality and the potential for indeterminacy in disposals. The Supreme Court believed that an individualised welfare approach could lead to indeterminate sentences in the name of treatment in circumstances where if adults had committed the offences, they would have been treated more leniently. Developments in the United States also influenced the English youth justice system. In England, the Criminal Justice Act 1982 required that legal representation be offered to the young person, that social inquiry reports be presented to assist the court and that sanctions be determinate and proportionate. The 1982 Act created youth custody sentences which were fixed by the courts and not by social workers. The 1982 Act expanded the use of detention centres and empowered the courts to incarcerate young offenders for periods exceeding three years.

The judgement in *In re Gault* was part of a broader contemporary liberal commitment to the protection of human rights (Cavadino and Dignan 2006, 216). However, if children are to be protected from the disastrous consequences of their offending behaviour, then youth crime prevention strategies have to be part of a much wider consideration of how justly life chances are distributed to our children. Youth justice cannot simply be about their just treatment within legal or formal systems of control, important though that may be; it has to be about the way life chances and opportunities are provided for children. It is therefore imperative that general social policy provides a coherent and comprehensive welfare safety net so that vulnerable children are protected from the adverse environmental, familial and socio-economic circumstances that can encourage criminal behaviour (Arthur 2002).

Since the 1990s, policy responses to juvenile offending in England and Wales have been founded on the image of young offenders as threatening and lawless as distinct from vulnerable, threatened and disadvantaged children (Goldson 1999). Young offenders have been conceptualised as violent predators warranting retribution, rather than as wayward children in need of a guiding hand. This trend reached fever pitch after the tragic killing of James Bulger in February 1993, when the then prime minister, John Major, declared that 'society needs to condemn a little more and understand a little less' (Major 1993). This harsher stance set the tone for refocusing policy and practice in relation to children in trouble upon punishment, retribution and the wholesale incarceration of children. New Labour, with its focus on individual and parental responsibility and its desire to cement its position on the law and order high ground, continued this trend (Muncie 1999). Legislation introduced since 1997 reflected an ideological conviction in favour of punishment in which more and more people, including children, are brought within the orbit of the criminal justice system for an ever-growing range of criminal behaviour. This stance is indicative of the Labour government's avowed attempt to 'talk tough on crime' (Goldson 1999). Thus, there emerged a new punitive bipartisanship around questions of crime and punishment (Loader 2006). For example, the Children Act 1989 brought about a radical separation between criminal justice and childcare concerns. The Children Act 1989 removed from the youth court the power to order a young person into the care of a local authority. Care and supervision orders can now only be made in the Family Proceedings Court, leaving the youth court to deal exclusively with criminal matters. The Criminal Justice and Public Order Act 1994 lowered the age at which children could be detained in custody for grave crimes, such as manslaughter or other crimes of violence, from 14 to 10 years of age. The 1994 Act also introduced a range of measures which extended the courts remand and sentencing powers to younger offenders by introducing secure training orders for 12- to 14-year-old persistent offenders, increasing the maximum length of detention in a Young Offenders Institution from 12 to 24 months for 15- to 17-year-olds and allowing the court to remand 12- to 14-year-olds.

In 1996 the Audit Commission report *Misspent Youth* was highly critical of the youth justice system in England and Wales. It concluded that 'The current system for dealing with youth crime is inefficient and expensive while little is being done to deal effectively with juvenile nuisance' (Audit Commission

1996, 96). The New Labour government responded to the Audit Commission's verdict on the youth justice system in the consultation paper *No More Excuses: A New Approach to Tackling Youth Crime in England and Wales* in which it suggested that up until 1997 youth offending had been greeted with excuses instead of action (Home Office 1997a, 1). *No More Excuses* proposed a 'root and branch' overhaul of the youth justice system and a breaking with the philosophy of the 1969 Act (Home Office 1997a, 9.2). Consequently, Section 37 of the Crime and Disorder Act established preventing offending by children and young people as the principal aim of the youth justice system and placed all those working in the youth justice system under a duty to have regard to that aim in carrying out their duties. Welfare concerns are also ominously absent from the Youth Justice Board's 'Strategic Objectives for 2008–11'. These objectives are (1) to prevent offending and reoffending by children and young people under 18 years, (2) to increase victim and public confidence and (3) to ensure safe and effective use of custody (Youth Justice Board 2008).

Prior to taking office as prime minister, Tony Blair expressed his view that 'duty' was at the heart of creating a strong society so that 'bonds of duty allows us to be much tougher and hard-headed in the rules we apply and how we apply them' (Blair 1995). This notion of 'duty' and responsibility underpins New Labour's approach to crime and disorder. New Labour emphasised the need for citizens to share risks and responsibilities with the state, reflecting a discourse which increasingly draws upon the lexicon of obligations rather than rights (Lister 1998, 313). New Labour's approach created a channel for shifting blame from the government to citizens and allowed for the welfare-paternalist approach to be replaced by a new crime prevention agenda. This approach to tackling youth offending places less emphasis on the social contexts of crime and measures of state protection and more on prescriptions of individual/family/community responsibility and accountability (Muncie 2005). Thus, the centrality of welfare issues in sentencing has been changed in favour of more retributive sanctioning that regards young offenders as utilitarian, rational-choice actors who should be held accountable for their behaviour. The primary aim of youth crime prevention signals a political preference for a punitive response to young people's behaviour (Pitts 2001; Muncie 2002) and potentially allows for welfare considerations to be circumvented. This crime prevention aim allows for young people to be portrayed as threats to public safety and the youth justice system is cast in the role of preventing this threat from being realised (Arthur 2010). Neoconservative principles of re-moralisation and authoritarianism allow the state to represent crime as indicative of the break-up of the moral fabric and cohesion of society. Shadow home secretary Tony Blair characterised youth offending as a descent into 'moral chaos' (Haydon and Scraton 2000). Consequently, the police need to be 'tough on crime' to substitute for the vanished social cohesion which had previously kept crime at bay. Crime prevention is provided as a means to micromanage behaviour in order to 're-moralise' the recipients (Muncie 2006, 782). In this representation, the young person's welfare needs can easily become a secondary concern (Smith 2006, 97–8; Mason and Prior 2008, 280).

In the white paper *No More Excuses*, the government stressed that it did not see any conflict between protecting the welfare of the young offender and preventing that individual from offending again, because 'preventing offending promotes the welfare of the individual young offender and protects the public' (Home Office 1997a, 2.2). However, this is not a view shared by the courts. In the case of *R v Inner London Crown Court, ex p N. and S.* ([2001] 1 Cr. App. R. 343) Lord Justice Rose, deputy chairman of the Sentencing Guidelines Council, examined Section 37 of the Crime and Disorder Act 1998 and stated that the need to impose a deterrent sentence may take priority over the provisions of Section 44(1) of the Children and Young Persons Act 1933, which requires the court to promote the welfare of individual offenders. Thus, despite the government's assurances in *No More Excuses* to protect the welfare of young people who engage in offending behaviour, Section 37 of the 1998 Act ignores the potentially corrosive impact of custodial life upon a young person's development (Stone 2001) and allows the youth court to impose a deterrent sentence with the aim of preventing young people in general from offending, but which does not necessarily serve the welfare of the individual offender. Michel Foucault believed that this emphasis on crime prevention has allowed the penal system to increasingly shift away from a concern with catching those responsible for crimes to identifying who might be at risk of deviance.

> Thus, the purpose of the sanction will not be to punish a legal subject who has voluntarily broken the law; its role will be to reduce as much as possible – either by elimination, or by exclusion or by various restrictions, or by therapeutic measures – the risk of criminality represented by the individual in question. (Foucault 1994, 198)

Impact of Pursuing a Crime Prevention Agenda

The crime prevention agenda has allowed for a shift in focus towards increasingly punitive forms of governance and behavioural regulation which envelop and obscure the relevance of socio-economic factors within a broader policy concerned with the incarceration and (re)moralisation of specific groups (Donoghue 2011). Neoliberal imperatives involve responsibilisation, managerialism, risk management and restorative justice. Effective processes of internalised control have also long been identified as a critical foundation for the stability of liberal states (Day Scalter and Piper 2000). The corrosive impact of these imperatives can be seen in four areas of the youth justice system: *doli incapax*, restorative justice, use of custody and making parents responsible for their children's behaviour, which areas will now be dealt with seriatim.

Doli incapax

Under successive New Labour administrations it has become increasingly common to treat young offenders as entirely rational, fully responsible young adults rather than children, thus justifying their subjection to the full rigours of the criminal law. This allows them to define social problems in terms of individual rather than state responsibility (Bell 2009). This portrayal of young people as fully responsible young adults has greatly undermined the potential of disposals which encourage an approach towards youth offending which concentrates predominantly on the welfare of young people (Bell 2011, 77–8). An example of this can be seen in the attitude of the New Labour government to the issue of children's capacity to commit crime. In *No More Excuses* the Labour government made several recommendations about improving the youth justice system (Home Office 1997a). One aspect of this radical reorganisation was to modernise 'the archaic rule of *doli incapax*'; the government believed that the 'notion of *doli incapax* is contrary to common sense' and is 'not in the interests of justice or victims or of the young people themselves' (Home Office 1997a, 4.4). Following this white paper, Section 34 of the Crime and Disorder Act abolished the presumption of *doli incapax*. Consequently, a child aged 10 can be considered as legally responsible for their actions as an adult. Such a child is no longer presumed incapable of evil. Thus, England and Wales now has a law

> which holds that a person is completely irresponsible on the day before his tenth birthday, and fully responsible as soon as the jelly and ice-cream have been cleared away the following day. (Smith 1994, 427)

Doli incapax reflected a concern that 'using criminal penalties to punish a child who does not appreciate the wrongfulness of his or her actions lacks moral justification' (Penal Affairs Consortium 1995, 5). The abolition of *doli incapax* removes an important principle which had acted to protect children from the full rigour of the criminal law. Bandalli argues that the abolition of *doli incapax* reflects a steady erosion of the special consideration afforded to children and is 'symbolic of the state's limited vision in understanding children, the nature of childhood or the true meaning of an appropriate criminal law response'

(Bandalli 2000, 94). Bandalli stressed that the presumption of *doli incapax* operated in a protective manner, 'shielding the child from the damage that might otherwise be done by being absorbed into the criminal justice system' and that its removal makes childhood irrelevant to criminalisation (Bandalli 1998). This portrayal of young people as fully responsible young adults has allowed England and Wales to take a markedly more punitive approach to this issue than comparable countries. The impact of the English approach is that young defendants with impaired mental capacity are exposed to the full rigours of the criminal justice system. This is exactly the type of situation in which the presumption could have acted as a safeguard.

Restorative justice

By 1997 New Labour wanted to incorporate restorative principles and practices into the new youth justice system in order to create a victim-centred system while also encouraging offenders to take responsibility for their actions and prevent future offending (Home Office 1997a). New Labour saw restorative justice principles as a vehicle for achieving its pledge to be 'tough on crime, tough on the causes of crime'. The main thrust of restorative justice in the English youth justice system is to promote more effective ways of preventing offending by young people by undertaking early interventions that seek to address the known causes of their antisocial and offending behaviour. These efforts aim to make young people accountable for what they have done by requiring them to undertake some reparation to the victim and/or the community. Statutory guidance outlines the forms of reparation that are considered appropriate as including letters of apology, restorative conferences and practical reparative activity related to the offence (Home Office 2000, 55). This process offers victims a chance to speak about how they have been affected by what has happened, to say what might repair the harm done to them and to ask questions and get answers from the one person who can answer them, namely, the offender. For offenders it offers the opportunity to take responsibility for what they have done, to apologise for the harm they have caused and to make amends.

Nikolas Rose (1999, 263) suggests that in a neoliberal society, one of the fundamental tasks of 'control workers', including police, is to identify 'the riskiness of individuals, actions, forms of life and territories'. The 'final warning' is a sanction which combines notions of deterrence via formal procedures that make clear the consequences of further criminal activity, and reform, from the inclusion of a requirement for referral to the Youth Offending Team (YOT) for assessment and a 'change' programme (Hine 2007). The final warning combines a formal verbal warning given by a police officer to a young person who admits guilt for a first or second offence, with an assessment to determine the causes of the young person's offending behaviour and a programme of activities designed to address these causes. A young person can only get one final warning, so that any further offending will usually go to court. Thus, the final warning ignores the possible benefits of a further warning. This inflexibility has ensured that the police have lost their discretion to deal with cases informally and has resulted in the youth court being inundated with petty cases. This rigid approach risks undermining efforts to divert large numbers of young people from the youth justice system and risks prematurely launching children into the criminal justice system. *R v Durham Constabulary and another ex parte R (FC)* ([2005] UKHL 21) involved a 15-year-old youth who had received a final warning for indecent assault. The House of Lords acknowledged the lack of flexibility in final warnings and felt that this was inconsistent with the objective of diverting children from the criminal justice system and that it seriously risked offending against the principle that intervention must be proportionate both to the circumstances of the offence and the offender. Also, final warnings remain on the Police National Computer for a period of five years and are cited in court hearings if a young person engages in subsequent offending. Compliance and non-compliance with a final warning programme is cited in Youth Offending Team court reports. Thus, a young person's engagement with a final warning programme can have a potentially detrimental effect on future sentencing options for the young person. Moreover, any young offender in court charged with an offence within two years of receiving a final warning is unable to be given a conditional discharge, unless the circumstances are exceptional. Instead, the young person will receive a penalty, probably a referral order, thus progressing further down the road to a serious criminal conviction.

In England and Wales, the restorative elements are peripheral to the work of the youth justice system. These local approaches to crime control operate in uneasy tension with harsher and more punitive approaches. They are additions rather than defining components of a youth justice system that is committed to punishment and incarceration. In Scotland and New Zealand, where the children's hearing and family group conference systems have both succeeded, the restorative justice arrangements are substitutes for court appearances and not additions to the system. Thus it is important that restorative justice processes are used as an alternative criminal justice response, rather than an additional one.

Use of custody

The Crime and Disorder Act 1998 created the generic custodial sanction of the Detention and Training Order (DTO). A DTO can be given to any 15- to

17-year-old for any offence considered serious enough to warrant custody and to 12- to 14-year-olds who are considered persistent offenders. The orders are for between 4 and 14 months. Half of the order is served in the community under the supervision of a social worker, probation officer or a member of a YOT and the other half is served in custody. The detention and training order was heralded as a measure to ensure that custody for children was a constructive experience with an appropriate focus on education and training (Home Office 1997a; Youth Justice Board 2000). The rationale behind the order is the belief that the increased emphasis on a clear sentence plan to tackle the underlying causes of offending and on community supervision after release from custody would provide a 'clearer, simpler, more flexible and more consistent custodial arrangement for young offenders' (Home Office 1997a, 6.20). However, it represents a substantial increase in the custodial powers of the youth court and a loosening of the conditions which must be satisfied before custodial orders can be imposed on children aged between 12 and 14 years (NACRO 2000). England and Wales lock up more young people than any other country in Western Europe (resonating with the adult criminal justice system; see Teague, this volume), and these young people are incarcerated in overcrowded conditions with little scope for rehabilitation and education. Large numbers of these young people sentenced to custody do not pose a serious risk to the community, and indeed, by leading to broken links with family, friends, education, work and leisure, they may become a significantly greater danger upon their release (Goldson and Peters 2000). The practice of imprisoning children also appears to run counter to the aim of preventing offending. When young persons are in custody, they are making no reparation to the victim or society. Child imprisonment makes little if any positive effect in preventing offending; patterns of reconviction with regard to children, following release from all forms of custodial institution, are exceptionally high (Goldson 2005, 82). Hagell and Hazell (2001) also noted with concern that child imprisonment compounds the likelihood of reconviction and that this has been a recurrent and enduring historical theme of youth imprisonment. In the early 1990s custody was described as 'an expensive way of making bad people worse' (Home Office 1990, 27) and Miller (1991, 181–2) acknowledged that 'the hard truth is that…juvenile penal institutions have minimal impact on crime [and if] most prisons were closed tomorrow, the rise in crime would be negligible'. These views echo those expressed by Mary Carpenter (1853, 13) in the nineteenth century, when she described prisons as being 'most costly, most inefficacious for any end but to prepare the child for a life of crime'. The current approach to using custody in the English youth justice system fails to address the underlying causes of offending, does not prevent offending, and is prohibitively expensive. Expenditure on custody accounts for almost

70 per cent of the Youth Justice Board's expenditures. The Crime and Society Foundation found that countries with higher rates of welfare investment are likely to enjoy lower rates of custody and conversely, countries with the highest rate of imprisonment, including the United Kingdom, all spend below average proportions of their GDP on welfare (Downes and Hansen 2006). Similarly, the Audit Commission stressed that if effective early intervention had been provided for just one in ten young offenders in custody, annual savings in excess of £100 million could have been achieved (Audit Commission 2004). Social investment in family offers a promising prospect for both reducing crime and maximising the human capital that the young represent. A progressive approach to youth crime prevention is ultimately bound up with the pursuing and resourcing of mechanisms for social justice. The government must ensure that social justice extends to all members of society. According to this view, the state must acknowledge that it, as well as the offender, has some responsibility for youth crime and that society can justifiably punish young offenders for their crimes only to the extent it has fulfilled its obligations to those young people and their families as members of society.

Making parents responsible for their children's behaviour

Punishing parents is part of a rationale which emphasises punishment and retribution in the context of the social moralisation of 'flawed parents'. However, the emphasis is placed on 'good' parenting as predicated upon individual responsibility, rather than supported and facilitated by state social responsibility (Donoghue 2011). The Crime and Disorder Act 1998 introduced the 'parenting order' which enables the court to require the parent of every convicted young offender to attend parenting programmes and, if necessary, to control the future behaviour of the young person in a specified manner. The parenting programmes deal with issues such as experiences of parenting, communication and negotiation skills, parenting style and the importance of consistency; praise and rewards and can also include a residential element. In effect, the parenting order requires a parent to attend counselling or guidance sessions once a week for a maximum of 12 weeks. Parents may also be required to apply control over their child; for example, they may be ordered to ensure that their child attends school or avoids associating with particular individuals who are adversely affecting their behaviour. The Anti-Social Behaviour Act 2003 empowers Youth Offending Teams (YOTs) to apply to the courts for parenting orders where the YOT suspects that the parent is not taking active steps to prevent the child's antisocial or criminal behaviour and it is clear that this behaviour will continue. Section 24 of the Police and Justice Act 2006 allows registered social landlords to apply for a parenting order when they have reason to believe that a child is engaging in antisocial behaviour. Accordingly, parents who have not committed any crime can receive a parenting order in response to their children who have not committed any crime (Holt 2008, 204).

In 1997 the Home Office consultation paper *Tackling Youth Crime* first detailed the underlying principle of the parenting order, which was to make 'parents who wilfully neglected their responsibilities answerable to the court' (Home Office 1997b, 32). This consultation paper was followed by the white paper *No More Excuses: A New Approach to Tackling Youth Crime in England and Wales* (Home Office 1997a), which stated that the government intended to make parents more responsible for their children's behaviour by making available sanctions for parents who evade their responsibilities. Laws that penalise parents for their children's behaviour cast parents as 'failures' and confront them with the prospect of financial penalties and potentially, imprisonment. Parental responsibility laws also serve to fragment the government's approach to both tackling youth crime and supporting families in crisis. In 1997 the government stated in *No More Excuses* that 'as they develop, children must bear an increasing responsibility for their actions, just as the responsibility of parents gradually declines' (Home Office 1997a). The government believed that to prevent offending and reoffending by young people, society must stop making excuses for youth crime. According to this view, children aged 10 years and above are generally mature enough to be held accountable for their actions and the law should recognise this. Yet, parental responsibility laws are built upon the idea that parents have caused their children to offend. Rather than parental responsibility decreasing when the child is held criminally responsible, both parent and child are held legally liable regardless of the actual or, indeed, presumed capacity of the child, and consequently there is no diminution in parental responsibility as the child gains responsibility (Hollingsworth 2007). Kempf-Leonard and Peterson express this contradiction succinctly.

> If youths are to be processed using adult criteria and held responsible for their delinquent actions as individuals capable of making rational decisions, it is an incompatible dichotomy to hold parents responsible for these capable youths as well. (Peterson 2002, 445)

Parental responsibility laws not only reduce the responsibility of the child, but they also obscure the fact that the government can be implicated in the causes of antisocial and criminal behaviour. The recognition that there may be a link between parenting and family circumstances and the chances that a child becomes involved in offending behaviour is not a new one. For example, Aristotle asserted that in order to be virtuous, 'we ought to have been brought up in a particular way from our very youth' (quoted in McKeon 1941). Nineteenth- and twentieth-century theorists concur with this view. From the concerns of those in the child-saving movement in the nineteenth century (Andry 1957; Bazelon 1976) to the present (Farrington 1996; Shoemaker 1995), the family has been regarded as a major influence in the presence or absence of youth offending behaviour. The American criminologist Travis Hirschi (1969) characterised the nature of the parent–child relationship as a 'bond of affection' whose strength can later determine the degree of resistance to breaking the law, 'the important consideration is whether the parent is psychologically present when temptation to a crime appears'. However, the fact that parental behaviour is related to youth offending does not provide sufficient reasons for imposing sanctions on parents. The challenges that confront children who are engaging in antisocial and offending behaviour, their families and the various professionals who work with them are complex, deep-rooted and multifaceted. Many youths entering the youth justice system have multiple serious problems in terms of their school achievement, psychological health, alcohol and drug abuse. The Labour government's response to youth offending ignores the complex patterns and interrelated problems that young people endure. These laws are both moralising and individualised. Children are characterised as perpetrators of antisocial behaviour and criminalised. Parents are cast as 'bad parents' and insufficient attention is paid to the ways in which parental capacity is affected by the financial and material circumstances within which parenting takes place (Lister 2008, 393). Thus, there is a need for prevention policies and interventions to avoid a narrow focus on parents and to take into account the family, social and contextual factors that are frequently associated with youth offending. Given the need to make families function better, the objective of youth crime prevention initiatives must be to develop and provide the environment, the resources and the opportunities through which families can become competent to deal with their own problems. The family should be assisted in guiding and nurturing the child through the provision of resources and support services which equip them to be good parents, reduce their isolation and promote the welfare of parents and their children.

Conclusion

New Labour wished to distance itself from the traditional 'liberal' politics of the Children and Young Persons Act 1969 and instead, embraced a mixture of neoliberal, free-market philosophies and traditional conservative values which prioritised the defence of the hierarchy and the desire to restore traditional morality. New Labour's 'Third Way' focused on an 'enabling state', with a firm emphasis on the individualised duties and responsibilities of citizens

(James and James 2001, 211). New Labour created a youth justice system which is increasingly characterised by a culture of control and an atmosphere of hostility towards children and young people. Interventions which are supposed to be directed towards preventing youth crime rely on punitive and custodial measures. For example, the abolition of *doli incapax* coupled with the low age of criminal responsibility, places England and Wales further out of step with most jurisdictions in the rest of Europe. The 1998 Act contains a range of orders such as the antisocial behaviour order, the child safety order and the child curfew, where there is no requirement for the commission of, or conviction for, a criminal offence. The 1998 Act places an increased emphasis on responsibility for offending, by both young persons and their families. The emphasis on individual responsibility has served to allow for crime to be disassociated from its social roots and masks the fact that the state and the law-abiding majority also have responsibilities (Jamieson and Yates 2009). Within a neoliberal operating context, young people are culturally positioned as learners who must be carefully guided towards suitable degrees of self-regulation in order to become legitimate citizens. This carries specific implications for how they are perceived and treated by agents of the state such as social workers and police (Kennelly 2011). This has allowed for a shift in focus away from the provision of universal welfare services towards targeted provision of resources and services to high-risk neighbourhoods and populations.

Welfarism has been increasingly criticised for encouraging state dependence, overloading the responsibilities of the state and undermining the ability of individuals to take responsibility for their own actions. Consequently, welfare concerns have been eroded by the individualisation of risk, earlier intervention, a focus on 'deeds' at the expense of 'needs', a prevailing discourse of responsibilisation and a growing penal populism. In England and Wales, the youth justice system combines a mélange of proactive welfare measures with overt reactive and punitive measures. It demonstrates an uneasy mixture of welfarist, actuarialist, and retributive impulses with an emphasis on responsibilisation and earlier intervention in the lives of young people and their families. However, the emphasis is very much on managing individual offenders rather than on addressing wider socio-economic constraints through the provisions of the social state. An effective youth crime reduction and prevention philosophy is one that addresses the life experiences of children and in which prevention is promoted through the collaborative and integrated activities of a range of services which they previously had been denied. Policy responses to youth offending should no longer be based upon a misguided notion of a threatening and lawless youth, but instead, should reflect the view that most young offenders have suffered a vulnerable, abusive and disadvantaged childhood. Arguably, the brave new world of the neoliberal state does not support such a policy.

Acknowledgement

Thanks to Dr Siobhan Daly for her helpful comments on the first draft of this chapter.

References

Andry, R. G. 1957. 'Faulty Parental and Maternal-Child Relationships, Affection and Discipline' *British Journal of Delinquency* 8: 34–48.

Arthur, R. 2002. 'Tackling youth crime: Supporting families in crisis'. *Child and Family Law Quarterly* 14 (4): 401–26.

———. 2010. 'Protecting the best interests of the child: A comparative analysis of the youth justice systems in Ireland, England and Scotland'. *International Journal of Children's Rights* 18 (2): 217–31.

Audit Commission. 1996. *Misspent Youth: Young People and Crime*. London: Audit Commission.

———. 2004. *Youth Justice 2004: A Review of the Reformed Youth Justice System*. London: Audit Commission.

Bandalli, S. 1998. 'Abolition of the presumption of *doli incapax* and the criminalisation of children'. *Howard Journal of Criminal Justice* 37 (2): 114–23.

———. 2000. 'Children, responsibility and the new youth justice'. In *The New Youth Justice*, edited by B. Goldson. Lyme Regis: Russell House.

Bazelon, D. 1976. 'The morality of the criminal law'. *Southern California Law Review* 49: 385–403.

Bell, E. 2009. '"Large, unpleasant thugs"? The Penal Responsibilisation of Young People in France and the United Kingdom'. *Revue Française de Civilisation Britannique* 15 (3): 115–32.

———. 2011. *Criminal Justice and Neoliberalism*. Basingstoke: Palgrave Macmillan.

Berlins, M. and G. Wansell. 1974. *Caught in the Act*. Harmondsworth: Penguin.

Blair, T. 1995. 'The rights we enjoy reflect the duties we owe'. *Spectator Lecture*, 22 March.

Bottoms, A. 1974. 'On the decriminalisation of the English juvenile court'. In *Crime, Criminology and Public Policy*, edited by R. Hood. London: Heinemann.

Brown, W. 2005. *Edgework: Critical Essays on Knowledge and Politics*. Princeton and Oxford: Princeton University Press.

Carpenter, M. 1853. *Juvenile Delinquents: Social Evils, Their Causes and Their Cure*. London: Cash.

Cavadino, M. and J. Dignan. 2006. *Penal Systems: A Comparative Approach*. London: Sage.

Cheshire, L. and G. Lawrence. 2005. 'Neoliberalism, Individualisation and Community: Regional Restructuring in Australia'. *Social Identities* 11 (5): 435–45.

Day Scalter, S. and C. Piper. 2000. 'Re-moralising the family? Family policy, family law and youth justice'. *Child and Family Law Quarterly* 12 (2): 135–52.

Donoghue, J. 2011. 'Truancy and the Prosecution of parents: An unfair burden on mothers?' *Modern Law Review* 74 (2): 216–44.

Downes, D. and K. Hansen. 2006. *Welfare and Punishment: The Relationship between Welfare Spending and Imprisonment*. London: Crime and Society Foundation.

Eekelaar, J. 2002. 'Beyond the welfare principle'. *Child and Family Law Quarterly* 14 (3): 237–49.

Farrington, D. P. 1996. *Understanding and Preventing Youth Crime*. York: Joseph Rowntree Foundation.

Foucault, M. 1994. 'About the Concept of the "Dangerous Individual" in Nineteenth-Century Legal Psychiatry'. In *Power: Essential Works of Foucault 1954–1984*, edited by J. B. Faubian. New York: The New Press.

Goldson, B. 1999. 'Punishing times for children in trouble: Recent developments and the Crime and Disorder Act 1998'. *Representing Children* 11 (4): 274–88.

———. 2005. 'Child imprisonment: A case for abolition'. *Youth Justice* 5: 77.

Goldson, B. and E. Peters. 2000. *Tough Justice, Responding to Children in Trouble*. London: Children's Society.

Gray, I. 2001. 'Neoliberalism, individualism and prospects for regional renewal'. *Rural Society* 11 (3): 283–96.

Hagell, A. and N. Hazel. 2001. 'Macro and micro patterns in the development of secure custodial institutions for serious and persistent young offenders in England and Wales'. *Youth Justice* 1 (1): 3–16.

Haydon, D. and P. Scraton. 2000. '"Condemn a little more, understand a little less": The political context and rights implications of the domestic and European ruling in the Venables-Thompson case'. *Journal of Law and Society* 27 (3): 416–48.

Hine, J. 2007. 'Young people's perspective on final warnings'. *Web Journal of Current Legal Issues* 2.

Hirschi, T. 1969. *Causes of Delinquency*. Berkeley: University of California Press

Hollingsworth, K. 2007. 'Judicial approaches to children's rights in youth crime'. *Child and Family Law Quarterly* 19 (1): 42–59.

Holt, A. 2008. 'Room for resistance? Parenting orders, disciplinary power and the production of the "bad parent"'. In *ASBO Nation: The Criminalisation of Nuisance*, edited by P. Squires. Bristol: Policy Press.

Home Office. 1927. *Report of the Departmental Committee on the Treatment of Young Offenders*. London: HMSO.

———. 1990. *Crime, Justice and Protecting the Public*. London: The Stationery Office.

———. 1997a. *No More Excuses: A New Approach to Tackling Youth Crime in England and Wales*. London: The Stationery Office.

———. 1997b. *Tackling Youth Crime*. London: The Stationery Office.

———. 2000. *The Final Warning Scheme – Guidance for Youth Offending Teams*. London: Home Office.

James, A. L. and A. James. 2001. 'Tightening the Net: Children, Community and Control'. *British Journal of Sociology* 52 (2): 211–28.

Jamieson, J. and J. Yates. 2009. 'Young People, Youth Justice and the State'. In *State Power Crime*, edited by R. Coleman, J. Sim, S. Tombs and D. Whyte. Sage: London.

Kempf-Leonard, K. and E. Peterson. 2002. 'Expanding Realms of the New Penology: The Advent of Actuarial Justice for Juveniles'. In *Youth Justice: Critical Readings*, edited by J. Muncie, G. Hughes and E. McLaughlin. London: Sage

Kennelly, J. 2011. 'Policing Young People as Citizens-In-Waiting: Legitimacy, Spatiality and Governance'. *British Journal of Criminology* 51 (2): 336–54.

Higgins, V. 2002. *Constructing Reform: Economic Expertise and the Governing of Agricultural Change in Australia*. New York: Nova Science.

Lister, R. 1998. 'Vocabularies of citizenship and gender: The UK'. *Critical Social Policy* 18 (3): 309–31.

———. 2008. 'Investing in children and childhood: A new welfare policy paradigm and its implications'. In *Childhood: Changing Contexts*, Comparative Social Research vol. 25, edited by A. Leira and C. Saraceno. Bingley: Emerald.

Loader, I. 2006. 'Fall of the "platonic guardians": Liberalism, criminology and political responses to crime in England and Wales'. *British Journal of Criminology* 46: 561–86.

Major, J. 1993. *Mail on Sunday*, 21 February, 8.

Mason, P. and D. Prior. 2008. 'The Children's Fund and the prevention of crime and anti-social behaviour'. *Criminology and Criminal Justice* 8 (3): 279–96.

McKeon, R. (ed.) 1941. *The Basic Works of Aristotle*. New York: Random House.

Miller, J. 1991. *Last One Over the Wall: The Massachusetts Experiment in Closing Reform School*. Athens, OH: Ohio University Press.

Ministry of Justice. 2010. *Breaking the Cycle: Effective Punishment, Rehabilitation and Sentencing of Offenders*. London: Ministry of Justice.

Muncie, J. 1999. *Youth and Crime – A Critical Introduction*. London: Sage.

———. 2002. 'A new deal for youth? Early intervention and correctionalism'. In *Crime Prevention and Community Safety: New Directions*, edited by G. Hughes, E. McLaughlin and J. Muncie. London: Sage.

———. 2005. 'The globalization of crime control – the case of youth and juvenile justice: Neo-liberalism, policy convergence and international conventions'. *Theoretical Criminology* 9 (1): 35–64.

———. 2008. 'The punitive turn in juvenile justice: Cultures of control and rights compliance in Western Europe and the USA'. *Youth Justice* 8 (2): 107–21.

NACRO. 2000. *The Detention and Training Order – NACRO Briefing*. London: NACRO.

Newburn, T. 2002. 'Atlantic crossings: Policy transfer and crime control in the USA and Britain'. *Punishment and Society* 4 (2): 165–94.

Penal Affairs Consortium. 1995. *The Doctrine of Doli Incapax*. London: Penal Affairs Consortium.

Pitts, J. 2001. *The New Politics of Youth Crime*. Basingstoke: Palgrave.

Rose, N. 1999. *Powers of Freedom: Reframing Political Thought*. Cambridge: Cambridge University Press.

Shoemaker, D. J. 1995. *Theories of Delinquency: An Explanation of Delinquent Behaviour*, 3rd ed. New York: Oxford University Press.

Smith, R. 2006. 'Actuarialism and Early Intervention in Contemporary Youth Justice'. In *Youth Crime and Justice*, edited by B. Goldson and J. Muncie. London: Sage.

Smith, T. 1994. '*Doli Incapax* under threat'. *Cambridge Law Journal* 53 (3): 426–8.

Stenson, K. 2001. 'The new politics of crime control'. In *Crime, Risk and Justice: The Politics of Crime Control in Liberal Democracies*, edited by K. Stenson and R. Sullivan. Devon: Willan.

Stone, N. 2001. 'Custodial sentences: aims and principles in youth justice, disparity and other complexities'. *Youth Justice* 1 (1): 42.

United States Government. 1967. *President's Commission on Law Enforcement and Administration of Justice: Task Force Report*. Washington: US Government Printing Office.

Youth Justice Board. 2000. 'Detention and training order – a better sentence for young offenders'. *Youth Justice Board News*, June.

———. 2008. *Corporate Plan 2008–11, Business Plan 2008/09: Supporting Young People, Making Communities Safer*. London: Youth Justice Board.

Chapter 7

INSTITUTIONALISING COMMERCIALISM? THE CASE OF SOCIAL MARKETING FOR HEALTH IN THE UNITED KINGDOM

Paul Crawshaw

Why can't you sell brotherhood and rational thinking like you sell soap?
(Weibe 1952, 679)

Introduction

Throughout this book there is reiteration that neoliberalism has become the dominant mode of social, political and economic organisation over the past three decades in the Western industrialised nations and beyond. As noted in the introduction, the purpose of the book is to substantiate this assertion and to add to the wealth of discussion and analysis which has already been contributed by further illustrating not only how this new doxa has profoundly shaped the macro political and economic organisation of nation states, but, further, to illuminate its operation at the micro level of institutions and organisations. In doing this, it is intended that the chapters presented add weight to Harvey's (2005, 3) assertion that as a mode of governance,

Neoliberalism…has pervasive effects on ways of thought to the point where it has become incorporated into the common sense way many of us interpret, live in, and understand the world.

This is to be achieved through critical analysis of the institutionalisation of neoliberal values and modes of thought in a variety of settings. The empirical focus of this chapter is the growing use of social marketing for health as a new public health methodology in the United Kingdom.

Public health is a complex discipline which draws on a range of cognate subjects and methodologies with the broad aim of protecting and improving the health of populations. It is the latter, health improvement, which has become the main focus of public health as it has been understood in the Western industrialised nations in the second half of the twentieth and first decade of the twenty-first centuries. Thus, despite its origins in, and a history predicated upon, social engineering and environmental interventions (from the sanitary innovations of the Graeco-Roman world to the great public health projects in the United Kingdom in the mid-nineteenth century), Western public health has more latterly focused upon individual lifestyles and promoting behavioural change in populations in order to reduce inequalities and bring about health improvement. This shift in practice and orientation is said to be a response to the so-called epidemiological transition from infectious or communicable diseases to chronic diseases as the main sources of morbidity and mortality in the industrialised global North. The focus upon lifestyle and behaviours has led to new interventions often predicated upon education and the promotion of individual agency in improving health with decreasing emphasis upon structural or environmental changes. These newer modes of governing the health of populations, described by some as characterised by a troubling politics of behaviour, have been identified as indicative of the emergence of 'health societies' (Kickbusch 2007), societies characterised by an ever-growing territorialisation of health alongside an almost limitless promotion of health reflexivity. Under these conditions, there have emerged myriad imperatives to be healthy from diverse sources including the media, government offices, non-governmental organisations (NGOs) and health agencies. Health has thus emerged as a new mode of governing populations, closely linked to particular moral imperatives regarding the individual and responsibility within late modern capitalist economies (Lupton 1995).

Commentators have noted that these imperatives are typically predicated upon the construction of the healthy subject (Crawshaw 2007), that is, the subject who is willing and able to take control of their own well-being and that of their families. As such, they assume a rational, civilised, risk-averse actor who is able to respond to health advice and act appropriately in the interests of avoiding morbidities and achieving longevity. It is clear that these assumptions are congruent with neoliberal rationalities which emphasise the role of the individual who has the freedom to choose from available resources to construct their own self-identity. The key sources of such directives have traditionally been health education and health promotion, complementary disciplines said to be respectively didactic and enabling.

Like its commercial cousin, social marketing aims to encourage particular behaviours in targeted (or in the parlance of both social and commercial

Figure 7.1.

marketing, segmented) individuals and communities. Where it differs, however, is that its main intention is to bring about these changes in order to achieve 'social good' (French and Blair Stevens 2005). It is here that some of the paradoxes and contradictions in embracing the concept of social marketing in public-health policy and practice become apparent. Although the achievement of social good is a claim reiterated throughout the literature (see, for example, French and Blair-Stevens 2005; Truss, Marshall and Blair-Stevens 2010), the focus of campaigns is typically, and explicitly, behavioural change in the individual, focused upon what are often described as 'merit' and 'demerit' behaviours.[1]

The key proposition of this discussion is that the introduction and growing influence of social marketing for health as a key component of governmental strategies for health improvement is indicative of a troubling neoliberalism within both broader health provision,[2] and more specifically, public health strategies and methodologies within the United Kingdom, whereby individuals are increasingly compelled, often through the media or distant governance mechanisms, to take responsibility for the management of their own health and well-being. These strategies are congruent with prevailing forms of economic, political and social organisation which defer to market and consumer-oriented modes of governance and reflect the dominance of capitalist logics of production, consumption and organisation. Considerable critical space has been given to concerns regarding the creeping privatisation of the UK National Health Service (see, for example, Pollock 2004) and recently, the UK Conservative–Liberal coalition government has put a bill in place which opens the door for a more explicitly privatised health service (Health and Social Care Bill 2010–11). Less attention has been paid to the introduction of neoliberal rationalities to public health practice in the United Kingdom.

Given attempts to create a 'health marketplace' in service delivery (Pollock 2004), it is perhaps unsurprising that marketing is heralded as a panacea for health improvement within modern public health discourses. Robertson (2001, 294–5) has noted that

> particular discourses on health emerge at particular historical moments and gain widespread acceptance primarily because they are more or less congruent with the prevailing social, political and economic order within which they are produced, maintained and reproduced.

The move towards more distant methods of intervention such as social marketing for health, which, although they may be initially based upon consultation or research with segmented or targeted populations, rely heavily upon the communication of particular messages which individuals will act upon to make improvements to their own health (see Figure 7.1). Reflecting a broader de-collectivisation of welfare (Rose 2001), these strategies have adopted methods of governance at a distance and become, it is argued, exemplars of neoliberal methods of governing late modern societies through inculcating self-management and individualisation of responsibility. In what follows, some critical discussion of the institutionalisation of neoliberalism in public health is offered. This is followed by the presentation of findings from a sample of 17 semi-structured qualitative interviews conducted with key stakeholders involved in either the strategic planning or operationalisation of social marketing within one locality in the northeast of England. These findings are considered in light of key theoretical propositions regarding responsibility and a growing neoliberalism within public health policy and practice in the United Kingdom and beyond.

From Environments to Lifestyle

Harvey (2010, 131) has proposed that the success of the neoliberal doxa has been to impose a powerful new 'mental conception of the world', a conception which others have argued (see Read 2009) ceases to be ideological but rather frames all human activity within the terms of reference of the market place, promoting competitive individualism and an understanding of social relationships as increasingly based upon models of the market with the individual posited as an enterprising subject, willing and able to construct a healthy self-identity under the guidance of distant expert discourses. Over two centuries, public health in the United Kingdom has been characterised by a number of key political shifts which have defined its approach to improving the health of populations. As Robertson (2001) notes, these are congruent with wider political trends. From the mid-nineteenth century's golden age of interventionism to the emergence of the new public health in late twentieth century, the philosophies and methods of public health have reflected wider political mores which have determined how policymakers and practitioners have attempted to improve the health of populations in response to shifting epidemiological patterns from infectious or communicable diseases to a more contemporary focus upon chronic illness and the often-cited role of lifestyle factors as determinants of these. Where the nineteenth-century reformers aimed to improve environments (sanitation, clean water) to combat the deadly effects of communicable diseases such as cholera, the role of public health in the late twentieth century became that of addressing issues of lifestyle and behaviour, with the intention of tackling modern epidemics of morbidity such as chronic heart disease and cancers. Enshrined in the Ottawa Charter of 1986, the focus has increasingly become individuals and their consumption practices as well as their dispositions towards particular behaviours such as participation in exercise, and so on. Over the past two decades, these discourses have gained momentum to the degree that in the Western industrialised nations, the main focus of public health work has become individuals and their behaviours, typically with an emphasis upon risk and its reduction among key populations (Petersen and Lupton 1996).

To achieve this, in the late 1970s, under the auspices of the new public health, a new discipline emerged in the form of health promotion. Health promotion was conceived as a means of improving the health of populations through focusing upon both individual and environmental determinants of health. Said to represent a qualitative shift from simplistic and didactic health education, as a project, it aimed, in line with the wider objectives of the new public health (Baum 2008), to both provide supportive environments in which people could lead healthier lives while simultaneously promoting healthier lifestyles and behaviours. It is the latter which has come under significant criticism from a variety of sources (see, for example, Crawford 1977 and 1986) because of its propensity for not only 'blaming the victim', but also its capacity to detract attention from wider social and economic determinants of health and the potential role of states in addressing structural barriers to healthy living. Despite this, health promotion has remained a powerful discourse in public health work in the Western industrialised nations into the twenty-first century, and has more recently been joined by a newer and closely related form of governance – social marketing for health.

Understanding Social Marketing (for Health)

The key claim of social marketing is that it aims to promote 'social good' (National Social Marketing Centre 2007) using the methods of commercial marketing. These methods include, customer/consumer orientation, setting of behavioural goals for a social good, use of a marketing mix to achieve those goals, audience segmentation to target customers effectively and use of the concepts of 'exchange' and of 'competition' (Robinson and Robertson 2010). Social marketing for health typically targets individuals and communities (the sick, but more often and most significantly for this discussion, the 'worried well'), with the aim of encouraging behavioural change, often with populations deemed to be 'at risk'. These objectives are achieved through a complex 'mix' of methods which includes recognising the relationship between the product, price, place and promotion characteristics in intervention planning and organisation (Lefebvre and Flora 1988). This mix is operationalised by beginning with specific target audiences as the basis of campaigns (segmentation), gaining full understanding of how audiences construct the product, considering the costs and benefits of behavioural change and understanding the place or settings in which both audiences will be targeted and in which changes will take place.

The adoption of social marketing as a strategy is driven by the observation that many of the health challenges facing Western societies have significant behavioural elements including obesity, alcohol misuse, infection control, recycling, saving for retirement and crime (French 2009, 1). These challenges are coupled, French (2009) argues, with growing resistance to state paternalism and its perceived propensity to breed dependency. Social marketing operates with 'consumers' as its starting point, guided by the nostrum that under the right guidance and with appropriate 'nudges' (Thaler and Sunstein 2009), individuals can and should take responsibility for well-being. Here, social marketing takes its place alongside a range of 'soft' or 'libertarian' paternalistic (Pykett 2011) approaches to behaviour change which have been embraced by current and recent UK governments. To achieve these ends, social marketing typically uses advertising and other forms of media to encourage behavioural change, alongside interventions. For example, Change4Life (http://www.nhs. uk/Change4Life/) was instigated by the UK's New Labour government in 2009 (and is being used by the current coalition government as the main driver for reducing obesity with the aim of improving children and families' diet and fitness (Jones et al., 2010).[3] The campaign (see Figure 7.1) combines advice and encouragement to engage in more physical activity with events which are free to access; for example, offering dance classes around the United Kingdom in the spring of 2010.

It is clear that through its adoption of the individual as the starting point for much of its work, and with an explicit mandate for behavioural change, social marketing has much in common with its cousin, health promotion, and as such is subject to many of the same longstanding criticisms; that is, placing responsibility for health upon individuals without acknowledging wider social, political and economic determinants (Crawford 1977 and 1986). As Griffiths et al. (2009, 269) have recently noted, the theories of social marketing and health promotion have much in common.

> Good health promotion and good social marketing have a shared and consistent core theory and practice base – they both have a driving concern with achieving social good through the use of ethical approaches that engage, mobilise and empower individuals and communities. They are both also behavioural, going beyond simple message based communications to find ways to help people achieve and sustain positive behaviours.

In both social marketing and health promotion, health and its attainment become a form of consumption (Bunton and Burrows 1995), as individuals are positioned as rational actors able to make judicious and informed choices from a range of options made available to them. It is perhaps unsurprising, then, that social marketing for health adopts commercial methods to promote well-being, premised upon targeting populations of reflexive agents capable of monitoring and managing their own health. The key contention of this discussion is that such strategies are indicative of prevailing neoliberal ideologies of welfare which posit solutions at the level of the individual. This in turn reflects a troubling turn towards the politics of behaviour in wider public policy.[1] The aim of what follows is to explore how this discourse of commercialisation may have become embedded within the rhetoric and practice of those charged with improving the health of populations at a local level.

In what follows, qualitative data from interviews with a range of professionals involved in either the strategic development or implementation and operationalisation of social marketing programmes and drawn from a range of organisations including primary care organisations and local authorities, is analysed to consider critically how social marketing is understood within contemporary public-health practice in the United Kingdom. The aims of social marketing are explored and its construction of individuals and their health as objects of intervention are considered. The overall aim is to consider how social marketing may reflect a troubling commercialisation of health work which is reflected across a range of forms of service delivery that have continued to embrace neoliberal modes of operation within an increasingly diverse 'health marketplace'. Respondents present a number of understandings and constructs of social marketing as a model for health improvement and reflect upon its wider role in bringing about behavioural change in individuals. The implications of adopting this as the primary focus for health interventions are critically appraised under what is proposed as a troubling neoliberal behavioural turn in public-health methodologies.

Methodologies

Data was collected in a locality in the northeast of England. A series of semi-structured qualitative interviews were carried out with professionals working in a range of health and health-related fields. Professionals were selected by the criteria that they had some involvement with social marketing for health at either a strategic or operational level. This led to the identification of a small initial sample with snowball sampling used for further recruitment. A total of 17 participants were recruited overall. Respondents ranged from those in senior local and regional public health directorate roles to operational leads for particular services, for example, smoking cessation. The data was anonymised and any extracts presented coded on the basis of being either operational (O), strategic (S) or both, for example, O1 represents respondent number 1, operational; S2 would be respondent number 2, strategic; O/S would be respondent number 3, operational/strategic.

Qualitative methods were used because of their potential to elicit in-depth understandings of respondents' experiences and constructions of social marketing for health as a phenomenon in public health practice (Marvasti 2004, 7). Interviews were conducted on the premises of the various organisations to which individuals were attached, in a room allocated specifically for these purposes. Data was collected by a research assistant using a topic guide developed in consultation with the project supervisor. As the overall focus of the data collection was to explore experience, understandings and constructions of social marketing for health, questions explored themes such as 'What do you understand by social marketing?' 'What are its key methods and methodologies?' 'What are its strengths and weaknesses as a method?' Interviews ranged in length from one hour to one hour and thirty minutes. The data was analysed using the conventions of thematic qualitative analysis (Miles and Huberman 1994). The analysis was conducted collaboratively between the research assistant and project supervisor. Ethical approval was granted by the relevant School Research Ethics Committee at Teesside University.

The Commercial and the Social

Respondents freely engaged the idea of social marketing and were often able to describe it in terms of a complex set of interrelated ideas intended to influence individual behaviours with the aim of promoting 'social good'. A consistent theme which emerged was the synthesis between social and commercial marketing.

> Social marketing links in very much with traditional marketing, so it's getting your message out there as much as possible, getting people to buy

into that message, so it's building the bridge between the product and the customer. (O1)

Here, and elsewhere, it was presented as unproblematic to approach social marketing as a means of operationalising or segmenting individuals and communities with perceived shared needs (e.g. new mothers) as customers or consumers within a market relationship in which they were to be sold a product, namely, more appropriate and 'healthy' behaviours (for example, breast feeding of infants). Respondents often described the key tenets of social marketing in considerable depth and consistently noted the link between commercial methodologies and the implications of this for new ways of working with individuals and communities, or service users, as they were often described.

> Social marketing relating to health is using marketing systematically to gain an understanding about population needs, lifestyle, their preferences, their beliefs in order to tailor an intervention or a new service or a pathway to meet their needs, and make it appealing to them so that the service fits them and you're not developing a service and then hoping it suits their needs. So it's using more of the marketing tools that traditionally commercial sectors used, but in a way to benefit people's health, rather than purchasing a commercial commodity. (O6)

Here, employing such methods was typically presented as unproblematic and, rather, was judged to be an 'evidence based' and pragmatic response to meeting the health needs of populations in a more comprehensive and 'bottom up' way. The implications of transferring ideas directly from the commercial sectors (a sector whose concerns are, of course, mainly the creation of increased surplus value) were not considered. Rather, the methods of commercial marketing were understood as something which could be learned from and imported directly into health settings.

> I think we can learn a lot from what the commercial sector have done in the sense of they really do understand their target audience, and that the link there, that where there's a lot in common. They don't try to sell their product to everybody. It's about using the consumer insight in order to market your intervention to do good for the populations' health. (O6)

Throughout the sample, respondents clearly expressed that they felt that social marketing was merely a logical extension of the discipline of commercial

marketing and that many lessons could be learned in order to target better
health improvement interventions and in accessing audiences effectively.

> Using the principles of marketing for social good. So ensuring that in a
> public health context when we are looking at the health of a population
> and designing interventions that we actually take into consideration
> the lifestyles, attitudes and beliefs, the cultures of people within that
> population so that we ensure that services are focused around their needs
> and take into consideration anything that may cause barriers to them,
> either changing their behaviour or entering into a service so it's kind
> of using the discipline in terms of communication marketing and how
> you would analyse those things, then use what solutions you would have
> applied to selling a product or a service, using those skills but for social
> good. (O5)

It was often recognised, as discussed earlier, that this was closely linked to the
more established methods of health promotion as an intervention. Here, the
adoption of healthy lifestyles and practices becomes a form of consumption
and, as these respondents note, audiences are segmented and their needs
met appropriately in order to make the selling of health as a commodity
more effective. In this way, there was clear evidence of social marketing
for health being understood as an adaptation of commercial methods; an
adaptation which was felt to be unproblematic in transferring approaches
designed to sell products to promoting the adoption of behavioural changes
in the complex social and environmental settings in which health identities
are constructed.

Respondents echoed the position of Hastings (2007), who, following
Weibe (1952), has questioned why it is that methods which are known to be
successful in commercial settings cannot simply be imported into the public
realm in order to achieve social good. In asking why it is that 'the devil should
have all the best tunes', Hastings (2007) proposes that it is by providing us
with the ability to make the right choices in particular settings that we can
change behaviours for the good of all. It is here that the institutionalisation
of a market model in public health practice is apparent. Respondents posit
marketing as an unproblematic (and often pragmatic) response to meeting
the needs of populations in more effective ways through techniques such as
segmentation. Consideration of the complexity and contradictions raised
by attempting to sell complex behavioural changes using the same methods
used to sell commercial products was not offered and social marketing was
presented as an effective methodology and important addition to the public
health arsenal.

Achieving 'Behavioural Goals'

French and Blair-Stevens (2005) are explicit in their directive that the aim of social marketing is to bring about behavioural change. Behaviour change is a key tenet of public health strategies to achieve many of its targets of reduction in chronic diseases (cardiovascular disease, cancers, diabetes). It aims to reduce an individual's likelihood of morbidity by changing behaviours which are said to increase their risk. Within this discourse, behaviours (alcohol consumption, tobacco use, diet, exercise) become risk factors for potential future morbidities, and complex profiling tools are used to make individuals aware of their likelihood (or risk) of future illness based upon current measures of health status (for example, blood pressure readings, cholesterol levels) and the behaviours (smoking, diet, exercise). For example, one aspect of the current NHS Health Check screening programme, based upon collection of the above data, is to provide 'well' individuals (aged 40–74) with a risk 'score' for their likelihood of experiencing a cardiovascular incident within the next ten years.[5] Appropriate advice is then offered to the individual on how this score can be reduced with appropriate behavioural changes and based upon the premises that

> everyone is at risk of developing heart disease, stroke, type 2 diabetes or kidney disease. But these diseases can often be prevented, and NHS Health Check can help you by assessing your risk and giving you personalised advice on how to reduce it… Take charge of your long term health, with the NHS Health Check. (NHS Choices, http://www.nhs.uk/)

The promotion of behavioural change is not limited to such semi-clinical encounters, however, but is apparent in wider public health marketing such as the Change4Life campaign (see Figure 7.1), which promotes the simple message of 'eat well, move more, live longer'. Here, although tied in with a variety of activities and interventions – offering dance classes around the United Kingdom in the spring of 2010 and being used as a recognisable branding to promote making healthier choices, for example, on fruit and vegetable in convenience stores – the emphasis is upon the individual choosing healthier behaviours. Respondents in this sample recognised that a key aim of social marketing is to bring about behavioural changes in individuals and described both how they understood this as a particular standpoint on health improvement and how it might be used to achieve this goal. It was universally acknowledged that behaviour change was the key aim of these interventions as a whole.

> Social marketing is used to support behaviour change in an audience segment. So it's basically selling a message or selling a behaviour change

to them in a way that they would respond to using a whole load of commercial principles like exchange principles. (S8)

Simultaneously, they were quick to recognise that this was a highly ambitious aim and that it was potentially one which could be much harder to achieve in social marketing than in commercial marketing. As one respondent who had experience of both sectors noted,

> It's easier to work in commercial marketing, because usually when you're selling a product to someone there's a reason for them to want it, whereas in social marketing, in particular social marketing in health, we're often asking people to do things that are not particularly going to be pleasant for them, so giving up smoking which especially if somebody's been smoking for a long period of time, there's a whole host of other factors that influence social marketing as opposed to commercial marketing like, you know, there's a lot less emphasis on, like, families and surroundings and the social networks when it comes to commercial marketing as opposed to social marketing. (S8)

Respondents stressed issues such as the challenges of achieving longevity in behavioural change in 'wicked' issues such as smoking and alcohol use when competing with some of the environmental and cultural pressures which they felt made these behaviours so deeply ingrained and persistent.

> I guess what marketing wants is behaviour change, but that there was some differences potentially in the competencies around (A) How you market something in a traditional sense in a marketing sense and (B) What you need to do in effective piece of social marketing work with local people because ultimately some of them in public health we want to use it as something that creates long term positive behaviour change in a vulnerable part of the population usually if you want to reduce inequality. (S3)

Although it was recognised that the role of social marketing was both to provide a greater understanding of the context in which health behaviours take place and align these with appropriate interventions, ultimately changing behaviours was felt to be something which individuals themselves were responsible for bringing about. It was often noted that if a greater understanding of both context and attitudes was available, if health beliefs could be understood more clearly, then it became possible to encourage people to change their behaviours.

You know, if we're doing smoking, we do exactly the same as if we're doing drugs and health, but I think we need to consider a little bit better what do the communities whose behaviour health beliefs and behaviours we're trying to influence [think], what are those health beliefs and, you know, what are the attitudes towards them and what can we do to support that change. (S5)

Here, it is clear that although a fuller understanding of the context of health beliefs and behaviours is felt to be vital to successful health improvement strategies, the main aim is to bring about changes in the behaviour of an individual in order to facilitate health improvement. In the current popular neoliberal parlance, behavioural change may be something which can be supported by the provision of appropriate choice architecture (Thaler and Sunstein 2009); however, ultimate responsibility lies with the individual taking messages on board and acting in a rational and risk-averse manner to increase their chances of future well-being.

Choice

Choice has become a key theme in health work in the United Kingdom (see NHS Choices discussed above) throughout the past decade. In the delivery of services, this has been epitomised by schemes such as 'Choose and Book', conceived to empower patients to have greater control over where and when they receive an approved treatment. Such initiatives represent part of a greater push for a patient-centred NHS. Some respondents referred to this as an important aspect of patient choice, although not always uncritically, recognising the social and environmental barriers to 'choice'.

The first thing is, do you understand the choices, but the second thing, are you in the position to exercise that choice. So, for example, Choose and Book is potentially a very good thing for patients. Right? You've got a choice to go to a number of hospitals. You choose as a patient, it's your right to choose as a patient and then we'll book you in then, so before you leave this surgery you know when your appointment is. Great for patients when it works; my concern is that will they understand the choices, and secondly, have the wherewithal to actually exercise any of those choices, because if you lived alone and you haven't got a car, then your choice is much more limited. You may understand the choices, but your choice is more limited. Really, it's pretty much restricted to which one you can get to. So you might have to wait longer in more pain. (S1)

Here, respondents identified some of the limitations of introducing choice as a blanket 'good' in service delivery without awareness of the potential inhibitors of such choices. Related more specifically to health improvement and the role of social marketing, respondents stressed the importance of basic health education in allowing people to make healthier choices.

> It's important to raise people's awareness of different issues, but it's also important to educate people so that they can understand and make changes to their lifestyles with well-informed choices, to make informed choices about their own health, so it's important that they're educated enough to make those informed choices and it's important that we educate people in order for them to make those informed choices and equally interventions you know we need to kind of give them a hook to engage with to begin with. (S8)

Here, the imperative for change rests upon a well-informed individual with the capacity to make the 'right' choices regarding their health and, often, that of their families. It is clear that such perspectives on health improvement assume a rational, calculating actor or individual who is willing and able to make appropriate choices and changes under the guidance of typically distant experts (Petersen and Lupton 1996). Elsewhere, choice was presented as something central in bringing about behavioural change, which stresses that individuals are given the right tools to make healthy choices, often regardless of wider social determinants. Social marketing was understood as key here, with a perceived potential to access 'hard to reach' groups, for example, persistent smokers concentrated within lower socio-economic groups.

> If we know how to engage with our so-called hard-to-reach and if we know that if we invested so much we'll get the message across then help them make healthier lifestyle choices, helping to engage with preventative services such as screening, stop smoking, engaging with their GPs earlier, so rather than waiting until they are actually blue-lighted into hospital, if we can demonstrate that we've got…we've found a communication channel and if we can then demonstrate outcomes that we endorse, then it would be a resource well spent, rather than trying to do a broad brush approach which we know over the years hasn't made a significant impact on those hard-to-reach groups. (S4)

Some respondents also recognised that social and environmental factors were in themselves key determinants of an individual's ability to choose and that these must be taken into account. There was clear understanding of the challenges of using social marketing methods to bring about behavioural changes and, ultimately, social good (French and Blair-Stevens 2005) where significant other factors impinged upon people's day-to-day lives and opportunities to be healthy. Socio-economic factors were highlighted,

> Well, if the wider determinants of your health are not right, if you don't have a job, if you don't have a decent home, if you don't have fabric and the infrastructure to make a positive behaviour change that is difficult, so I do think, you know, holistically, all those things need to be in relative order and a good place before anybody's going to have the most supreme and excellent lifestyle. (S7)

Some respondents consistently returned to these wider determinants of lifestyle, choice and behaviours and ultimately argued that although social marketing had become a key tool in public health methodologies overall, its limitations must be recognised for populations experiencing high levels of social inequality, inequalities that it has been consistently acknowledged require 'social action' (Marmot 2010). As one respondent commented regarding smoking and diet for mothers living in areas of high deprivation (a feature of the locales in which this research took place),

> Anybody who lives in a deprived area knows people smoke for different reasons. Take, for instance, the young mum who's maybe got three small children and not much money, you know she's kinda thinking 'oh my god, what can I get for the tea' and what she chooses is probably going to be something that's cheap, not necessarily nutritious, full of salt, full of whatever because that's what she can afford. When she gets them to bed, her reward is to sit down and have cigarettes. (O/S2)

Rose (2001, 18) argues that in the twenty-first century it is a well-regulated body and an outward concern for health which have become the most significant organising principles of a life of prudence, responsibility and choice. If Rose is accurate in his contention, it is perhaps unsurprising that the discourse of choice has so profoundly permeated public health work and become a key tenet of strategies such as social marketing, premised as they are upon facilitating 'better' choices and allowing individuals to take 'control' over their long-term health and well-being. As some data presented above highlights, however, choice is a highly complex and contested area, with many variables impacting upon the ability to choose healthier options, behaviours and strategies such as socio-economic status, education, and so on.

Lifestyle Change and Responsibility

The theme of responsibility for health improvement and the role of social marketing in positioning populations as determiners of their own health emerged consistently throughout the sample, with respondents expressing a variety of perspectives.

> It's the balance between rights and responsibilities and it's the balance between what is and isn't the deal here and what can be expected and, you know, what services we can provide and should provide and where are we nanny stating and where are we morally and ethically judging. There is an element of responsibility for us all, you know, and there is an element in taking that responsibility that some of us are in much better places to take on that responsibility than others, so I suppose when we look at what Michael Marmot is saying about social gradients and social inequality and it's the social justice issue. (S3)

Here and elsewhere, respondents stressed that responsibility for health resided with the individual who should respond appropriately to health messages and attempts to 'enable' their well-being and that of their families. This finding has been echoed in other studies of populations' constructions of their own responsibility for their health (see Crawshaw and Newlove 2011). Although respondents like the following suggested that the aim of such work should be to allow individuals to recognise that they have the potential to take more control and responsibility, there was recognition that this must be understood in the context of wider social and environmental determinants of health.

> It's not a lay the blame [thing] and saying you absolutely must and we are the experts telling you that you'll be all damned if you don't. It's not about that, it's about saying, you know, come on now, you've got it within you, you've got the opportunity here, but I think you can't expect social marketing strategies on their own to be sufficient to start behaviour change if somebody's fundamentals aren't right. (O4)

Respondents were cautious of the potential of discourses of responsibility leading to victim blaming, which is a criticism long levelled at health promotion (Crawford 1977 and 1986). It was recognised that individual lifestyle changes were part of a wider matrix of determinants of health and that these were potentially profound in shaping people's potential to make healthy choices.

In some respects, yes, but if you look at Dahlgren and Whitehead's wider determinants of health model, you will see from that that individual lifestyle changes are only part of the problems. You need to look at the bigger picture. All of the things that influence your individual lifestyle changes are influenced by things like your educational attainment, your employment status, your housing conditions, what foods you can even access, you know, your agricultural area, sanitation, the economic climate. All of these things are in the macro environment that you don't have any particular control over and necessarily influence your health choices as an individual, which is where public health has a role and a responsibility to provide and to support the environment of the individual to support them in making those informed, educated choices around their own lifestyle and health and where we can support that and where we can educate people and give them and incentive to do so, it's our responsibility to do that, so I guess the answer to your question is potentially no. (S8)

At this point, respondents recognised the power of social class in determining to what degree individuals are willing and able to take responsibility for their own health and that of their immediate families. Socio-economic factors were reiterated as determining how much responsibility for health could be taken and overall it was felt that this presented some real challenges for public health interventions.

You have your individual choices shaped by the environment in which you're living. So whilst for me, comfortably middle-class with a car and all the rest of it, [I] can quite easily go and buy vegetables from the supermarket, for example, but if I was in some council estate without a car and the nearest place that I can buy fresh veg is, you know, three bus rides away and my kids don't eat fresh veg, therefore it's a bit of a waste, then am I really going to go and try hard to try and get fresh veg on the table? Probably not, you know. (S5)

Education was identified as a key factor, inextricably linked to socio-economic status, which was said to shape dispositions to health and health behaviours, morbidity and mortality.

You know, it's not just about people making those choices; it's about knowing their choice to make and the benefits of the choices. Yeah, personal circumstances on things like, I don't know, like breast feeding, there should be, you know, some women genuinely don't know that's better and, you know, I think it's hard from an educated, middle-class perspective to understand why people make some choices that… you've got to understand their perspective and the value they place on life for example. For example, their life might be so rubbish that smoking and dying 15 years early doesn't bother them. (O/S3)

People who are better educated tend to make better choices in terms of their health needs, for example, professional people. You'd find nowadays that smoking rates among those groups are very low, very low. That's because for people to achieve those positions, [they] are well educated, they tend to have more control of their lives and have greater self-esteem and they tend to be in a position to make choices which are healthy choices over time, one of which will be to choose not to smoke or if they've smoked when they were younger, to have the ability to understand it's not a good thing to do and to choose to try and stop. (S1)

Longstanding tensions between individual responsibility and the role of the state in maintaining health (Minkler 1999) are played out with respondents expressing the often-contradictory debates which arise. Respondents often argue (following Minkler 1999) for a balanced and ecological model that stresses individual responsibility for health within a broader social responsibility, ultimately reiterating the core values of health promotion of providing enabling environments in which individuals can exercise 'healthy' choices. Despite this, it is clear from the data collected that these professionals working in public health believe that there remains a powerful role for individual responsibility, in spite of the recognition that this is equally shaped and inhibited by structural and systemic factors.

Discussion

The National Social Marketing Centre (2007) proposes that the role of social marketing for health is to 'enable consumers to critically interpret mass-media messages in order to make informed decisions' and 'to gain greater control over the factors that influence their health'. French and Blair-Stevens (2005) take this one step further to argue that social marketing is the systematic application of marketing, alongside other concepts and techniques, to achieve specific behavioural goals for a social good. Both definitions belie ambitious goals for social marketing as a methodology with the potential to bring about significant health and wider social improvement. Both are also predicated on bringing about behavioural changes in the individual.

It is here that many of the challenges and contradictions of social marketing lie. The reiterated goal of 'social good' is to be achieved not through attempts to promote or engineer systemic or structural changes (e.g. campaigns for more progressive taxation, attempts to mobilise particular interests groups around specific issues), but rather through encouraging people to make better choices within their own lives. To achieve this, the individual must be reflexive, rational and overall, enterprising in recognising where and how they can make the 'right' choices and appropriate changes in order to improve their own health and well-being. Recent Foucauldian analysis has suggested that the key feature of the social and political organisation of neoliberal economies is the operation of forms of governance premised upon the reorganisation of social relations on the basis of the self as enterprise (McNay 2009). Here, the focus of government becomes the governance of the self outside of the state, typically mimicking the political rationality of the market, whereby the individual is positioned as entrepreneur and the self as an enterprise to be formed in direct response to the imperatives of neoliberal choice, itself provided through a system of markets and incentives to achieve self-actualisation through judicious navigation of a series of regulated freedoms (Rose 1999). These conditions, Lazzarato (2009, 110) argues, have led to the formation of a new kind of individual: 'the subject who is an 'entrepreneur of him-/herself' who is meant to fit into the frame of society as an enterprise society.

The discussion presented above illuminates how social marketing for health has been taken on board as a new form of governance judged to be capable of importing commercial methods into new sectors and areas of public life with the aim of improving lives and creating social good. The key contention of this discussion is that such shifts are indicative of the institutionalisation of market-driven, neoliberal imperatives into diverse areas of social and welfare provision. Harvey (2005, 3) has powerfully suggested that neoliberalism has become incorporated and accepted into the common-sense way in which many of us view the world. Read (2009, 2) goes further to suggest that neoliberalism represents not merely a new ideology, but a transformation of ideology, as it is generated not from the state or a dominant social class, but from the experience of buying and selling commodities from the market, which is then extended across other social spaces, 'the market place of ideas', to become an image of society. Foucault (2009, 268) suggests that 'neo-liberals apply economic analysis to a series of objects, to domains of behaviour or conduct which were not market forms of behaviour or conduct: they attempt to apply economic analysis to marriage, the education of children and criminality'. Governmental health strategies administered through discourses of social marketing fit neatly within such domains of conduct which were not previously market forms of behaviour, but which have emerged under more and more explicit attempts to construct 'health marketplaces' in the United Kingdom and beyond.

Consequently, more recent public health strategies bear less and less resemblance to the interventionism and social engineering of the Victorian reformists (Rosen 1993), nor even the aims of the new public health movement to engage communities and improve environments (Ashton and Seymour 1988). Rather, they operate with governmental rationalities which aim to inculcate regimens of self-discipline (and entrepreneurship) in diet, exercise and the regulation of consumption of risky substances such as alcohol and tobacco, reflecting a wider behavioural turn and an implicit shift from the social to the individual as the target of interventions. These in turn reflect a more explicit institutionalisation of neoliberal values and methods within public-health practice. The data presented in this chapter explores a range of professional understandings and constructions of social marketing strategies with critical issues, such as the importing of commercial methodologies into the 'social' endeavours discussed, the aim of behavioural change examined and issues of choice and responsibility explored. Respondents acknowledge that health behaviours are acted out in complex settings, with, often, considerable pressure from external factors which may be deleterious to well-being. However, a key theme becomes the power of commercial methods in identifying, engaging, and influencing individuals and communities in their health choices and behaviours. Overall data presented here indicates how the pseudo-commercialism of social marketing for health is accepted unproblematically by a sample of those working in the field of public health as a methodology for improving the health of populations. Respondents do recognise the challenges of influencing health behaviours in complex real-world settings; however, this is underpinned by a belief in the potential of appropriate marketing to work effectively with targeted populations and bring about sustainable behavioural changes.

From the UK Black Report of 1979 onward, a stream of evidence has been produced locally and globally which has consistently highlighted the role of external and environmental and socio-economic factors in determining health and systematically constructing structural inequalities between social groups stratified on the basis of income. Recent studies have continued to emphasise the social determinants of health and the economic and structural basis of health inequalities (see, for example, Dorling 2011; Marmot 2010; Wilkinson and Pickett 2009). Despite this, by embracing methodologies such as social marketing, public health work continues to plough a behavioural furrow, focusing upon the capacities of individuals to change rather than on the possibilities for change to structural and systemic dynamics. In this way, it is argued that public health discourses have come to reflect a wider neoliberalism apparent within public policies in the United Kingdom and beyond which posit the enterprising individual as a route to combating social evils and a wider promotion of social goods. If this is the case, methodologies such as social marketing for health come to represent little more than, at best, resignation to the unlikelihood of the implementation of bolder, structural changes to improve health as recommended by commentators such as Marmot (2010) or, at worst, a wilful and ideologically driven disregard for the weight of evidence of the social determinants of health which, of course, runs counter to modes of market organisation and the promotion of the enterprising self as the key tenets of neoliberal democracies.

Notes

1 For example, taking regular exercise is a merit behaviour, but smoking tobacco would constitute a demerit behaviour.
2 On the 13 October 2011 a new set of UK coalition government documents were released detailing a comprehensive and unified social marketing programme to target a number of key public health areas between 2011 and 2014.
3 See Department of Health, *Change4Life: Three year social marketing strategy* (London: Department of Health, 2011) and Department of Health, *Healthy lives, healthy people: A call to action on obesity in England* (London: Department of Health, 2011).
4 See Science and Technology Committee Report on behaviour change published by the House of Lords in 2011.
5 See the appropriately titled NHS Choices http://www.nhs.uk/Pages/HomePage.aspx

References

Ashton, J. and H. Seymour. 1988. *The New Public Health*. Buckingham: Open University Press.

Baum, F. 2008. *The New Public Health*. Melbourne: Oxford University Press Australia and New Zealand.

Bunton, R. and R. Burrows. 1995. 'Consumption and health in the 'epidemiological' clinic of late modern medicine'. In *The Sociology of Health Promotion: Critical Analysis of Consumption, Lifestyle and Risk*, edited by R. Bunton, S. Nettleton and R. Burrows, 206–22. London: Routledge.

Crawford, R. 1977. 'You are dangerous to your health: Ideology and politics of victim blaming'. *International Journal of Health Services* 21 (3): 423–39.

———. 1986. 'Individual responsibility and health politics'. In *The Sociology of Health and Illness: Critical Perspectives*, edited by P. Conrad and R. Kern, 369–77. New York: St Martins Press.

Crawshaw, P. 2007. 'Governing the healthy male citizen: Men, masculinity and popular health in Men's Health magazine'. *Social Science and Medicine* 65: 1605–18.

Crawshaw, P. and C. Newlove. 2011. 'Men's understanding of social marketing and health: Neo-liberalism and health governance'. *International Journal of Men's Health* 10 (2): 136–52.

Dorling, D. 2011. *Injustice. Why Social Inequality Persists*. Bristol: The Policy Press.

Foucault, M. 2009. *The Birth of Biopolitics*. Basingstoke: Palgrave.

French, J. 2009. 'The nature, development and contribution of social marketing to public health practice since 2004 in England'. *Perspectives in Public Health* 129: 262–7.

French, J. and Blair-Stevens, C. 2005. *Social Marketing Pocket Guide*. London: National Consumer Council.

Griffiths, J., Blair- C. Steven and R. Parish. 2009. 'The integration of health promotion and social marketing'. *Perspectives in Public Health* 129 (6): 268–71.

Harvey, D. 2005. *Neo-liberalism: A Very Short Introduction*. Oxford: Oxford University Press.

————. 2010. *The Enigma of Capital*. London: Profile.

Hastings, G. 2007. S*ocial Marketing: Why Should the Devil Have All the Best Tunes?* London: Butterworth-Heinemann.

Jones, R., J. Pykett and M. Whitehead. 2010. 'Big Society's Little Nudges: The Changing Politics of Healthcare in an Age of Austerity'. *Political Insight* 1 (3): 85–7.

Kickbusch, I. 2007. 'Responding to the health society'. *Health Promotion International* 22 (2): 89–91.

Lazzarato, M. 2009. 'Neoliberalism in action: Inequality, insecurity and the reconstitution of the social'. *Theory, Culture and Society* 26 (6): 109–33.

Lefebvre, R. and J. Flora. 1988. 'Social marketing and public health intervention'. *Health Education Quarterly* 15 (3): 299–315.

Lupton, D. 1995. *The Imperative of Health: Public Health and the Regulated Body*. London: Sage.

Marmot, M. 2010. *Fair Society, Healthy Lives: The Marmot Review*. London: The Marmot Review

Marvasti, A. 2004. *Qualitative Research in Sociology*. London: Sage.

McNay, L. 2009. 'Self as enterprise: Dilemmas of control and resistance in Foucault's The Birth of Biopolitics'. *Theory, Culture and Society* 26 (6): 55–77.

Miles, M. and A. Huberman. 1994. *Qualitative Data Analysis*. London: Sage.

Minkler, M. 1999. 'Personal responsibility for health? A review of the arguments and evidence at the century's end'. *Health Education and Behaviour*, February, 126–41.

National Social Marketing Centre. 2007. 'NSMC: About us'. Available at http://www.thensmc.com/ (accessed April 2011).

Petersen, A. and D. Lupton. 1996. *The New Public Health: Health and Self in the Age of Risk* London. Sage.

Pollock, A. 2004. *NHS Plc: The Privatisation of Our Health Care*. London: Verso.

Pykett, J. 2011. 'The new maternal state: The gendered politics of governing through behaviour change'. *Antipode* 44 (1): 217–38.

Read, J. 2009. 'A Genealogy of Homo Economicus: Foucault, Neoliberalism and the Production of Subjectivity'. In *A Foucault for the 21st Century: Governmentality, Biopolitics and Discipline in the New Millennium*, edited by S. Binkley and J. Capetillo. Newcastle: Cambridge Scholars Publishing.

Robertson, A. 2001. 'Biotechnology, political rationality and discourses on health risk'. *Health: An Interdisciplinary Journal of Social Studies in Health and Medicine* 5 (3): 293–309.

Robinson, M. and S. Robertson. 2010. 'The application of social marketing to promoting men's health: A brief critique'. *International Journal of Men's Health* 9 (1): 50–61.

Rose, N. 1999. *Powers of Freedom: Reframing Political Thought*. Cambridge: Cambridge University Press.

————. 2001. 'The politics of life itself'. *Theory, Culture and Society* 18 (6): 1–30.

Rosen, G. 1993. *A History of Public Health*. Baltimore: Johns Hopkins University Press.

Stead, M., G. Hastings and L. McDermott. 2006. 'The meaning, effectiveness and future of social marketing'. *Obesity Reviews* 8 (1): 189–93.

Thaler, R. and C. Sunstein. 2009. *Nudge: Improving Decisions about Health, Wealth and Happiness*. London: Penguin.

Truss, A., R. Marshall and C. Blair-Stevens. 2010. 'A history of social marketing'. In *Social Marketing and Public Health: Theory and Practice*, edited by J. French, C. Blair-Stevens, D. McVey and R. Merritt, 19–28. Oxford: Oxford University Press.

Weibe, G. 1952. 'Merchandising commodities and citizenship on television'. *Public Opinion Quarterly* 15: 679–691.

Wilkinson, R. and K. Pickett. 2009. *The Spirit Level: Why More Equal Societies Almost Always Do Better*. London: Penguin.

Chapter 8

NEOLIBERAL POLICY, QUALITY AND INEQUALITY IN UNDERGRADUATE DEGREES

Andrea Abbas, Paul Ashwin and Monica McLean

Introduction

In this chapter we analyse two contradictory framings of 'a high-quality undergraduate education' and reveal how neoliberal higher education policy is in danger of increasing inequality in England.[1] The first framing, which is found in policy documents, sees the marketisation of the higher education system as essential to high quality. It views student employment as the key measure of high quality and suggests that disadvantaged students would prefer to pursue degrees that focus on employment training rather than study academic disciplines. The English university system is class-divided and most disadvantaged students, along with members of the lower middle class, attend lower-ranking universities (Roberts 2009).[2] The policy documents definition of high quality has implications for curricula in these universities. The second framing is in current social science students' accounts of what they value about the education they are receiving. These students, who are from diverse backgrounds and are based in higher- and lower-ranking universities in England, value the ways that engaging with disciplinary knowledge transforms them personally, empowers them socially and prepares them for employment.

Basil Bernstein's (2000) term 'pedagogic rights' provides a definition of 'a high-quality undergraduate education' that helps us evaluate these two very different perspectives. 'Pedagogic rights' signifies what higher education should contribute to democratic societies. Two elements of 'pedagogic rights' (enhancement and inclusion) map what students say they gain from studying social science at four universities which have been given pseudonyms to protect the identity of departments and students (see section on methodology). If neoliberal policies are successful, students in lower-ranking universities may be deprived of these rights, which come from learning social sciences. Enhancement and inclusion are necessary for students to acquire Bernstein's third pedagogic right (participation) which denotes political empowerment; but equal participation also requires that graduates from all universities access opportunities to exercise political power. The policy documents' definition of high quality, which is presented as increasing fairness for disadvantaged students by improving employment, will not give more political power to students in lower-ranking universities.

This chapter contributes to academic analysis of the potential and limitations of higher education quality systems in tackling national and global inequality (Amaral and Rosa 2010; Brennan et al. 2010; Abbas and McLean 2007, 2010; Morley 2003). It provides a pertinent example of the limits of neoliberal policies' economised conceptions of high-quality undergraduate education (Gidley et al. 2010) in a specific national context and answers calls to bring empirical data and social theory to bear on the policy problems associated with quality systems (Blackmur 2010). We achieve this by applying Bernstein's concept of pedagogic rights to students' descriptions of a high-quality undergraduate social science education. This sheds light on what is to be gained from disciplinary education and what is at stake if certain sections of society lose access to this type of education.

We begin by exploring how current literature links neoliberalism, higher education quality systems and inequality. Next, we describe recent changes to higher education funding in England, which appears set to alter conceptions of high-quality undergraduate degrees and to modify the role of quality systems. We follow this with an overview of our methodology. We then develop our argument by comparing the notion of quality within policy documents and, empirically, with students' perspectives. Bernstein's definition of pedagogic rights helps to frame and conceptualise students' views. We conclude by discussing how this concept might help to develop a more socially just way of evaluating pedagogic quality than the neoliberal framework offered by the government documents.

Neoliberalism, Quality and Inequality

It is imperative to evaluate the impact of changing higher education policies on the most disadvantaged students, because in England and globally, universities have only relatively recently begun to play an explicit role in tackling inequalities associated with class, ethnicity, age and disability (Reay,

Crozier and Clayton 2009a, 2009b) and they need to build on the limited success they have had so far. The specific problems they face in trying to do this must be understood in their national and global contexts (Gidley et al. 2010). Literature on the English university system draws attention to the role of universities in producing middle class and upper class advantage (Reay et al. 2009a, 2009b) and the need to track universities' role in creating new and unjust hierarchical divisions in novel social, economic and political contexts. Roberts (2009) suggests that English universities may be involved in creating new divisions within an expanding middle class. Middle class students have taken up most of the new university places which have accrued since the 1980s, but the upper middle classes (who attend a few elite universities and occupy the best paid and most politically powerful jobs) have continued to benefit most from higher education. All other middle class groups have significantly lower levels of participation and the inclusion of those from disadvantaged groups remains comparatively limited and is largely restricted to lower-ranking universities.

Two consecutive British governments have represented their goals for an expanded higher education system as both economic and social.[3] They claim that it is important to tackle social inequality by having more disadvantaged students participating in higher education (Blair 2004; Willetts 2011). It is suggested that individual students and the country will benefit economically from it. However, critics are sceptical as to whether the neoliberal policies these governments have introduced are motivated by a desire to tackle inequality (Ainley 2004; Canaan 2008). The British government has imitated countries like the United States and Australia in claiming that the cost of funding a mass higher education system is too expensive for the state and that marketisation and privatisation are necessary for growth to continue (Slaughter and Rhoades 2004). Neoliberalisation has been represented as the only option for extending the benefits of higher education to a wider population (Collini 2010). However, higher education is a business worth billions of dollars (the General Agreement on Trade in Services (GATS), legally framed education as a product that can be traded between nations (Knight 2003), and critics suggest that the prime motivation for privatisation is to allow businesses to profit from the expanded global demand for knowledge and education (Abbas 2011). These contradictory claims about neoliberalisation make it imperative that evidence is gathered to evaluate the impact of neoliberal policies on equality.

Governments and higher education organisations have tended to see quality assurance procedures as vehicles for equality, ensuring that all students receive acceptable standards of teaching (Cheung and Tsui 2010). However, the effectiveness of quality processes depends on how 'high quality' is conceptualised and measured (Blackmur 2010). A critical body of research suggests that the underlying meaning of high quality currently underpinning quality systems is based on the interests, values and practices of the powerful, and that as a consequence, they tend to maintain inequality rather than ameliorate it (Abbas and McLean 2007, 2010). Much of the evidence for the role of quality in (re)producing inequality comes from an analysis of league tables (the most widely used and cited form of quality data), showing that nationally and globally, institutional wealth and students' social backgrounds, rather than quality, determine league table positions (Singh 2010). When 'quality' is equated with league table ratings, it has an ideological function: less wealthy students, universities and nations do badly in the tables, which represent them as failing. From this perspective, the high value attached to high-ranking institutions like Oxford and Cambridge results from their historical association with the upper middle classes rather than the quality of the education. The fact that so many British politicians, well-known media figures and business elites went to these universities constructs a powerful cultural myth about the quality of the education received there and their 'excellence' is taken for granted. Research that critically explores the qualitative differences between undergraduate curricula, pedagogies and students' experiences in differently ranked universities supports this viewpoint, because it finds that that the variation in quality reported in league tables might be spurious (Abbas and McLean 2007; Brennan et al. 2010).

The lower-ranking universities have been pivotal in the expansion of the university system in England and in widening access to universities to the lower middle classes and students from disadvantaged backgrounds (Crozier, Reay, Clayton and Colliander 2008). In 1992, when former polytechnics (classified as lower-ranked universities) were granted university status, new quality systems were introduced to try to ensure equal standards across the higher education sector (Harvey 2005). Quality assurance processes apply to the whole sector but their impact is stronger in lower-ranked universities. While governments have gained increasing control over almost all universities by rewarding and punishing them through financial (dis)incentives and quality information is used to inform these decisions, the power that institutions feel the government has varies according to the wealth and status of the university (Naidoo 2004). Universities with large independent sources of wealth and large numbers of overseas students are less malleable. The financially poorest universities, which attract most disadvantaged students, are the most susceptible to changing notions of high quality because they are obliged to chase the financial incentives.

Governments' conceptions of what counts as a high-quality education are important because they shape what universities offer, what students study and what contribution graduates can make to society (Barnett 1992). Current academic research often defines existing quality systems as a problem, suggesting that they (1) are a mechanism for control rather than improvement and say little about university learning and teaching, (2) provide crude and distorted measures, (3) undermine learning and teaching by making universities spend too much time and money producing quality data, (4) hinder communication that could help develop good teaching because reporting success becomes the focus and (5) encourage game-playing rather than genuine improvements (Morley 2003; Blackmur 2010; Gibbs 2010; Harvey and Williams 2010). However, it is important to have some way of evaluating and communicating about what universities do and what students and other stakeholders can expect from them.

Recent Developments in English Higher Education

The conceptualisations of quality that we explore in policy documents were initially developed by the previous Labour government (1997–2010) and are more recently being elaborated and implemented by the British Conservative–Liberal Democrat coalition government (elected in May 2010) in their first 18 months in office. There is a radical speeding up of neoliberalisation (Collini 2010), and institutions, educators and students are increasingly encouraged to conceptualise higher education (HE) as providing a service (the education) and a product (the degree) which students consume. The changes are positioned as necessary to save the state from financial ruin (McGettigan 2011). Beginning in the academic year 2012–13 universities' funding will become more strongly dependent on the choices of students. The debt that students acquire in order to pay their fees is about to triple because money that was once paid to universities through government agencies (80% of the teaching budget) will now be borrowed by students who will pay back the fees to the state after they have graduated, that is if they earn over a pre-specified amount. The government argues that access for disadvantaged students will be improved because they will not have to pay back the money borrowed if they don't earn sufficiently high salaries afterwards. There will also be some grants and additional support for students from poorer backgrounds, particularly the few who qualify for highly ranked universities. However, critics argue that disadvantaged students will be put off by the large debt and government number capping will ensure there will be fewer places available in the lower-ranked universities which are much more frequently attended by these students.

There has been a gradual shift in the English university system. An elite publicly funded university system that paid the fees of very few, predominately upper middle class, home students (5 per cent of the school leaving population in the 1960s), taught alongside fee paying international elite students, has given way to a mass system in which an increasing proportion of the fee is paid by students and approximately 45 per cent of school leavers attend full-time undergraduate courses (Brennan et al. 2010). The nature of what is taught has also changed. Initially, universities educated students in traditional disciplines and trained higher professionals (doctors and lawyers); now, there is a wider range of academic disciplines and a diverse range of more vocationally orientated degrees. In this context, there has still been an official sense that English universities work to a similar standard (ensured by a cross-institutional, external examining system and explicit statements of standards by quality assurance processes) and that they aim for broadly similar outcomes for their students, for example, by all working to subject benchmarks. However, there has also been an unofficial but prevalent understanding that students in high-ranking universities get a better education. The new changes to funding, the policies examined for this chapter and the forthcoming higher education white paper (due in the summer of 2011) appear set to modify definitions of 'high quality'. Early indications from the government elected in 2010 are that they will represent a speeding up of an existing neoliberalism rather than a change of policy direction. Hence, the definition of high quality we reveal here is likely to be informing the future role of higher education.

Methodology

The empirical data underpinning this chapter is drawn from a mixed-method project called Pedagogic Quality and Inequality in University Undergraduate Degrees funded by the Economic and Social Research Council which is systematically exploring differences in quality between four differently ranked social science departments.[4] It has produced a wide range of data sets from each department and an analysis of relevant national and international documents.[5] For this chapter, we analyse national documents, 98 interviews with first-year students from diverse backgrounds (50 in lower-ranking universities and 48 in higher-ranking universities; 60 are the first in their family to go to university),[6] and 32 follow-up interviews with a subset of these students in their second year (18 in lower-ranked universities, 16 in higher-ranked universities; 21 are the first in their family to go to university).[7]

Edderhall and Draystone are post-1992 universities which are persistently ranked in the bottom quartile, and Yaddon and Nilesbrough are pre-1992 universities persistently ranked in the top quartile of the main league tables for English universities.

We selected policy documents that illuminate the current and future directions of higher education policy.

1. Two major white papers published by the last Labour government
   a. Department for Education and Skills (DfES) 2003
   b. Department for Business Innovation and Skills (BIS) 2009
2. A policy document which sets out a view of how higher education might expand (Department for Universities, Innovation and Skills (DIUS) 2008)
3. Some initial indications of the position of the new coalition document from two impact assessments
4. A letter to the Higher Education Funding Council for England (HEFCE)
5. Some guidance published by the Office for Fair Access (BIS 2010a, 2010b, 2010c, 2011)

One-hour semi-structured interviews explored students' experiences and perceptions of their first and second years at universities, including what they value about their university education. Biographical interviews using a life grid methodology (Wilson, Cunningham-Burley, Mulburn and Masters 2007) preceded the one-hour interviews and gave a broader insight into the role of higher education in students' lives. The second-year repeat interviews built on our familiarity with the students. All data sets have been analysed using NVivo software (Bazeley 2007) and our analytical process has involved research team members generating coding themes and using rigorous cross-validation processes and inter-coder reliability checks (Driedger, Gallois, Sanders and Santasso 2006).[8]

High Quality in Policy Documents and Students' Perspectives

In this section we outline and contrast, in government documents and in student interviews, the core ideas that constitute a high-quality undergraduate education. Fundamentally, the government and students present two markedly divergent understandings of what undergraduates should gain from higher education. High quality in the policy documents highlights the importance of students making choices based upon different forms of post-graduation employment and proposes that a marketised system, increased privatisation, institutional diversity, diverse funding, competition for students, clear information about institutions and degrees, 'fairer' access to elite institutions, employment-focused curricula (in lower-ranking institutions), and employment-focused evaluations of quality (in terms of employment outcomes) are integral to achieving this. There is no mention of the content of curricula or the role of disciplines in achieving these goals, but implicitly and explicitly, the documents indicate that higher-ranking institutions will continue to teach academic disciplines, and vocational curricula should be taught in lower-ranking institutions. By way of contrast, the overwhelming majority of current first- and second-year social science undergraduates in our study conceptualised high quality in terms of the degree to which universities facilitate personal transformation. Several factors were identified as fundamental to this process and central to high-quality provision: interesting and challenging disciplinary knowledge (curricula), appropriate learning opportunities (pedagogy), social, learning and living spaces which facilitate relationships that support an effective transformation (infrastructure and location), and the degree to which personal transformation turned them into effective, valuable and employable people. This prioritisation of personal transformation was shared by students regardless of which university they went to.

In order to present and contrast these two conceptualisations of high-quality undergraduate degrees, we begin with the representation in the policy documents which is framed in terms of a high-quality university system; in relation to high-quality educational provision; and finally, according to how high quality benefits the wider society. Next, we flesh out Bernstein's (2000) notion of pedagogic rights, because this provides us with conceptual tools to help us evaluate and frame what students value. We examine those elements of the student data which focuses on high-quality provision and high-quality benefits to wider society. Finally, we consider the implications of the students' perspectives for the high-quality university system presented in the policy documents.

Documentary Analysis

A high-quality higher education system

The current quality system was ostensibly set up to ensure that all students get a similar standard of teaching. In the policy documents we analysed, good teaching is represented as important to high quality for all students. In 2003 it is indicated that rewarding teachers would improve teaching.

> It (the higher education system) must also be supported by clear expectations about the standards that every university must meet, so that no student has to put up with poor teaching. There must also be clear and visible rewards for the best, to spread good practice in the system, as well as sending important signals both to students and to institutions about the value of teaching in its own right. (Department for Education and Skills (DfES) 2003, paragraph 4.1, 47)

However, none of the documents really discuss what good teaching entails and in later documents, the way of ensuring good teaching changes. It is implied that it will emerge from a correctly organised marketised system. According to the documents, the marketised system should be made up of a diverse range of providers of higher education which includes existing universities, further-education colleges and private organisations. It should also be funded from a wide range of sources including state funding, private capital, student fees and alumni contributions; and it should be organised to mirror a commercial market with different providers competing for student fees by providing high-quality teaching and curricula at a low cost. Competition between the institutions is represented as ensuring that the best institutions flourish and poor-quality institutions change or close. Competition is presented as wholly positive and there is no mention of inherent difficulties, such as the inevitably poor state of universities whose finances are declining because of their poor market position.

Student choice is represented as pivotal to high quality and to driving overall direction of the current system.

> Their (students') choices and expectations should play an important part in shaping the courses universities provide and in encouraging universities to adapt and improve their service. (Department for Business Innovation and Skills (BIS) 2009, 70)

> Well-informed student choice will be the most powerful force for change over the next decade. (BIS 2009, 79)

Students are represented as being driven by employer choices (of students for jobs) and it is assumed that both student and employer choices will be based upon the information provided by universities (rather than on status or reputation) that will accurately mirror the quality of what is provided.

> By requiring course content and outcomes to be more transparent, students and employers will be enabled to make informed choices that increase competition between institutions. No student should ever be misled into believing that a course will deliver employment outcomes that it will not. (BIS 2009, 4)

Previous research suggests many problems with these assumptions; for example, a range of complex factors influences students' choices of university and these tend to push students from disadvantaged backgrounds and the lower middle classes towards lower-ranked institutions (Hernandez-Martinez, Black, Williams, Davis, Pampaka and Wake 2008; Christie 2009; Mangan et al. 2010). However, this is not seen as a difficulty; universities are implicitly positioned as having created the main obstacle to high quality – providing misleading information.

Despite the government's purported faith in student choice to create a system that will ensure universities prioritise high quality degrees, it also wants to shape the system and influence what students and universities do. Hence, it is a controlled market. This diminishes the students' role in shaping higher education provision. For example, government will prioritise funding for degrees which it believes will contribute to the nation's economy.

> We will give new priority to the programmes that meet the need for high-level skills, especially for key sectors including those identified in the New Industries New Jobs strategy of April. This will mean enhanced support for the 'STEM' subjects – degrees in the sciences, technology, engineering, and mathematics – and other skills that underwrite this country's competitive advantages. (BIS 2009, 12)

The documents position the national economy as needing particular (largely yet to be conceptualised and written) degrees that will emerge from a high-quality marketised system.

High-quality undergraduate provision

High-quality educational provision is characterised as being constituted by institutions which have diverse and distinct focuses. To elaborate implicitly and explicitly, the documents suggest that a variety of institutional identities and curricula will emerge from institutions differentiating themselves and their products in niches of the student-consumer market. It expects universities to ensure that their degrees result in employment by co-constructing degrees with potential employers. Diversification in modes of delivering degrees is also important for high-quality provision (e.g. two-year degrees, online degrees and shorter vocational training courses). There might be a mix of courses. Some universities should focus on training local workforces, specialising in two-year degrees and diverse delivery for employees, while others concentrate on international research and teach academic disciplines.

High-quality contribution to wider society

In the documents, two particular contributions to wider society define what constitutes high quality: providing a trained and economically valuable workforce and furthering social equality (sometimes termed 'fairness').

Employability skills and knowledges have increased in importance over the time span of the policy documents analysed. In DfES (2003), universities are encouraged to build employability skills into what they already do.

> Higher education already makes a huge contribution to the development of the higher-level technical skills that are so vital. Many of the newer universities have a strong vocational focus and have led the way in developing new courses aimed at supplying students with the skills and knowledge they need for jobs in the new, expanding areas of the economy.
>
> As well as improving vocational skills we need to ensure that all graduates, including those who study traditional academic disciplines, have the right skills to equip them for a lifetime in a fast-changing work environment. (DfES 2003, paragraph 3: 23: 44)

However, in BIS (2009) there is a strong sense that all undergraduate education should change its purpose to being mainly focused on preparing students for employment.

> [I]t is a top concern for business that students should leave university better equipped with a wider range of employability skills. All universities should be expected to demonstrate how they prepare their students for employment, including through training in modern workplace skills such as team working, business awareness, and communication skills. (BIS 2009, 13)

Equality is also constructed as a central aim throughout the documents, but again its meaning and the strategies to achieve it have changed over time. In DfES (2003) the government proposed that it should ensure equality by guaranteeing all students good teaching.

> All students have the right to good teaching, and some may not be able to exercise their choices as easily as others... So as well as making sure that students can make well-informed choices, we must seek to guarantee good-quality teaching for everyone. (DfES 2003, paragraph 4: 13: 49)

And by facilitating participation for disadvantaged students,

> The Government's commitment to fair access will not waver. All those who have the potential to benefit from higher education should have the opportunity to do so. This is a fundamental principle which lies at

the heart of building a more socially just society, because education is
the best and most reliable route out of poverty and disadvantage. (DfES
2003, paragraph 6.1: 8)

In BIS (2009), there is a considerable shift and 'non-traditional' student-
consumers are constructed as a distinct market segment – workers in need of
training.

We will give priority to growing a diverse range of models of higher
education most attractive to non-traditional students. These include
options such as part-time and workplace-based courses aimed particularly
at mature students or those from non-conventional backgrounds. (BIS
2009, 11)

Here, the notion that employment-focused degrees are more appropriate
than disciplinary degrees for disadvantaged students is apparent. The
move can be seen in different elements of the documents. For example,
DfES (2003) portrays further education colleges (FECs) as important in
delivering access courses, which are underpinned by academic disciplines
and foundation degrees, which can be vocational or academic. However, in
BIS (2009), FECs importance lies in offering a local, accessible and flexible
higher education that is more responsive to business needs. The link between
low-ranking institutions (FECs lay below former polytechnics in higher
education hierarchies) and more disadvantaged students means that this
statement is making assumptions about students' backgrounds and the type
of higher education they want.

   High-ranking universities' curricula are assumed to be already high quality
and they are instead encouraged to focus on ensuring fair access.

We need to treat these world-class institutions for what they are, and the
institutions themselves need to recognise their own obligations to UK
undergraduates, in terms of excellent teaching and fair access on merit
and potential, regardless of family background. (BIS 2009, 21)

The overt aim to increase equality is undermined by implicit and explicit
assumptions about different students. The policy documents' definition of
high quality focuses on the level of the national system, and so long as there is
an overall achievement of economic prosperity for the nation, it does not seem
to care that diverse students would gain access to different types of knowledges
and curricula.

Pedagogic Rights

We briefly elaborate the term pedagogic rights here, because we use it to conceptualise the student data and to contrast the underlying values represented in students' accounts with those in the policy documents. Bernstein (1974 and 1990) developed a host of interrelated concepts over a long career. We present a more comprehensive overview of how the critical application and development of these concepts might help us understand quality and inequality in higher education elsewhere (McLean, Abbas and Ashwin 2010). Bernstein (2000) sees higher education as important in constituting effective, fair and inclusive democracies, but believes that it will only contribute successfully if all students feel they have a stake in their education and if higher education is organised and executed in a way that will help them to realise it. He suggests that for this to occur, three interrelated pedagogic rights need to be accessed by students: enhancement, inclusion and participation. Enhancement denotes the development of individual confidence, which arises when students can think independently. This is gained by learning and accessing particular kinds of knowledge which Bernstein suggests shapes consciousness. Confident personal action is facilitated by acquired knowledge, which helps create independent thoughts and actions. This independence of thought and action is necessary to 'inclusion', which refers to the ability to participate in society and to speak out in an autonomous way. Participation occurs when students (or perhaps more usually, graduates) can participate politically and can influence what happens in society. Bernstein implies that all students should be gaining access to pedagogic rights regardless of where they study and access to this type of education should be spread equally across society.

Students' Perspectives

High-quality provision

In contrast with the view suggested by the policy documents, students appear to value similar provision regardless of their institution or background. Their conceptions of high-quality provision focus on whether it facilitates a transformation of their identities and ways of seeing the world and, as Bernstein's concept of enhancement suggests, knowledge (learning academic disciplines) dominates their conceptualisations of high-quality provision. Social science gives them access to enhancement by giving them new insights into society and allowing them to have independent thoughts.

> Knowledge, it has made me question things, challenge things. Instead of just saying 'Yes, alright then', it has made me query things: 'No, that does

not sound logical, that does not sound right'. I think more clearly than I have ever done before. It has changed me. (Draystone, Year 1)

Before university…I never kind of knew anything about any of this, I never quite realised how much influence outside factors have on the individual. You assume that you're autonomous, but then in reality, everything affects the way you are, so I think it's made me a lot more angry about things, when I see on the news some new policy that they would enact and…the evidence shows that that's completely the wrong way to do things. (Yaddon, Year 2)

These students' claims that they have changed their relationship with the world are typical. Students believe that universities should help them to develop their own opinions, and to be able to question, challenge, and argue.

Because you have to take a stand, you can't sit on the fence, you have to have an argument. And you have to either agree or disagree with something. I like that aspect to it. (Nilesbrough, Year 1)

In this way, they appear to be confirming the importance of enhancement and demonstrating the confidence it gives them, and they attribute it to their social science education.

Students' understanding of high-quality knowledge and learning and teaching provision seems unrelated to the economised view provided by the policy documents. The students focus upon the conditions needed to achieve learning the discipline: reading, writing, discussion and developing the appropriate skills.

I've learned to write a lot faster, I think, at university. During the lectures… you have to scribble it down quickly before you forget it. Generally, I think [reading] academic texts is the greatest skill I've learnt, and it's how to use them properly rather than having that fear of… or…thinking it's all above you and you can't really understand; but reading and actually understand[ing] what they're saying and simplifying it in a way to let it make sense to you. (Yaddon, Year 1)

They appreciate tutors' efforts to facilitate learning, whether it is being funny, or showing passion for the discipline, or trying out new teaching methods. They also emphasise the importance of good relationships with students and with other tutors in the learning process.

I really enjoy the seminars because they're interactive, I love interaction, you know, asking questions and raising a topic and then someone challenging you – it's just really interesting and insightful as well because someone could raise something and you think, 'I didn't know that, I didn't really understand that'. (Draystone, Year 2)

In the first year, everyone was shy and nervous and didn't want to speak out of turn, so the lecturers were sort of trying to encourage us on and build up our confidence to talk. But this year, we've all been a lot more involved... And I feel that the lecturers, the tutors [are] getting us going, I feel that they're taking in our arguments and respecting our opinions as well. (Edderhall, Year 2)

Students' accounts imply that high-quality provision is about facilitating enhancement (personal confidence through knowledge) and through teaching methods that will encourage them to strive for it.

Students claim that the transformation they seek also requires 'good enough' resources and facilities, including physical locations and social spaces that maximise opportunities to make friends, a campus/location that students can identify with and find attractive (whether a bustling city or a beautiful campus), and, they want to be able to study sufficiently near to or far from home according to their needs (for some, this is about being able to continue existing living arrangements; for others it is about the right combination for the individual to promote the growth of independence from family and friends and to allow contact). If there are insufficient books, or students don't have opportunities to make friends, there are problems. Students want to be able to read what they need to read, discuss their ideas with peers and develop the personal space needed to develop independent thinking. Students' diverse views on location provided some support for the government's notion that varied provision is important; for example, opportunities to study locally or away from home. However, dissimilarity between students is not a 'natural phenomenon' and there is a danger in seeing student-consumers as being equally free to choose. It is unjust to represent a student who has chosen to study near home in order to care for a relative, or study part-time for financial reasons, as making a 'free' choice similar to students with wealth and personal freedom. In sum, the picture of a high-quality provision drawn by the social science students we interviewed is that which provides an environment in which they grapple alongside tutors and other students with the knowledge and performance of discipline in order to transform themselves, or in Bernstein's terms, they try to gain access to enhancement.

High-quality contribution to wider society

Students from all four universities concur with policymakers that one of the goals of university is to provide them with skills and knowledge that will equip them for post-university working life. However, their notions of being transformed into workers are more holistic than being trained for a job. Students believe that the social sciences are a basis for going into work that helps people. A high proportion indicate that they want to *use* their degrees to exercise their expanded minds and to contribute to the improvement of society. Students believe their discipline gives them knowledge relevant to their future working lives.

> When you are helping people from different cultures, you can understand the problems and where they are coming from. Especially, a lot of women who have been oppressed, I feel I have been apprised [by] education and I think I would like to be an advocate for those women. (Draystone, Year 2)

However, Bernstein's term 'inclusion' is more apposite than 'participation', because while for students having, in Dewey's (1916) words, their 'minds developed' as integral to developing employment skills, the amount of participation (the ability to influence politically) will depend upon the social arenas they access. For most students, this will depend upon employment.

Feeling confident and able to participate socially is also aided by students having a degree they are proud of. Independent of what employment they might secure, many students (in particular those who are the first in their families to go to university) point to how a degree makes them and their families proud.

> You feel like you're doing something with your life. I feel like I'm working towards getting a better future for myself. I'm proud to say that I'm a university student and you get to develop your ideas and your learning habits... And I think it gives me a sense of worth. I think I am going to get my degree and my parents will be proud and I can say that I have a degree. (Draystone, Year 1)

Generally, students do not allow external measures of quality which, as stated above, already undermine the value of their degrees, to undermine their pride and the sense that they have a good education. External measures of quality, rather than the quality of their education, provoke either satisfaction or disgruntlement. Students at high-status universities appreciate the 'social cachet' they will bring to the labour market. Some students at Edderhall and Draystone, both post-1992 universities, indicate that they think it unfair that their university is not seen publicly as 'good'. However, they do not experience their education as not good. So, at the lower status universities, students' conception of quality is at odds with the league tables, which undermine the potential of these students after university. While it is not the focus of this chapter to discuss comparative quality, it is worth noting here that so far in our project, variation in pedagogic quality is not by institution; that is, university status does not appear to be related to the quality of teaching and learning.

Concluding Discussion

Contrasting these two markedly different views of what constitutes high-quality undergraduate education reveals that inequality will be perpetuated if the neoliberal approach to high-quality undergraduate education is implemented and disciplinary undergraduate degrees are restricted. Interpreting students' perspectives through the lens of Bernstein's notion of pedagogic rights helps to conceptualise what is at stake. Some students are in danger of losing their right to experience personal transformation (enhancement), their social empowerment (inclusion) and their potential for participation. Disadvantaged students and the lower middle classes are more negatively impacted by the policy definition of high quality, which is attempting to make employability, knowledge and skills central to undergraduate education. The social science knowledge discussed here, which is valued by students from all backgrounds and institutions, could be distributed according to wealth and social status and reinforce and exacerbate existing inequalities. There is already some evidence that this is happening in response to the funding changes (Morgan 2011).

At the moment, social science undergraduate education can be seen as an equalising force. In a related publication (Ashwin, Abbas and McLean 2012), we have challenged Bernstein's view that universities in England currently distribute different forms of knowledge to social students of different status. Bernstein's notion of the pedagogic device suggests that access to social science knowledge is stratified within society, and this implies that the students in our study who are from lower-ranking universities would be getting access to different and less powerful forms of knowledge. However, despite some differences between institutions (as an example, in terms of particular curricula or forms of assessment), our early analysis suggests that our first- and second-year students are getting access to similar forms of knowledge. Here, we have suggested that this also gives these students access to the first two pedagogic rights (enhancement and inclusion). As outlined above, Bernstein positions access to knowledge as essential for equality because it shapes consciousness and the ability to act autonomously and to contribute socially and politically. This chapter adds to evidence from the United States (Giroux 2001) suggesting that neoliberal policies undermine disciplinary-based undergraduate education and

Bernstein's concepts have helped us to explain why this unequal distribution of knowledge may lead to increased inequality. Our analysis also indicates that the contribution that other disciplines make to societies should be made explicit in order to understand the impact of neoliberal policies.

The neoliberal definition of high quality is strongly focused on how students are employed after obtaining their degrees. Bernstein's notion of participation suggests that this could be important for alleviating inequalities. However, even this element of neoliberal policy is in danger of exacerbating existing inequalities. Our student accounts demonstrate that current undergraduates in all four institutions are developing the potential to participate politically in society and that many wish to use their newly found knowledge to think independently and to have political influence. Disadvantaged and lower middle class students are not likely to have the strong social and political connections which help them gain access to such arenas, so they are dependent on employment to do this. If degrees in lower-ranking universities are too tailored to employer's immediate needs, the long-term need for greater equality will be compromised because students will not gain access to the powerful knowledge described above. While neoliberal policies will aim to encourage a few 'gifted students' from disadvantaged backgrounds to attend elite institutions, this strategy will not tackle overall levels of inequality. The social, cultural and economic factors underlying student choices will not be tackled if disadvantaged students attend universities that try to teach curricula which focus on the needs of the local economy, unless they also incorporate knowledge which promotes independent thought and overall development. In addition, lower-ranking universities are likely to be further undermined, because they tend to be more locally focused and graduate employment statistics might be more dependent on the local economy than the quality of degrees. These and a host of other problems suggest that the marketised system proposed by the neoliberal policy documents will not tackle inequality. Bernstein's notion of pedagogic rights provides an alternative way of thinking about what undergraduate education can contribute to the personal, social and political life of students and the nation.

Notes

1 We focus on England rather than the United Kingdom because Scotland, Ireland and Wales have some policy independence which allows them to modify the effects.
2 The hierarchical divisions within the English university system are characterised in a number of different ways (Brennan et al. (2010) provide a discussion). We use the terms higher-ranked and lower-ranked here because our discussion is focusing on the role of quality systems and the ranking of universities.
3 The British government is responsible for policy for the English higher education system.

4 This work was supported by the Economic and Social Research Council (Grant Number: RES-062-23-1438).
5 Further information about the project is available at the project website http://www.pedagogicequality.ac.uk/.
6 Fifty-two per cent of first year students are white British, 9 per cent are black British, 6 per cent are Bangladeshi British, 28 per cent are a mixture of mixed race British, black African, Chinese, East Asian and white other; 69 per cent are female (reflecting the gender balance of the disciplines), 16 per cent are mature (over 24) and 9 per cent have disabilties.
7 Nineteen are white British, 2 black British, 2 Bangladeshi British and 11 are are a mixture of mixed race British, black African, Chinese, East Asian and white other, 22 are female and 12 male, 7 are mature (over 24) and 6 have disabilities.
8 We thank Xin Gao and Alison Kington for their meticulous work in coding the interviews. We thank Ourania Fillipakou for first-year interviews and for her work on the policy documents, and Martina Daykin for her tireless support in organising all of the interviews.

References

Abbas, A. 2011. 'A new revolution in higher education policy in England?' In *Freedom, Equality and the University*, edited by C. Kościelniak and J. Makowski. Warsaw: Instytut Obywatelski.

Abbas, A. and M. McLean. 2007. 'Qualitative research as a method for making just comparisons of pedagogic quality in higher education: A pilot study'. *British Journal of Sociology of Education* 28 (6): 723–37.

———. 2010. 'Tackling inequality through quality: A comparative case study using Bernsteinian concepts'. In *Global Inequalities and Higher Education: Whose Interests Are We Serving?*, edited by E. Ulterhalter and V. Carpentier. London: Palgrave Macmillan.

Ainley, P. 2004. 'The new market state and education'. *Journal of Education Policy* 19 (4): 497–514.

Amaral, A. and M. J. Rosa. 2010. 'Recent Trends in Quality Assurance'. *Quality in Higher Education* 16 (1): 59–61.

Archer, L. and C. Leathwood. 2003. 'Identities, inequalities and higher education'. In *Higher Education and Social Class: Issues of Exclusion and Inclusion*, edited by L. Archer, M. Hutchings and A. Ross. London: Routledge Falmer.

Ashwin, P., A. Abbas and M. McLean. 2012. 'Using the pedagogic device to understand relations between disciplinary knowledge practices and teaching-learning processes in higher education'. In *Reconceptualising Tribes and Territories in Higher Education: Practices in the 21st Century*, edited by P. Trowler, R. Bamber and M. Saunders. London: Routledge.

Barnett, R. 1992. *Improving Higher Education: Total Quality Care*. Buckingham: SRHE and Open University Press.

Bazeley, P. 2007. *Qualitative Data Analysis with NVIVO*. London: Sage.

Bernstein, B. B. 1974. *Theoretical Studies towards a Sociology of Language*. London: Routledge and Kegan Paul.

———. 1990. *The Structuring of Pedagogic Discourse*. London: Routledge.

———. 2000. *Pedagogy, Symbolic Control and Identity: Theory, Research, Critique*. Lanham, MD and Oxford: Rowman and Littlefield.

BIS. 2009. *Higher Ambitions: The Future of Universities in a Knowledge Economy*. Available at http://webarchive.nationalarchives.gov.uk/+/http://www.bis.gov.uk/wp-content/uploads/publications/Higher-Ambitions.pdf (accessed 11 May 2012).

————. 2010a. *Interim Impact Assessment: Urgent Reforms to the Funding of Higher Education and Student Finance*. Department for Business Innovation and Skills. Available at http://www.bis.gov.uk/assets/biscore/higher-education/docs/i/10–1310-interim-equality-impact-assessment-he-funding-and-student-finance.pdf (accessed 11 May 2011).

————. 2010b. *Government Letter to Higher Education Funding Council for England* (HEFCE), Department for Business, Innovation and Skills. Retrieved from http://www.bis.gov.uk/assets/biscore/higher-education/docs/h/10–1359-hefce-grant-letter-20-dec-2010.pdf (website discontinued).

————. 2010c. *Guidance to Director of Fair Access*. Department for Business, Innovation and Skills. Retrieved from http://www.bis.gov.uk/assets/biscore/higher-education/docs/g/11–728-guidance-to-director-fair-access (website discontinued).

Blackmur, D. 2010. 'Does the Emperor Have the Right (or Any) Clothes?: The Public Regulation of Higher Education Qualities over the Last Two Decades'. *Quality in Higher Education* 16 (1): 67–9.

Blair, T. 2004. The prime minister's speech to the IPPR thinktank and Universities UK joint conference on higher education reform, 14 January.

Brennan, J., R. Edmunds, M. Houston, D. Jary, Y. Lebeau, M. Osborne and J. T. E. Richardson. 2010. *Improving What is Learned at University: An Exploration of the Social and Organsiational Diversity of University Education*. London: Routledge.

Canaan, J. 2008. 'Higher Education'. In *The Era of Globalization and Neoliberalism: Structure and Agency in the Neoliberal University*, edited by J. Canaan and W. Shumar. New York: Routledge.

Cheung, P. P. T. and C. B. S. Tsui. 2010. 'Quality Assurance for All'. *Quality in Higher Education* 16 (2): 169–71.

Christie, H. 2009. 'Emotional journeys: Young people and transitions to university'. *British Journal of Sociology of Education* 30 (2): 123–36.

Collini, S. 2010. 'Browne's Gamble'. *London Review of Books* 32 (21): 3.

Crozier, G., D. Reay, J. Clayton and L. Colliander. 2008. 'Different strokes for different folks: Diverse students in diverse institutions – experiences of higher education'. *Research Papers in Education* 23 (2): 167–77.

David, M. E. 2009. 'Introduction to the Dilemmas of Widening Participation'. In *Improving Learning by Widening Participation in Higher Education*, edited by M. E. David. London: Routledge.

Department for Business, Innovation and Skills. 2009. *Higher Ambitions*. Available at http://webarchive.nationalarchives.gov.uk/+/http://www.bis.gov.uk/higherambitions (accessed 11 May 2011).

Department for Education and Skills. 2003. *The Future of Higher Education*. Available at http://www.bis.gov.uk/assets/biscore/corporate/migratedd/publications/f/future_of_he.pdf (accessed 11 May 2011).

Department for Universities, Innovation and Skills. 2008. *A New 'University Challenge': Unlocking Britain's Talent*. Available at http://www.bis.gov.uk/assets/biscore/corporate/migratedd/publications/u/university-challenge.pdf (accessed 11 May 2011).

Dewey, J. 1916. *Democracy and Education: An Introduction to the Philosophy of Education*. New York: Macmillan.

Driedger, S., M. Gallois, C. B. Sanders and M. Santasso. 2006. 'Finding Common Ground in Team-Based Qualitative Research Using the Convergent Interviewing Method'. *Qualitative Health Research* 16 (8): 1145–57.

Gibbs, G. and the Higher Education Academy. 2010. *Dimensions of Quality*. York: The Higher Education Academy.

Gidley, J., G. P. Hampson, L. Wheeler and E. Bereded-Samuel. 2010. 'From Access to Success: An Integrated Approach to Quality Higher Education Informed by Social Inclusion Theory and Practice'. *Higher Education Policy* 23: 123–47.

Giroux, H. A. 2001. 'Vocationalizing Higher Education: Schooling and the Politics of Corporate Culture'. In *Beyond the Corporate University: Culture and Pedagogy in the New Millennium*, edited by H. A. Giroux and K. Myrsiades. Lanham, MD: Rowman and Littlefield

Harvey, L. 2005. 'A History and Critique of Quality Evaluation in the UK' *Quality Assurance in Education* 13: 263–76.

Harvey, L. and J. Williams. 2010. 'Fifteen Years of Quality in Higher Education'. *Quality in Higher Education* 16 (1): 3–36.

Hernandez-Martinez, P., L. Black, J. Williams, P. Davis, M. Pampaka and G. Wake. 2008. 'Mathematics students' aspirations for higher education: class, ethnicity, gender and interpretative repertoire styles'. *Research Papers in Education* 23 (2): 153–65.

Knight, J. 2003. 'GATS, Trade and Higher Education: Perspective 2003 – Where Are We? Report for the Observatory on Borderless Higher Education.

Mangan, J., A. Hughes, P. Davies and K. Slack. 2010. 'Fair access, achievement and geography: Explaining the association between social class and students' choice of university'. *Studies in Higher Education* 35 (3): 335–50.

McGettigan, A. 2011. 'Commentary: "New Providers": The creation of a market in higher education'. *Radical Philosophy* 167 (May/June): 2–8.

McLean, M., A. Abbas and P. Ashwin. 2010. 'Working Paper 1: "Pedagogic Quality and Inequality: Bernsteinian Conceptual Framework"'. Available at http://www.pedagogicequality.ac.uk/documents/Working_Paper1_FINAL_March_2010.pdf (accessed 11 May 2011).

Morgan, J. 2011. 'London Met Course Closures May Prove Costly'. *Times Higher Education*. Available at http://www.timeshighereducation.co.uk/story.asp?storycode=416278 (accessed 11 May 2011).

Morley, L. 2003. *Quality and Power in Higher Education*. Maidenhead: Society for Research into Higher Education and Open University Press.

Naidoo, R. 2004. 'Fields and institutional strategy: Bourdieu on the relationship between higher education, inequality and society'. *British Journal of Sociology of Education* 25 (4): 457–71.

Reay, D., G. Crozier and J. Clayton. 2009a. '"Fitting in" or "standing out": Working class students in UK higher education'. *British Educational Research Journal* 36 (1): 107–24.

———. 2009b. '"Strangers in paradise?" Working class students in elite universities'. *Sociology* 43 (6): 1103–21.

Roberts, K. 2009. 'The Middle Class, the Working Class, and the Expansion of UK Higher Education'. Presented at 'New Labour, Social Mobility and Higher Education', conference held at Manchester Metropolitan, 3 March.

Singh, M. 2010. 'Quality Assurance in Higher Education: Which Pasts to Build on, What Futures to Contemplate?' *Quality in Higher Education* 16 (2): 189–94.

Slaughter, S. and G. Rhoades. 2004. *Academic Capitalism and the New Economy: Markets, State and Higher Education*. Baltimore, MD: Johns Hopkins University Press.

Willetts, D. 2011. Ron Dearing Lecture: 'Universities and Social Mobility'. University of Nottingham, 17 February.

Wilson, S., S. Cunningham-Burley, K. Mulburn and H. Masters. 2007. 'Young people, biographical narratives and the life grid: Young people's accounts of parental substance use'. *Qualitative Research* 7 (1): 135–51.

Chapter 9

RELIGION AND CRIMINAL JUSTICE IN CANADA, ENGLAND AND WALES: COMMUNITY CHAPLAINCY AND RESISTANCE TO THE SURGING TIDE OF NEOLIBERAL ORTHODOXY

Philip Whitehead

Introduction

Throughout its notorious history and accompanying robust longevity, capitalism has spewed its floodwaters upon human bodies and institutional formations. Capitalism has not only survived since the late eighteenth century, but has done so despite periodic crises (Arrighi 2010), the critique of alternative ideologies and its questionable moral and social impacts. Even its deleterious effects upon individuals and families, the ravaging of local communities, the capacity to inflict human suffering through inequality and poverty, have not distracted from its relentless ability to renew itself. Capitalism survived the crisis decade of the 1970s as President Reagan and Prime Minister Thatcher fashioned a neoliberal resurgence with an evangelical fervour expressed in the refrain, 'There Is No Alternative'. The most recent crisis, which erupted in 2007, precipitated by banking malfeasance (Crouch 2011; Duménil and Lévy 2011), added to the murky deposits and pushed the water mark even higher so that the election of a Conservative–Liberal coalition government in England and Wales in May 2010 signalled a critical moment for the capitalist–neoliberal meat grinder. The optimistic forecast is that the Liberal component of the two-party governmental coalition will act as a moderating influence upon the Neocons, so that things will not be as bad compared to the situation if the Conservatives governed alone. This is the Liberal Democrat 'neutralisation of worst fears' thesis. In marked contrast, the gathering storm warning is that by 2015 the neoliberal upsurge will have unleashed destructive forces into the social body on the back of financial restructuring that produces economic benefits for the few (or even fewer), at the cost of greater socio-economic insecurity for the many (or even more). State restructuring beyond the recession will primarily ensure the survival of the neoliberal leanest and fittest – the 'it will be as bad as feared' thesis – because government spent taxpayers' money to bolster rather than destroy the marauding beast of neoliberalism.

State restructuring, downsizing the public sector, reducing the deficit and balancing the budget are the neoliberal prerequisites for restoring economic confidence in the markets and attracting global investors. Consequently, the Big Society is being inveigled to take up the slack engendered by the retreating state. This has profound implications for the operational functioning of the criminal and youth justice systems in the form of the rehabilitation revolution which is prising open offender services to competition between the public, private, and voluntary sectors (Ministry of Justice 2010). On the one hand, it is possible to theorise that criminal justice reforms attendant upon the Big Society and rehabilitation revolution are functional for neoliberalism, a contemporary expression of the Marxist base–superstructure paradigm. On the other hand, one can advance the position that unexpected opportunities are opening up for the voluntary sector to contribute to, if not challenge and change by the cogency of its ideas (resonating with Weber more than Marx), the contours of state-directed current debates.

It should be acknowledged that egregious changes have occurred within the criminal and youth justice domains since the 1980s, a consequence of embedding a bureaucratic-punitive (conflating Weber and Durkheim) paradigm which has expanded the institution of the prison to accommodate the neoliberal excluded, as well as modernising probation services (Arthur, this volume; Bell 2011; Garland 2001; Straw 2009; Teague, this volume; Wacquant 2009; Whitehead 2010; Whitehead and Arthur 2011; Wilkinson and Pickett 2009). This paradigm shift constitutes a Foucauldian epistemic turn, a discrete cultural code around which criminal justice organisations have reshaped their responses, which can be illustrated as follows:

- Offenders have been reduced to units of risk for actuarial purposes to facilitate more effective management and control of future behaviours (Feeley and Simon 1992).
- Attenuated aetiological and sociological analyses, which constitute a shift of emphasis to punishing *what* offenders have done rather than analysing and understanding *why* (Whitehead 2011b).
- Probation services have been modernised to manage offenders in the community and on prison licence *from a distance* because offender managers

have been transformed into office-based computer operators, bureaucratic technicians who have less face-to-face personal contact with people who offend (House of Commons Justice Committee 2011; Whitehead 2007, 2010; Whitehead and Statham 2006).

Furthermore, these transformational dynamics have generated new organisational rationalities which have impacted upon axiological perspectives, released depersonalised forces and corroded debates centred on the pursuit of criminal and social justice.

Accordingly, the purpose of this chapter is to explore and also map the scope for the voluntary sector in general, and the faith sector in particular, to critique and challenge neoliberal orthodoxy for criminal justice reformation. Rather than functional and instrumental collusion, I argue the case for the independent faith sector to position itself in the vanguard of protest and resistance to the criminal justice developments adumbrated above. Furthermore, this chapter will be illuminated by presenting findings from original empirical research conducted in Ottawa, Canada, during the fall of 2010 on the relatively new religious phenomenon of community chaplaincy. After elucidating the methodological imperative, I proceed to describe the origins of community chaplaincy in Canada before turning to a contemporary epiphany in Ottawa. I then cross the Atlantic to its appearance in England and Wales. Even though it remains possible to identify deposits of religion within criminal justice (Whitehead 2010), its resurgence in the form of community chaplaincy is worthy of close attention, not least because of a limited literature on the subject. Furthermore, the purpose and scope of this chapter will be enhanced by proceeding from empirically informed insights, to establish a platform for critical reflection for those involved in what is a potentially significant yet under-researched field of enquiry. To facilitate this objective, an exploratory typology will be constructed before clarifying the rationale of community chaplaincy within the criminal justice systems of Canada, England and Wales, and its latent potential to challenge the prevailing neoliberal orthodoxy which will move the field forward into more critical terrain.

Methodology

The scope of this investigation is empirically informed as well as theoretically driven because during September 2010 I visited Ottawa, the capital of Canada in the province of Ontario.[1] Six months before this investigative journey, contact was established with the Correctional Service of Canada (CSC), headquartered in Ottawa, to inform them of the research I was undertaking during 2010–11 on community chaplaincy in England and Wales.[2] Accordingly, a planned visit to Canada was deemed instructive to learn about community chaplaincy in its country of origin and that this would be enhanced by conversations with those involved in its organisation and delivery. Therefore, during a ten-day period I was enabled to undertake 13 interviews with people differentially involved in community chaplaincy; 11 were located in Ottawa and 2 in British Columbia, Western Canada. This would not have been possible without the assistance of a member of staff at CSC who brokered these contacts. These 13 interviews included four members of the staff at CSC as well as a community chaplaincy coordinator in Ottawa, where it is known as MAP – mentorship-aftercare-presence. Other interviews included a representative of Alpha, a Christian organisation that has contact with serving prisoners, a prison chaplain at a detention centre in Ottawa, visits to the founder and director of Jericho Road Ministries that provides accommodation for ex-prisoners, in addition to the Harvest House drug recovery program. My understanding was further informed by participating in a video conference with one of only two full-time community chaplains in Canada and a telephone interview with the coordinator of Circles of Support and Accountability (CoSA), which also operates a religiously based operational model.[3] I was also invited to attend an 'offender-friendly church', which provided opportunities to discuss pertinent matters with the pastors. Significantly, on my final day I discussed relevant matters with the Reverend Dr Pierre Allard, the initial inspiration of community chaplaincy in Canada. The interviewees comprised nine males and four females who were selected on the basis that they would be representative of community chaplaincy in Ottawa. Prior to this visit, I extracted information from open-source websites on community chaplaincy in Canada; additional documentary evidence was provided before and during my stay, and I kept a daily diary of observations, visits, contacts and conversational asides outside of the structure of interview situations. Even though it has not been possible to quantify how many people are involved in the work of community chaplaincy in Ottawa, I reiterate that I relied on CSC staff to facilitate what were considered to be significant contacts. The importance of the interviews is that they provide insights into an under-researched topic and enrich the descriptive sections of this paper. Because the religious question in general and community chaplaincy in particular constitute my ongoing research activity in England and Wales, visiting Canada was indubitably informative.

Unravelling the Canadian Gene Code of Community Chaplaincy

In 1972 the Reverend Dr Pierre Allard was a prison chaplain at Dorchester Penitentiary, located near Moncton in New Brunswick, when conditions in

Canadian prisons were harsher than subsequently (Cayley 1998, 118). It was explained that prisoners were isolated, existing in 'a world apart', so that the inchoate vision of community chaplaincy was shaped by a commitment to build bridges between the prison and the wider human community. Specifically, these bridges would be erected by faith-motivated volunteers establishing contact with serving prisoners. It was also acknowledged that prison chaplains could 'not go it alone', but required volunteers to share responsibility for what is often difficult work with prisoners, many of whom have experienced unpropitious family backgrounds and are seized by a surfeit of personal problems (Griffiths, Dandurand and Murdoch 2007).

By 1980 the initial vision of community involvement with prisoners was extended to the period beyond release. Therefore, it is possible to trace the beginnings of community chaplaincy some 30 years ago to Moncton, New Brunswick in Eastern Canada, when a released prisoner was invited to the Allard's home for dinner. This was the inspiration for what became faith-orientated volunteers supporting people leaving prison. The vision was theologically grounded in the injunction to serve others and concretely expressed in a commitment to build community, a place called home and a sense of belonging for ex-prisoners. Fundamentally, it is a vision of faith in action with a group of people who were part of the human community before incarceration, and who often return to the same locality beyond release. Community chaplaincy does not dilute the classical criminological postulate of offender responsibility and behavioural accountability, but it does affirm that communities of faith have a responsibility for all citizens, which includes offenders. This is a theologically informed criminology which blends offender rational choice with the notion of shared well-being and mutuality. Expressed theologically, 'No element in the Body is dispensable or superfluous; what affects one affects all, for good and ill, since both suffering and flourishing belong to the entire organism not to any individual or purely local grouping' (Williams 2010, 25).

In 1987 Dr Allard was appointed chaplain general, remaining so for 11 years, during which time community chaplaincy received further support. It is important to clarify that the concept is not restricted to or synonymous with ordained ministry. There are only two full-time ordained community chaplains in Canada employed by CSC (the federal level), one of whom discussed pertinent matters with me through video conferencing facilities because of the distance between Ottawa and his location in British Columbia (the other is located in Toronto). Rather, the dominant operational model of community chaplaincy in Canada incorporates a much wider definition because it involves people of faith who are not ordained offering support to ex-prisoners. This model has arguably more flexibility than the formal structures and strictures attendant upon ordained ministry; it has emerged from and is sustained by grassroots support; and the operational dynamic is more bottom-up than top-down. It also encourages people of different faith traditions, the employed and retired and those more familiar with the criminal justice system than others, to make a difference in the lives of ex-prisoners when they exit the prison system by volunteering their time and personal capital.

A Contemporary Epiphany in Ottawa

Thirty years after community chaplaincy began in New Brunswick, numerous projects are scattered throughout Canada,[4] providing a faith-orientated support structure between incarceration and the community. Accordingly, I observed community chaplaincy in Ottawa, which has been coordinated by MAP since 2000. MAP is constituted as a non-profit, faith-based organisation comprising two coordinators who provide training to people from faith communities who volunteer their services to prisoners exiting the prison system of Eastern Ontario. It was explained that most volunteers are professional people with 'passion in their hearts'. The primary function of MAP is to provide a supportive presence to people leaving prison by assisting them to lead a new life by addressing their diverse needs, which are classified as *physical* (housing, employment, training and education), *social* (family, health, addictions, violence and anger) and *spiritual* (prayer, the need to belong and providing a church home). One of the MAP coordinators explained that community chaplaincy surrounds the released offender with 'things in the community they never had before', and its operational structure is as follows:

First, the two MAP coordinators, located in office accommodations several miles from downtown Ottawa, receive referrals on prisoners considering involvement with community chaplaincy beyond release. Referrals are made by the prison chaplain at the Ottawa-Carleton Detention Centre (OCDC), a provincial facility which holds approximately 500 inmates, and Alpha, a volunteer Christian organisation which visits OCDC prisoners on weekends to explore the 'meaning of life'. Referrals are also made by chaplains in prisons beyond Ottawa (Kingston, Kitchener and Gravenhurst federal institutions) in addition to which, inmates' families have been known to contact MAP. The 85 per cent males and 15 per cent females referred have numerous physical, social and spiritual needs in addition to bearing the scars of addictions and troublesome family backgrounds. An expression of faith by serving prisoners is not a prerequisite, but all those referred are assessed by the MAP coordinators.

Second, upon release, MAP surrounds the 'focal member', as the released prisoner is known, with support provided by three volunteer coaches drawn from diverse faith communities in Ottawa. MAP expects focal members to be active members of the coaching team for at least three months after leaving prison, but then support is available indefinitely. Focal members must remain committed to staying out of prison and accept help from their coaches at weekly meetings. Additionally, focal members are able to telephone their coaches in 'crisis situations' and relationships are 'based on the offender wanting to stay in touch'. Even though MAP has clear expectations of its focal members, the principle of voluntarism is fundamental. Consequently, community chaplaincy operates independently of the formal structures and statutory requirements of state apparatuses through its parole and probation officers. While some of its funding is provided contractually by CSC, MAP is supported by grants from private foundations and individual donors. Within this operational context, coaches surrounding the focal member provide a listening ear, support, and act as role models in the art of law-abiding citizenship.

Third, it is possible to signpost focal members towards a range of services available in Ottawa. These services are facilitated by the Ottawa Inner City Ministries and include drop-in centres, the provision of meals and clothing, mental health services, shelters for men and women and resources provided by the Salvation Army, Elizabeth Fry and John Howard organisations. I visited Jericho Road ministries and the Harvest House drug recovery facility. All these are illustrative of partnership arrangements between MAP, volunteer coaches and local faith-based community resources. However, there is some distance to travel before all the churches in Ottawa display the 'offender friendly' tag. It may be noted that there is a Prison Network Group (PNG) at OCDC and an Ex-Offender Friendly Faith Community Initiative (EFFCI). One respondent said that 'PNG has worked hard to identify faith communities that we know we can confidently refer people to and so we've got 30 to 35 faith communities, churches, in this area. We offer to train them and work with them to mentor ex-offenders. In fact, we are always looking for new churches and Mosques where we can refer people to.'

Since its inception in 2000 MAP has supported over two hundred people leaving prison and by 2009 had 25 volunteer coaches. However, it has trained many more coaches with a view to building tolerance towards offenders and ex-prisoners within the community. There are claims in various chaplaincy and Alpha documents concerning the effectiveness of community chaplaincy to reduce recidivism, but these are anecdotal rather than the result of rigorous quantitative empirical research. A rigorous evaluation of community chaplaincy remains to be undertaken in Canada, England and Wales, specifically the impact of faith-based measures upon recidivism (Whitehead 2011).

Crossing the Atlantic to England and Wales

If the gene code of community chaplaincy can be traced to Moncton in 1980, it subsequently crossed the Atlantic, where the first community chaplain was appointed at Swansea in 2001. It is also suggestive that the renaissance of the religious question in the criminal justice system of England and Wales was occurring at this time, associated with the emergence of the National Offender Management Service (NOMS) (Whitehead and Statham 2006). NOMS established the conditions whereby public, private, and voluntary sector organisations can contest for the business of providing services to offenders, a principle enshrined within Offender Management Act 2007. Even though the competitive dynamics of NOMS may enhance levels of performance in public sector organisations, New Labour governments between 1997 and 2010 increasingly encouraged the voluntary sector, which includes multifaith traditions, to get more involved. For example, during the autumn of 2003 the Home Office established the Faith Communities Unit, which was responsible for the document 'Working Together'. It was asserted that

> the Christian Churches have had an immense historic influence in shaping society, and make significant contributions in a wide range of areas such as community development, education, social inclusion and heritage. For these reasons, the Churches have made and continue to make a particular and distinctive contribution to the development and implementation of Government policy in certain areas. (Home Office 2004, 7)

It was also affirmed that government cannot promote citizenship, reduce reoffending, or promote community cohesion by itself, which is why it must seek alliances with, as one example, The Faith and Voluntary and Community Sector Alliance (NOMS 2005). One specific manifestation of partnership is community chaplaincy, which provides a bridge between prison and the community.

> It takes prisoners from the gate and supports them as they start their new lives, building the links between churches and the community. There are now 10 community chaplaincies in existence and 11 more in development. Community chaplaincy is not the creation of Government. It has grown up from the grass roots, and we must nurture it. It is an initiative to which many faith groups, not just Christian, are contributing. (Clarke 2005, 7)

By 2010 the newly created Community Chaplaincy Association of England and Wales had established its own website providing details of projects located at

Feltham, Wandsworth and Wormwood Scrubs, and Basic Caring Communities in London, Leicester, Manchester, Birmingham, Buckinghamshire, North Staffordshire, Durham, Exeter, Lewes, Swansea and Leeds. In fact, more are being planned to create a national network of support for released prisoners which utilises the resources of local churches as well as other faith traditions, volunteers and mentors.[5] The vision, which resonates with the Canadian gene code, is to help ex-prisoners to achieve successful re-entry by offering support and services to free themselves from crime and build a brighter future in the community. Furthermore, this initiative is timely because it resonates with the Big Society articulated by the Conservative–Liberal coalition government formed in May 2010. Therefore, one should not underestimate the importance being attached to community chaplaincy within the context of state, and accompanying criminal justice reformation which is currently gathering impetus.

Community chaplaincy is separate from, but linked to, multifaith chaplaincy arrangements within the prison system in England and Wales. Some are located within prison establishments and others outside the gate. Critically, most community chaplaincies in England and Wales utilise volunteers to achieve numerous objectives: to support people at the point of release from prison to lead a crime-free life, build safer communities, protect the public and reduce the number of victims. Moreover, these objectives will be achieved by responding to the accommodation needs of ex-prisoners, providing opportunities to achieve the requisite skills to enhance employment opportunities by signposting towards other organisational resources, advising on finances, benefits, substance abuse, physical and mental health issues, transforming attitudes, thinking and behaviours, providing pastoral counselling and supportive relationships consistent with the values traditionally associated with faith communities. In June 2010 justice secretary Ken Clarke announced a rehabilitation revolution that will make better use of the latent expertise waiting to be liberated in the voluntary sector, and that non-governmental organisations (NGOs) will be paid by results to reduce crime. Consequently, this is the prevailing context within which community chaplaincy is being encouraged to realise its vision of helping ex-prisoners to lead a crime-free life. It is also the context within which to interrogate what constitutes a potentially significant development within criminal justice in Canada and England and Wales.

Critical Interrogation: Constructing an Exploratory Typology

Given the lengthy historical relationship between religion, prisons, criminal justice and penal policy, the contemporary manifestation of community chaplaincy requires attention. The next step proceeds beyond empirically informed description to critical engagement to elucidate what is a complex theoretical and empirical landscape. To facilitate this task, a typology will be constructed which acknowledges Tittle and Welch (1983), who addressed numerous theoretical strands when explaining the connections between religion and deviance, which include a functionalist perspective where religion promotes conformity, differential association where morally acceptable and law-abiding behaviour can be the outcome of exposure to a surfeit of religious and moral influences, a psychological–sociological dynamic that forges links between childhood, family stability and the place of religion in socialisation, and religion as an ideological tool in the hands of the powerful to control troublesome populations.

Subsequently, Tom O'Connor (2004a, 2004b) explored the historical context for the association between religion, culture and rehabilitation in the United States, where religion has been influential in shaping society since the Puritan influx of the 1600s. In doing so, he questioned the constructs of Tittle and Welch (1983) for guiding research and the impact of religion on offending. Accordingly, O'Connor's refinements integrate criminological theory and religious perspectives by assimilating social learning theory, which suggests that people can learn new behaviours inspired by faith-orientated role models, social attachment conducive to controlling behaviour through the positive influence of the family, work, peers, and beliefs associated with religion and church attendance, and religious *metanoia* – a Greek term meaning a change of heart and behaviour – not as a one-off salvific event, but a lifelong process; and the principles of the What Works project, which supports the effective practice agenda. It is also of interest to allude to the 'Hellfire Hypothesis' of Hirschi and Stark (1969), which stated that religion deters criminality by the threat of supernatural sanctions as well as the efficacy to create new social identities beyond the prisoner label (Maruna, Wilson and Curran 2006).

After acknowledging Tittle and Welch (1983) and O'Connor (2004a, 2004b), I now turn to construct a typology of religion and crime within which to stimulate discussion on community chaplaincy. It is not possible within the scope of this chapter to integrate the full range of theoretical perspectives on religion, including classical and contemporary social theory (Furseth and Repstad 2006; Harrington 2005). Nevertheless, the assembled typology combines disparate elements which allow pertinent themes of a more critical nature to surface. Notwithstanding an absence of methodologically rigorous research on recidivism and community chaplaincy, there is, by contrast, a copious research literature on religion and crime which will be considered first.

Religion Reduces Recidivism – Or Does It?
Some Research Evidence

Within the scope of two articles O'Connor (2004a, 2004b) acknowledges a copious research literature which addresses the question, does religion work as a correctional intervention? After clarifying that there's more research on juveniles than on adults, Knudten and Knudten (1971) reviewed the literature from 1913–70 before arriving at the conclusion that rigorous research is lacking in the religion and corrections field. Later, Tittle and Welch (1983) reviewed 65 studies, but only 10 did not show a significant negative relationship between religion and deviance. Ellis (1985) included 32 studies of which 5 revealed no effect and 27 a reduced effect. Sumter (1999) examined 23 published studies of which 5 showed no effect, but 18 demonstrated evidence of a statistically significant inverse relationship between religion and deviance. However, there are methodological difficulties, so caution is required when evaluating these data. Johnson, Li, Larson and McCullough (2000) completed a systematic literature review of articles pertinent to religion and delinquency published between January 1985 and December 1997. Out of 40 studies, one suggested religion increased delinquency, one failed to specify an effect, three demonstrated a mixed effect, five showed no effect, but 30 demonstrated negative or reduced effects. Again, methodological weaknesses are acknowledged. Subsequently, Baier and Wright's (2001) systematic review of the effect of religion on crime included 60 studies published between 1969 and 1998 and concluded that there is evidence that religion can have a positive effect on reducing crime. Hirschi and Stark (1969) may well have been unexpectedly gloomy when advancing the view that religion does not act as a deterrent, but 'Our findings give confidence that religion does indeed have some deterrent effect' (Baier and Wright 2001, 16).

It is imperative to acknowledge Aos, Miller and Drake (2006), who reviewed the evidence on what works (and what does not) from 291 evaluations in the United States and other English-speaking countries over a period of 35 years. This review is significant because it constitutes 'the most succinct and methodologically sound summary of the research to date' (O'Connor and Duncan 2008, 88). Pertinently, it includes six evaluations of faith-based interventions, five of which were grouped together because they promoted Christianity among prisoners to reduce recidivism beyond the prison walls. Aos et al. (2006) concluded that four out of five studies did not have a programme effect (O'Connor, Su, Ryan, Parikh and Alexander 1997; Burnside, Adler, Loucks and Rose 2001; Trusty and Eisenberg 2003; Johnson 2004). One reason for this could be that they were not adequately aligned to the principles of What Works (O'Connor and Duncan 2008; O'Connor, Duncan and Quillard

2006). By contrast, Wilson, Wilson, Drummond and Kelso (2005) did find a programme effect.

Because research studies contained in various literature reviews vary in methodological rigour, caution is required when claiming that religion prevents, deters or reduces crime. Nevertheless, the phenomenon of religion cannot be ignored, because religious affiliations and sensibilities are conducive to promoting morally and legally acceptable behaviour (Johnson 2004). Prisoner involvement in religious activities can contribute to psychological well-being (Clear and Myhre 1995), and faith-based interventions with prisoners utilising bible study, prayer, pastoral and spiritual counselling, can have positive benefits (even though we are not sure precisely *how* faith-based measures work). Additionally, the research findings on the religiously inspired Circles of Support and Accountability for sex offenders in Canada are impressive (Wilson, Cortoni and McWhinnie 2009). Accordingly, there are empirical reasons for guarded optimism that cultivating religious sensibilities, in addition to faith-based interventions informed by the principles of What Works, can have rehabilitative impacts. Finally, Byron Johnson (2011) has conducted the most extensive systematic review of 272 studies published between 1944 and 2010. After considering the type of study, sampling methodology, the number of respondents from youths to adults, location of study and religious variables (religious attendance, bible study, religiosity, etc.), Johnson (2011, 78) claims that 'Consistent with previous systematic reviews, the vast majority of these studies (90 per cent) find religion and religious involvement to be associated with decreases in various measures of crime and delinquency'. Therefore, this literature offers encouragement to community chaplaincy that it could make an instrumental difference when prisoners are released from the prison system. At this point, I exit the research environment and step into three sociological streams which pose more complex intellectual challenges when exploring the connection between religion and crime. Before doing so, and as mentioned above, these are not the only theoretical perspectives in the marketplace of ideas (Furseth and Repstad 2006; Harrington 2005), but they do represent different lines of sociological enquiry.

Three Sociological Lines of Enquiry: Durkheim, Marx and Foucault

Émile Durkheim (1858–1917) made significant contributions to numerous sociological themes, including the sociology of religion. He advanced the view that the roots of religion are not located in a spiritual dimension of reality (community chaplaincy would disagree), but rather, in the collective needs of society so that 'God is merely the symbolic expression of society' (Durkheim 1912, 171). Notwithstanding his aetiological position, *The Elementary Forms of Religious Life* explains that religion functions to strengthen social bonds and as such, integrates individuals into the social whole. Durkheim suggests that the sociology of religion yields important insights into those collective values deemed necessary for the maintenance of society constituted as a moral entity. Therefore, religion, as a Durkheimian social fact, contains the efficacy to constrain behaviour and engender respect for the sacred-moral order of society.

For Marx (1818–1886), as well as Durkheim, religion is a human construction. By contrast, whereas Durkheim postulates the aetiology of religion within collective sentiments that function to benefit the social whole, Marx's materialist analysis suggests that religion is an epiphenomenon attached to the ideological superstructure which is shaped by narrow economic interests. Accordingly, religion benefits the ruling class by mystifying and obscuring the 'real' nature of society under capitalism, which engenders injustice, inequality, differential opportunity structures and conflict. Within this analytical framework, it is postulated that regardless of life's difficulties, God is always present; he suffers alongside human beings, but all will be well, if not in this world, then most certainly in the next (Raines 2002). Therefore, religion is delusional (Freud would add 'infantile'), promotes false consciousness, benefits one class at the expense of another and prevents the transformation of economic arrangements responsible for social ills as well as the necessity for the drug of religion. However, in addition to religion constituting an instrument of injustice, it can also constitute a protestation against injustice (Furseth and Repstad 2006, 31).

Among the many complex philosophical, sociological and linguistic issues addressed by Michel Foucault (1926–1984), there are allusions to religion, where the default position is that it constitutes a repressive apparatus of the state. It has been stated that the 'political force of religious discourse, in its power to silence and its power to demand an utterance, is the key theoretical operation on which Foucault's "religious question" can be examined' (Carrette 2000, 42). Even though religion does not receive a book-length treatment in the Foucauldian corpus, it is a disturbing presence in its association with politics, power and social control. If religion functions to strengthen consensual social bonds conducive to maintaining the moral order in Durkheim and an ideology functional to controlling subordinate classes in Marx, Foucault presents a darker vision. Here, its dystopian tone is associated with deposits of power, a strategic technique for quelling rebellious minds and silencing recalcitrant bodies, culminating in the formation of disciplined habits and routines, which is a prerequisite of capitalist modernity. Foucault, with Nietzsche lurking in the background, always wants us to root out the prevailing structure of domination and genealogical power dynamic.

Economic Responsibility and Value for Money

Governments are entrusted to spend taxpayers' money efficiently and effectively, a pressing fiscal objective on the back of global financial crises which erupted in 2007 and alluded to earlier. For illustrative purposes, what began under New Labour governments in England and Wales is currently being pursued with alacrity under the current Conservative–Liberal alliance elected in May 2010. This means that all departments of state from health, defence and education, to the Home Office and Ministry of Justice, must reduce their operating costs. Where the Ministry of Justice is concerned, plans are afoot to cut services in prisons, probation and the criminal courts by 23 per cent by 2015. Additionally, since 1995 Canada has reduced its federal costs on health care, education, and housing in its pursuit of market-orientated values; criminal justice services will also be affected by budget reductions from 2012 (Broadbent 2009; Harvey 2005). Nevertheless, the imperative to reduce spending in the state–public sector provides opportunities for the private as well as voluntary sector, where one encounters charities, disparate faith communities and, of course, community chaplaincy. Therefore, the influence of religion in general, and community chaplaincy in particular, are arguably being encouraged to get more involved in the criminal justice system, ostensibly to reduce central government expenditure, a message congenial to neoliberal administrations in England and Wales and in Canada.

Personalism

The doctrine of personalism (Mounier 1952), supportive of the gene code and contemporary epiphanies of community chaplaincy, advocates that human beings are of intrinsic value and irreducible worth, including offenders and ex-prisoners. This theologically inspired humanitarian perspective is attractive to the vision of community chaplaincy, for as one respondent in Ottawa commented, the 'men and women I know, and this sounds crazy, but in society's eyes they ask, "You care for inmates, you care for prostitutes?" "Well, yea, I do".' Alpha and MAP representatives in Ottawa explained that they 'walk alongside' the offender and create a cohesive web of support, so that 'the guys know that we care about them'. Furthermore, the full-time community chaplain in British Columbia told me that his mission is to assist 'offenders and their families as they rebuild their lives after incarceration. And the way we do it is by mobilizing faith communities to care and support them in that reintegration and rebuilding process.' Community chaplaincy endows human relationships with theological significance because of the notion of mutuality mentioned above (Williams 2010), in addition to which, empirical research suggests that relationships built upon care and support create the context for pro-social modelling, which facilitates desistance (McNeill and Weaver 2010).[6] In other words, pro-social modelling 'emphasizes the importance of demonstrating respect for individuals by being punctual, reliable, courteous, friendly, honest and open' (Chapman and Hough 1998, 16), the very characteristics that offenders value in their supervising officers. Therefore, by meshing personalism with pro-social modelling, a modus operandi is established for the transformation of antisocial attitudes, which resonates with the rationale of community chaplaincy.

Justice

David Harvey (2010) situates the human condition within the changing fortunes of capitalism, which since the 1750s has experienced periodic crises (see the introduction to this volume). When analysing the economic frailties of the 1970s crisis decade followed by neoliberal responses in the United States, the United Kingdom and Canada, this is described as a class project to restore power to economic elites. Neoliberalism endorses reducing the size of the state, deregulating economies, competitive markets and private rather than public sector solutions, coupled with individual and family responsibility. But it is a blessing and a curse: a blessing because it generates the resources for civilised life to be maintained; a curse because its differential impacts perpetuate inequality, insecurity and poverty amongst the most vulnerable sections of the community where ex-prisoners are located (Broadbent 2009). Therefore, even though religious communities have a duty of care towards the individual (a personalist ethic), they also have a moral responsibility to challenge economic policies which engender social insecurities illustrative of a malfunctioning political economy. The links between neoliberalism and social dislocations, including criminality and deviance, are well documented (Wacquant 2009; Wilkinson and Pickett 2009). Nevertheless, part of the neoliberal narrative is that poverty and inequality are issues of 'personal behaviour and dependency rather than about economic equality and justice. The problem is not structure or environment but individual failing and dysfunction' (Crudas and Rutherford 2010, 58). In summary, the elements comprising this typology, which draws upon the research literature, sociological theory, neoliberal economic imperatives, the ethic of personalism, and politics of social justice, can be presented in Table 9.1 as follows:

Table 9.1. Typology on religion and crime to explore the rationale of community chaplaincy

Type	Advocates	Main Features
Research	Johnson et al. 2000; Baier and Wright 2001; O'Connor, 2004a, 2004b; Aos et al. 2006 Johnson 2011	The central research question is: *Does religion work as a correctional intervention?* Some research deserves critical respect, but there is an absence of rigorous quantitative empirical research on specific faith-based measures concerning community chaplaincy in Canada, England and Wales.
Social bonds	Durkheim	Religion functions to promote social bonds by integrating the individual into the social whole, which constrains behaviour.
Ideology	Marx Raines 2002	Religion benefits the ruling bloc by obscuring the *real* nature of society under capitalist/neoliberal economic arrangements, but it can also be a source of protest.
Repression	Foucault Carette 2000	Religion, a repressive apparatus of the state, is implicated in strategies of power, discipline and control of human beings.
Economics	Neoliberal policies	Reduce the costs of the state-public sector by enlarging civil, voluntary, and faith sectors responses in a more marketised criminal justice domain. This is consistent with the Big Society and Rehabilitation Revolution in England and Wales.
Personalism	Mounier 1952	People have intrinsic worth, meaning and value. Supportive and caring relationships, the context for pro-social modelling, can facilitate crime reduction as well as being intrinsically significant.
Justice	Williams and Elliot 2010	Religion has a moral duty to transform economic policies that produce criminal and social injustice, contingent upon capitalism and neoliberalism, through theologically informed political engagement, protest, and resistance.

Discussion

While it is possible to theorise the interrelated dynamics of religion, crime and criminal justice from competing standpoints, illustrated by this typology, where does this leave community chaplaincy specifically? Its distinctive gene code, supported by empirical insights gleaned from Ottawa, in addition to research undertaken in England and Wales (see note 2), establishes a cogent case for providing unconditional support to people leaving prison. Furthermore, community chaplaincy does not eschew the objective of crime reduction through relationships, but, arguably, it remains to develop political engagement to promote social justice within a neoliberal environment. I now turn to discuss all three perspectives with a view to mapping what arguably constitutes the rationale of community chaplaincy in contemporary criminal justice domains, which moves the field forward in Canada and England and Wales.

Unconditional Support for People Leaving Prison

Criminal justice systems are comprised of contested rationalities, one of which is an *instrumental* mode of thought (the prevailing orthodox rationality). This means that governments expect their criminal justice organisations such as prison and probation to be effective instruments for achieving specific goals, primarily rehabilitative transformation and social control. Even though voluntary sector organisations and faith communities cannot avoid being immured within this instrumental rationality (*zweckrational*), particularly when the Big Society rehabilitative revolution is advocating payment by results, the argument is that it does not define the essence of community chaplaincy. Accordingly, the substantive point for emphasis is that empathy, understanding, building supportive relationships and setting a good behavioural example to ex-prisoners are not solely undertaken as a means to an end, but rather an end in itself. Accordingly, there is a moral rationality (*wertrational*) demand upon community chaplaincy to provide unconditional support regardless of the impact upon recidivism.[7] The dominant story line of reducing crime is as understandable as it is desirable, but the distinctive contribution of community chaplaincy operates within a moral- and value-driven framework that transcends conditional instrumentalism. It is this orientation which differentiates faith-orientated contributions from that of other organisational domains in an increasingly market-driven and payment-by-results field of criminal justice providers. Community chaplaincy is enjoined to serve the 'other' as neighbour, and to do so unconditionally regardless of who they are, what they have done or what the outcome might be. This resonates with Weber's concept of *value rational* social action in *Economy and Society* as putting into practice their convictions of what seems to them to be required by duty, honour, the pursuit of beauty, a religious call, personal loyalty or the importance of some cause no matter in what it consists, regardless of possible cost to themselves. (Weber [1922] 1968, 25)

Furthermore, the Platonic and Kantian idealist tradition advances the ontological position that there is a structure of reality beyond the phenomenal world of appearances. In other words, the world we inhabit is not 'real' because it is subjected to Heraclitean flux. By contrast, true reality is the domain of an unchanging realm of noumena, which cannot be known but only inferred from its manifestation in moral demands. According to Rudolf Steiner, 'There is only one access to these higher truths. This access is given in the voice of duty, which speaks within us emphatically and distinctly "You are *morally obliged* to do this and that"' (1973, 103; emphasis in original). Therefore, the personalist, theologically informed and value-driven rationality of community chaplaincy is not primarily a vocation for the pursuit of instrumental or governmental reason, but rather, to respond to the moral demands of the 'other' because it is the right thing to do as an end in itself.

Reduce Reoffending through Supportive Relationships

The desistance paradigm within the correctional literature emphasises that this is a process rather than isolated salvific event which addresses individual and social factors, facilitated by family and friends, as well as engagement with professionals. Importantly *supportive relationships* are a critical element of this process, which has recently been reinforced by the comment that 'the desistance paradigm understands rehabilitation as a relational process but achieved in the context of relationships with others' (Maruna and LeBel 2010, 81). The literature on the salience of relationships within the therapeutic and rehabilitative process is notably significant and the pertinent elements can be distilled as follows: This literature draws attention to the importance of human relationships which contain genuineness, warmth, approval, acceptance, encouragement, empathy and sensitivity (Lishman 1994; Rogers 1961; Traux and Carkhuff 1967). In fact, Martin Davies (1985) stated that the social worker must get two things right: the quality of the relationship and the achievement of results. Next, when reflecting on the process of casework throughout probation history, Peter Raynor (2002, 1173) asseverates that it was a process 'of therapeutic work in which the offender's needs and motivation, characteristically hidden by presenting problems, could be revealed through a process of insight facilitated by a relationship with a probation officer'. Additionally, desistance from crime is facilitated by relationships based on trust (McNeill 2003); the personal qualities of the worker, including the ability to form relationships, can be more important in shaping outcomes than specific methods employed in supervision (Smith 2006). Pro-social modelling delivered through establishing quality relationships is a constitutive element of What Works and an effective practice agenda (Underdown 1988) Intriguingly, the Ministry of Justice green paper on *Breaking the Cycle* asserts that 'Evidence indicates that the relationship between an offender and the person managing them is an important factor in successful rehabilitation' (2010, 24). The nucleus of community chaplains and associated volunteers in Canada and in England and Wales, are well placed to contribute to the desistance paradigm through building supportive relationships with ex-prisoners. Arguably, this strikes to the essential contribution of community chaplaincy; it is their métier. Even though the primary rationale of community chaplaincy is not instrumental efficacy but value rationality, this does not mean that it does not contribute to instrumental objectives. There is a remaining third element to consider.

Political Engagement and Social Justice

David Harvey (2005 and 2010) locates the vagaries of the human condition within the changing fortunes of a capitalist economic system. The immediate post-war period may well have been shaped by the Keynesian settlement (Whitehead and Crawshaw, both in this volume), but the crisis of the 1970s precipitated a neoliberal resurgence which pervaded the United Kingdom, the United States, Canada and other countries. There are those who argue that there is no alternative to a capitalist economic system, primarily because it generates the wealth to make the world go round. However, the advocates of this system are confronted with its differential impacts, illustrated by unequal opportunities, persistent inequality and social insecurities embedded in the most vulnerable sections of the community, where one is most likely to locate offenders and ex-prisoners. Furthermore, the links between neoliberalism and social dislocations including crime, deviance and harsh punishments are well documented (Bell 2011; Garland 2001; Reiner 2007; Wacquant 2009; Wilkinson and Pickett 2009). Neoliberal ideology elevates the economic successes of the few over social cohesion and security for the many, which is an indictment of its functioning within the glorification of a competitive, Darwinian survival-of-the-fittest marketplace. Nevertheless, when reflecting on the moral demands of justice there is a tradition of biblical, prophetic and theological engagements with social and economic questions which, in turn, can be extrapolated to critique contemporary material conditions within which ex-prisoners live, move and have their being. Consequently, as the size of the state is reduced and it withdraws from public places and spaces and the

Big Society expands, the potential impacts of these developments for criminal and social justice must trouble faith communities in general and community chaplaincy in particular. Therefore, analysis and response can be facilitated by reflecting upon the following tradition.

For illustrative purposes, the situation in Northern Israel around 760 BC to 750 BC precipitated a prophetic response. The pertinent prophetic biblical text from this period is Amos (Jones 1968, 17), which discloses marked contrasts between the nouveau riche and the poor, as well as corrupt practices in the courts, marketplace and aristocratic society. It was to this situation that the prophetic voice enunciated the logos of social justice to those in positions of leadership. Much later, in the twentieth century, William Temple ([1942] 1976) pondered the relationship between Christianity and the complexities of the social order. Next, in the 1960s religion was a significant feature in the civil rights movement within the United States, and then during the 1970s and 1980s liberation theology engaged with unjust political, social and economic conditions that pertained in Latin America. Finally, also in the 1980s, but this time in England and Wales, *Faith in the City*, a report published in the UK in Autumn 1985, authored by the Archbishop of Canterbury's Commission on Urban Priority Areas, criticised Thatcherite neoliberal policies and in doing so, was allegedly dismissed by one cabinet minister as a Marxist text. It is also claimed that Prime Minister Thatcher herself remarked that 'There's nothing about self-help or doing anything for yourself in the report' (Wyatt 1999, 22). Accordingly, there was a growing divide between rich and poor in the 1980s to which *Faith in the City* (Archbishop of Canterbury 1985), articulated a critical response, a divide which has been allowed to grow ever wider since (Dorling 2010).

Faith in the City gave faith communities a voice in the inner city, as it demanded justice on behalf of the poor and disadvantaged as the victims of socio-economic policies through integrating theology, spirituality and political engagement. It spoke of the common good, which resonates with a more recent collection of essays on ethics, economics and justice (Williams and Elliott 2010). Consequently, there is a long-standing tradition of theological engagement with the impacts of unjust socio-economic forces. These are the forces to which all of us are differentially related for good or ill; they generate employment and unemployment, material comforts and poverty, opportunities and inequalities, prospects for some and relegation of others to a marginalised existence where daily experience is one of hopelessness and despair. As much as diverse faith communities and community chaplaincy must offer unconditional support to ex-prisoners as an end in itself and make a valid contribution to the instrumental goal of reducing recidivism through supportive one-to-one relationships, there is also the moral imperative to engage with the pressing demand of social justice. Any dilution of this dualised *individual-support* and *social-justice* responsibility risks religion in general, and the rationale of faith communities, and community chaplaincy in particular, being reduced to a narrow ideological apparatus of the state that legitimates prevailing political, social and economic arrangements. In other words, there is the perennial danger that doing good towards the individual perpetuates criminal and structural social injustice because of a failure to take account of the macro impacts of neoliberalism and the corresponding social circumstances of ex-prisoners before they enter prison and later, following their release.

Conclusion

The purpose of this chapter is to explore and map the scope of the voluntary sector in general and the faith sector in particular and to critique and challenge criminal justice reformation within the parameters of neoliberal orthodoxy through the lens of community chaplaincy in Canada, England and Wales. This brings into view the *religious question* in contemporary criminal and penal policy, which has been approached empirically and theoretically, facilitated by the construction of the typology in Table 9.1. Even though the rehabilitation revolution and Big Society in England and Wales offers the prospect, albeit modestly, of rebalancing the managerial–bureaucratic episteme associated with the modernising turn of New Labour from 1997 to 2010, it is much more difficult to envisage the attenuation of the punitive upsurge since the early 1990s (Bell 2011). Going soft on crime is not on the agenda in both countries because it would signal political ruin for current and aspiring governments, and constitute a hostage to electoral fortune – its ideological and symbolic functionality is too important. Accordingly, the punitive trajectory will continue to spin its course, a trajectory which has ripped out the personalist heart and soul from the complex dialectics of criminal justice organisational structures.

It is within this rapidly changing environment since the early 1980s in Canada, then 2001 in England and Wales, that community chaplaincy has supplied its value-rational gene code of unconditional support to people exiting custodial institutions and positioned itself to contribute to reducing recidivism through supportive relationships; yet, it remains to take the decisive step to maximise political engagement to advance the cause of criminal, social and restorative justice. Accordingly, the 37 projects scattered across (mainly) Eastern Canada, and 18 projects in England and Wales (as of June 2011) are imbued with a theology of mutuality (Williams 2010), person-centred relationships, unconditional assistance and the ethic of personalism, the very impulses indubitably corroded by the politics of punitive and bureaucratic modernisation. But these value-rational impulses are the distinctive 'mental conceptions' (Harvey 2010, 237) by which community chaplaincy can mediate the worst excesses of the politics of punitive exclusion to restore a semblance of balance to criminal justice operations. Furthermore, the manifestation of these impulses provides an answer to the religious question which is located within the interstices of the formal state system and the emergence of the Big Society in England and Wales.

However, the question that remains intellectually troublesome concerns the efficacy of community chaplaincy to mediate the worst excesses of criminal justice expressions, the scope to promote a discernible transformation in the present direction of travel. It is a troubling question because even though community chaplaincy continues to expand its influence (26 projects in Canada in 2006, 37 by June 2011; 1 project in England and Wales in 2001, 18 a decade later), it lacks the power to pull the levers of governmental reason that will impact upon the policies of the Ministry of Justice within the National Offender Management Service, and tougher criminal justice commitments in Canada located within the Omnibus Crime Bill, which was re-launched in the House during the week beginning 19 September 2011. Non-governmental organisations, including faith organisations, are unquestionably committed, ameliorative, influential and composed of dedicated staff, but because they don't have power, they operate within the parameters of governmental constraints. Accordingly, the current position bears witness to moderate influence rather than transformational cogency; the muffled voice rather than the prophetic exclamation of protest and resistance; the cloud that hovers on the distant horizon; existing at the periphery rather than the centre of operational decision making.

The argument most certainly not being advanced is that community chaplaincy exists in a cul-de-sac of a one-dimensional, mono-causal, economically determinist view of criminal justice operations (it can't change anything, because it simply supports existing socio-economic arrangements). Rather, I advance a more flexible Weberian possibility of the way in which processes and events can be shaped by the complex interactions of competing spheres – the political sphere, economic forces, and the efficacy of ideas and values. If this means anything to community chaplaincy, then it must transcend unconditional support and rehabilitative relationships to rise to the challenge of political engagement. If this next step is taken, it could begin to challenge the deleterious forces of neoliberalism that hinder the pursuit of criminal and social justice. This will mean an uncomfortable journey of collision, protest and resistance, not collusion; of forming alliances with other organisational domains in the voluntary sector (see Chapter 10); of mapping a strategy to obtain a seat on the appropriate governmental policy-making boards to increase its sphere of influence where it can speak to and argue with structures of power. Arguably, community chaplaincy has no alternative but to pursue this course of action because it is demanded by its theological gene-code which operates within a tradition of social justice. The neoliberal dynamic may present itself as the end of history, as the only game in town, whose tenets have colonised economic policy in many countries as well as criminal and penal policy in Canada and England and Wales (Wacquant 2009). But because community chaplaincy belongs to the voluntary-charitable sector, is located *in* but is not essentially *of* the state's criminal justice system, then it is ideally placed to exert its influence to challenge the surging tide of neoliberal orthodoxy. In fact, being *in* and not *of* the formal system is its strength, because independence provides a field of opportunities not available to the state-directed statutory sector. Is it prepared for the challenge in Canada, and in England and Wales, to provide answers to the *religious question* by defining its specific contribution to the field of criminal justice and penal policy?

Notes

1 Canada, as well as other countries, including England and Wales, can be described as neoliberal Broadbent (2009); Harvey (2005). Moreover, Stephen Harper, leader of the Conservative Party, was reelected prime minister at the general election in Canada during 2011. One of the policy commitments is to develop a tougher criminal justice system, which was very much in the news when I revisited Canada during September/October 2011, because of the reintroduction of the Omnibus Crime Bill. This bill proposes a greater emphasis on punishment, tightens up procedures for young people, expands mandatory minimum sentences, cracks down on drugs that could result in more prison sentences, and imposes more restrictive parole procedures so that more prisoners will leave custody without state support (with implications for community chaplaincy). This bill is intriguing because there is no crime epidemic in Canada (*Corrections and Conditional Release Statistical Review, Annual Report 2010*).

2 There is a paucity of research on community chaplaincy in Canada and in England and Wales. However, in addition to the author undertaking a research visit to Canada in September 2010 and September/October 2011, research commenced in England and Wales in November 2010 (Whitehead 2011a). The aim of this research was to establish an exploratory understanding of community chaplaincy and the space it currently occupies in the state's criminal justice system in England and Wales at the end of its first decade (2001–2011). This exploration was pursued through visiting six community chaplaincy projects where 22 interviews were conducted over six months (November 2010–April 2011) on what is arguably a significant yet under-researched phenomenon. This data reveals a person-centred, theologically informed, value-driven, and voluntary-charitable organisation which operates within a multifaith ethos. It offers supportive relationships to men, women and young people (Feltham Young Offender Institution) at the point they leave custodial institutions. Some who leave custody are the subject of licence conditions which stipulate regular contact with probation; others are not subjected to statutory requirements. Even though projects are distinguishable from other organisational domains by their faith ethos, this does not mean that all

volunteers who work for community chaplaincy are people of faith or that they belong to faith communities (whereas in Canada most if not all volunteers are drawn from faith communities). Nevertheless, community chaplaincy projects require that volunteers are aware of and sympathetic to their distinctive faith orientation. Community chaplaincy does not attempt to proselytise offenders; rather, supportive relationships are offered unconditionally to people of faith and none when they leave custody.

Community chaplaincy, because of its faith orientation and value-driven nature, is more vocation than job, which facilitates added value. It also offers hope to people who, as a consequence of their offending, have acquired the negative status of being labelled offender, prisoner or even ex-prisoner. It operates with a person-in-situation mentality to counterbalance those punitive, de-humanising and depersonalising tendencies which have colonised criminal justice over recent years. Its vision is to walk with marginalised and excluded ex-prisoners on a difficult journey because of accumulated problems compounded since unpropitious childhood experiences of family conflict, insecurity, vulnerability, impoverished education, unstable work record, substance abuse, precarious finances and substandard accommodations. To people immured in such adverse social circumstances, community chaplaincy is a conduit of hope and support as they return to an uncertain future in the community. Arguably, within the contemporary rehabilitation revolution, community chaplaincy has exemplified the Big Society for a decade, but concerns were expressed about what these concepts actually mean. The voluntary sector in general, and the faith sector in particular, may well receive encouragement to get more involved in the criminal justice system by central government, but adequate resources are required and funding is a pressing issue for community chaplaincy projects. These are some of the key research findings in England and Wales which were presented to the Community Chaplaincy Association Management Board at their quarterly meeting in Cheltenham on 12 July 2011.

3 Kelly Richards and Philip Whitehead have undertaken collaborative work on Circles of Support and Accountability which, like community chaplaincy, also began in Canada.

4 There were 22 locations in 2006 and then 37 in June 2011 (Cuff 2006), but most are located in Ontario. It should also be acknowledged that there are different models of community chaplaincy operating in Canada, reflecting the vagaries of local conditions and operational structures. In other words, not all projects conform to the Ottawa model described above.

5 In March 2011 there were 18 projects in England and Wales comprising 50 paid staff and 487 volunteers. Furthermore, during 2010 community chaplaincy provided support to 1,354 people exiting custodial institutions; in 2011 it was 1273.

6 It is possible to summarise the desistance literature which draws attention to the importance of human relationships within this process as follows. According to McNeill and Weaver (2010) empirical research has established the following principles: desistance is an individual process because each person is different; motivating people and facilitating hope are crucial elements; desistance can only be pursued within the context of human relationships; support and develop the strengths and resources that can be found within offenders and ex-prisoners; respect human agency and self-determination, which means working with and alongside offenders; blend personal capital (individual skills, knowledge, and resources) with social capital (the development of relationships, networks of support, family and community links). This is as relevant for statutory sector probation work as voluntary sector community chaplaincy projects. Furthermore, there is a discussion in *Religion, Spirituality and Desistance* on page 68 which is pertinent for community chaplaincy.

7 Within Weber's methodology of social science, which includes *verstehen* and the heuristic device of ideal types, he constructs a typology of social action. Human beings constantly make decisions about the what, how and why of behaviour, and ascribe meaning to their own and others' behaviours. Accordingly, in *Economy and Society*, Weber's typology has the following elements: *Traditional action* – behaviour which is undertaken automatically, habitually, routinely without thinking; *Affectual* – where behaviour is driven by the emotions; *Value rational (wertrational)* is when human action is orientated around a specific value. Here, Weber states that human actors seek to 'put into practice their convictions of what seems to them to be required by duty, honour, the pursuit of beauty, a religious call, personal loyalty or the importance of some cause no matter in what it consists, regardless of possible cost to themselves' ([1922] 1968, 25). Finally, *Instrumental rationality (zweckrational)* is where the means and ends of human action are rationally calculated and carefully weighed. If rationalisation is the historical process by which society is increasingly orientated to planning, calculation, technical procedures and efficiency, then rationality is the degree to which these features dominate social action more than, for example, religious values, within organisational and institutional spheres.

References

Aos, S., M. Miller and E. Drake. 2006. *Evidence-Based Adult Corrections Programs: What Works and What Does Not*. Olympia, WA: Washington State Institute of Public Policy, 1–19.

Archbishop of Canterbury. 1985. *Faith in the City: A Call for Action by Church and Nation*. General Synod of the Church of England, London: Church House Publishing.

Arrighi, G. 2010. *The Long Twentieth Century: Money, Power and the Origins of Our Times*, new and updated ed. London and New York: Verso.

Baier, C. and B. Wright. 2001. '"If you love me, keep my commandments": A meta-analysis of the effect of religion and crime'. *Journal of Research in Crime and Delinquency* 38 (1): 3–21.

Bell, E. 2011. *Criminal Justice and Neoliberalism*. London: Palgrave Macmillan.

Broadbent, E. 2009. *Barbarism Lite: Political Assault on Social Rights is Worsening Inequality*. Ottawa: Canadian Centre for Political Alternatives.

Burnside, J., J. Adler, N. Loucks and G. Rose. 2001. *Kainos Community in Prisons: Report of an evaluation*. RDS OLR 11/01, presented to Research and Development and Statistics Directorate. London: Home Office.

Carrette, J. R. 2000. *Foucault on Religion: Spiritual Corporality and Political Spirituality*. London and New York: Routledge.

Cayley, D. 1998. *The Expanding Prison: The Crisis in Crime and Punishment and the Search for Alternatives*. Toronto: Anansi Press.

Chapman, T. and M. Hough. 1998. *Evidence Based Practice: A Guide to Effective Practice on Behalf of Her Majesty's Inspectorate of Probation*. London: Home Office.

Clarke, C. 2005. *Where Next for Penal Policy?* London: Prison Reform Trust.

Clear, T. R. and M. Myhre. 1995. 'A Study of Religion in Prison: The International Association of Residential and Community Corrections Alternatives'. *Journal on Community Corrections* 6 (6): 20–25.

Crouch, C. 2011. *The Strange Non-Death of Neoliberalism*. Cambridge: Polity Press.

Crudas, J. and J. Rutherford. 2010. 'The Common Table'. In *Crisis and Recovery: Ethics, Economics and Justice*, edited by R. Williams and L. Elliott. Houndmills: Palgrave.

Cuff, D. 2006. *National Chaplaincy Evaluation: Community Engagement Report*. Canada: Correctional Service of Canada.

Davies, M. 1985. *The Essential Social Worker: A Guide to Positive Practice*, 2nd ed. Aldershot: Gower.

Dorling, D. 2010. *Injustice: Why Social Inequality Matters*. Bristol: The Policy Press.

Duménil, G. and D. Lévy. 2011. *The Crisis of Neoliberalism*. Cambridge, MA and London: Harvard University Press.

Durkheim, É. 1912. *The Elementary Forms of Religious Life*. Oxford and New York: Oxford University Press.

Ellis, L. 1985. 'Religiosity and Criminality: Evidence and explanations surrounding complex relationships'. *Sociological Perspectives* 28: 501–20.

Feeley, M. and J. Simon. 1992. 'The new penology: Notes on the emerging strategy for corrections'. *Criminology* 30 (4) 449–74.

Furseth, I. and P. Repstad. 2006. *An Introduction to the Sociology of Religion: Classical and Contemporary Perspectives*. Aldershot: Ashgate.

Garland, D. 2001. *The Culture of Control: Crime and Social Order in Contemporary Society*. Oxford: Oxford University Press.

Griffiths, C. T., Y. Dandurand and D. Murdoch. 2007. 'The Social Reintegration of Offenders and Crime Prevention'. Research report 2007–2. Ottawa: National Crime Prevention Centre.

Harrington, A. 2005. *Modern Social Theory: An Introduction*. Oxford and New York: Oxford University Press.

Harvey, D. 2005. *A Brief History of Neoliberalism*. Oxford: Oxford University Press.

———. 2010. *The Enigma of Capital and the Crises of Capitalism*. London: Profile Books.

Hirschi, T. and R. Stark. 1969. 'Hellfire and Delinquency'. *Social Problems* (17): 202–13.

Home Office. 2004. *Working Together: Cooperation between Government and Faith Communities*. London: Home Office Faith Communities Unit.

House of Commons Justice Committee. 2011. *The Role of the Probation Service*. Eighth Report of Session 2010–12, vols 1–2, HC 519–I and HC 519–II. London: The Stationery Office.

Johnson, B. R. 2004. 'Religious Programs and Recidivism among Former Inmates in Prison Fellowship Programs: A Long-Term Follow-Up Study'. *Justice Quarterly* 21 (2): 329–54.

———. 2011. *More God, Less Crime: Why Faith Matters and How It Could Matter More*. West Conshohocken, PA: Templeton Press.

Johnson, B. R., S. de Li, D. B. Larson, and M. McCullough, 2000. 'A Systematic Review of the Religiosity and Delinquency Literature'. *Journal of Contemporary Criminal Justice* 16 (1): 32–52.

Jones, E. 1968. *Profiles of the Prophets*. Oxford: The Religious Education Press.

Knudten, R. D. and M. S. Knudten. 1971. 'Juvenile Delinquency, Crime, and Religion'. *Review of Religious Research* 12 (3): 130–52.

Lishman, J. 1994. *Communication in Social Work*. Basingstoke: Macmillan.

Maruna, S. and T. LeBel. 2010. 'The desistance paradigm in correctional practice: From programmes to lives'. In *Offender Supervision: New Directions in Theory, Research and Practice*, edited by F. McNeill, P. Raynor and C Trotter. Abingdon: Willan.

Maruna, S., L. Wilson and K. Curran. 2006. 'Why God is often found behind bars: Prison conversions and the crisis of self-narrative'. *Research in Human Development* 3 (2–3): 161–84.

McNeill, F. 2003. 'Desistance-Focused Probation Practice'. In *Moving Probation Forward: Evidence, Arguments and Practice*, edited by W. H. Chui and M. Nellis. Harlow: Pearson Education.

McNeill, F. and B. Weaver. 2010. *Changing Lives? Desistance Research and Offender Management*. Glasgow: Scottish Centre for Crime and Justice Research.

Mears, D. P., C. G. Roman, A. Woolf and J. Buck. 2006. 'Faith-Based Efforts to Improve Prisoner Re-entry: Assessing the Logic and Evidence'. *Journal of Criminal Justice* 34 (4): 351–67.

Ministry of Justice. 2010. *Breaking the Cycle: Effective Punishment, Rehabilitation and Sentencing of Offenders*. London: Ministry of Justice.

Mounier, E. 1952. *Personalism*. Notre Dame, IN: University of Notre Dame Press.

NOMS. 2005. *The Reducing Reoffending Faith and Voluntary and Community Sector Alliance*. London: Home Office.

O'Connor, T. P. 2004a. 'What Works: Religion as a Correctional Intervention, Part 1'. *Journal of Criminal Corrections* 14 (1): 11–27.

———. 2004b. 'What Works, Religion as a Correctional Intervention, Part 2'. *Journal of Criminal Corrections* 14 (2): 4–26.

O'Connor, T. P. and J. B. Duncan. 2008. *Religion and Prison Programming: The Role, Impact, and Future Direction of Faith in Correctional Systems*. Offender Programs Report, March/April, 81–96.

O'Connor, T. P., J. B. Duncan and F. Quillard. 2006. 'Criminology and Religion: The Shape of an Authentic Dialogue'. *Criminology and Public Policy* 5 (3): 559–70.

O'Connor, T. P., Y. Su, P. Ryan, C. Parikh and E. Alexander. 1997. *Detroit Transition of Prisoners: Final Evaluation Report*. Silver Spring, MD: Centre for Social Research, 1–25.

Raines, J. 2002. *Marx on Religion*. Philadelphia: Temple University Press.

Raynor, P. 2002. 'Community Penalties: Probation, punishment, and "what works"'. In *The Oxford Handbook of Criminology*, 3rd ed., edited by M. Maguire, R. Morgan and R. Reiner. Oxford: Oxford University Press.

Reiner, R. 2007. *Law and Order: An Honest Citizen's Guide to Crime and Control*. Cambridge: Polity Press.

Rogers, C. 1961. *On Becoming a Person: A Therapeutic View of Psychotherapy*. London: Constable.

Smith, D. 2006. 'Making sense of psychoanalysis in criminological theory and probation practice'. *Probation Journal* 53 (4): 361–76.

Steiner, R. 1973. *The Riddles of Philosophy*. Herndon, VA: SteinerBooks.

Straw, J. 2009. 'Probation and community punishment'. Speech given to trainee probation officers at the Probation Study School, University of Portsmouth, 4 February.

Sumter, M. T. 1999. 'Religiousness and post-release community adjustment'. Executive summary, unpublished doctoral dissertation, Florida State University, Tallahassee.

Temple, W. [1942] 1976. *Christianity and Social Order*. London: Shepheard-Walwyn.

Tittle, C. R. and M. R. Welch. 1983. *Religiosity and Deviance: Towards a Contingency Theory of Constraining Effects*. Chapel Hill: University of North Carolina Press.

Traux, C. B. and R. R. Carkhuff. 1967. *Towards Effective Counselling and Psychotherapy*. Chicago: Aldine.

Trusty, B. and M. Eisenberg. 2003. *Initial Process and Outcome Evaluation of the Inner Change Freedom Initiative: The Faith-Based Prison Program in TDCJ*. Austin, TX: CJ Policy Council.

Underdown, A. 1998. *Strategies for Effective Offender Supervision: Report of the HMIP What Works Project*. London: HM Inspectorate of Probation.

Wacquant, L. 2009. *Punishing the Poor: The Neoliberal Government of Social Insecurity*. Durham, NC and London: Duke University Press.

Weber, M. [1922] 1968. *Economy and Society: An Outline of Interpretive Sociology*, 3 vols, edited by Guenther Roth and Claus Wittich. New York: Bedminster Press.

Whitehead, P. 2007. *Modernising Probation and Criminal Justice: Getting the Measure of Cultural Change*. Crayford: Shaw and Sons.

―――. 2010. *Exploring Modern Probation: Social Theory and Organisational Complexity*. Bristol: The Policy Press.

―――. 2011a. *Evaluation Report of Research at Six Community Chaplaincy Projects in England and Wales*. Middlesbrough: Teesside University and Community Chaplaincy Association.

―――. 2011b. 'Breaking the Cycle or Re-cycling Errors: Critical comment on proposals for criminal justice reform'. *Critical Social Policy* 31 (4): 628–39.

Whitehead, P. and R. Arthur. 2011. '"Let No One Despise Your Youth": A sociological approach to youth justice under New Labour 1997–2010'. *International Journal of Sociology and Social Policy* 31 (7–8): 469–85.

Whitehead, P. and R. Statham. 2006. *The History of Probation: Politics, Power and Cultural Change 1876–2005*. Crayford: Shaw and Sons.

Wilkinson, R. and K. Pickett. 2009. *The Spirit Level: Why More Equal Societies Almost Always Do Better*. London: Allen Lane.

Williams, R. 2010. 'Knowing Our Limits'. In *Crisis and Recovery: Ethics, Economics and Justice*, edited by R. Williams and L. Elliott. London: Palgrave Macmillan.

Williams, R. and L. Elliott (eds). 2010. *Crisis and Recovery: Ethics, Economics and Justice*. London: Palgrave Macmillan.

Wilson, R. J., F. Cortoni and A. J. McWhinnie. 2009. 'Circles of Support and Accountability: A Canadian National Replication of Outcome Findings'. *Sexual Abuse: A Journal of Research and Treatment* 21 (4): 412–30.

Wilson, L. C., C. Wilson, S. R. Drummond and K. Kelso. 2005. 'Promising Effects on the Reduction of Criminal Recidivism: An Evaluation of the Detroit Transition of Prisoner's Faith Based Initiative'. Draft report.

Wyatt, W. 1999. *The Journals of Woodrow Wyatt*, vol. 1. London: Pan Books.

Chapter 10

MARKETS, PRIVATISATION AND JUSTICE: SOME CRITICAL REFLECTIONS

Philip Whitehead and Paul Crawshaw

Today, we do not know what we have to do, but we have to act now, because the consequences of inaction could be catastrophic. (Žižek 2011, 480)

There's Something Different Going On – Have You Noticed?

We are in the vice-like grip of an acute paradox. At the critical moment when neoliberal capitalism has entered its latest crisis, the relentless pursuit of profitable markets on the back of neoliberal dogma is infiltrating an expanded set of organisational domains. At the precise historical juncture when lessons could be assimilated to modify if not rid the world of a failed and failing political economy where money is the ultimate standard of value, desperate attempts are being made to resuscitate an ailing system by prescribing more of the same rather than deciding that enough is enough. However, the unfolding catastrophe which is being played out in the global market place of ideas and material conditions, manifested in an ecological crisis, struggles over raw materials, deepening and widening social divisions (Žižek 2011), has not gone without challenge, protest, or resistance. The Occupy Movement in Madrid during May 2011, with eruptions on Wall Street in September, subsequently established its presence in other cities and countries. In fact, one of us was directly affected by the movement when travelling from Ottawa to Toronto on Saturday, 15 October 2011 to return from Canada to the United Kingdom. Further the tented village in the precincts of St Paul's in London received a good deal of media attention as well as disquiet from the established church since the autumn of last year. The Occupy Movement is protesting against the effects of capitalism/neoliberalism in generating poverty, inequality, injustice, rising unemployment and differential life chances between the 1 per cent and 99 per cent globally. The fundamental question asked by this dispersed but collective movement is: How can it be right, fair or just that an economic system is capable of inflicting so much damage onto the lives of human beings by allowing extremes of wealth to be concentrated in the hands of the few at the expense of the many? One of the aims of the movement is to highlight the deleterious effects of a money-driven political system, which resonates with the concerns of this book when turning from a macro analysis to organisational structures, which includes: criminality, punishment, prisons and probation within the criminal justice system; illegal markets and policing the neoliberal state; youth justice, health and education and the voluntary and faith sectors. Arundhati Roy has acknowledged that Occupy provides a Durkheimian expressive outlet for the ventilation of deep concerns at the frustrations felt by the failures of neoliberalism. In an interview for the United Kingdom's *Guardian* newspaper on Wednesday, 30 November 2011, she asserted that

> the whole privatisation of health and education, of natural resources and essential infrastructure – all of this is so twisted and so antithetical to anything that would place the interests of human beings or the environment at the centre of what ought to be a government concern – should stop.

Accordingly, the motif that straps together the disparate chapters in this book was established initially by Whitehead and Crawshaw during a series of exploratory discussions in 2009, later taken forward by a group of academics located within the Social Futures Institute at Teesside University and ably enriched by colleagues from other universities. All of us have been simultaneously guided and troubled by considering how contributors operating within different fields could make a distinctive contribution to a subject precipitating deep concern, nationally and internationally, as these chapters illustrate. The neoliberal surge, which signalled the latest phase of capitalist political economy (Duménil and Lévy 2004 and 2011), began during the 1970s before rapid expansion in the 1980s. It is a central contention of this book that the irrepressible dynamic of neoliberalism is currently being institutionalised within an expanded set of organisational spheres. This process has been underway for over 30 years in different countries and paradoxically, has been given fresh stimulation by the economic crisis which began in 2007. As the crisis rumbles on, the paradox becomes more defined and we enter a qualitatively different phase that allows us to accentuate the following features:

- The year 2007 signalled the latest round of global economic convulsions which began in the United States, but the contagion has spread far wider (Duménil and Lévy 2011, 38).
- The general election in the United Kingdom during May 2010, as an example, was proceeded by establishing the ground rules for a period of restructuring which involves forging new relationships between the neoliberal political economy, the functioning of the state, the citizenry, and particularly the public sector, the latter guided by the seemingly irrefutable nostrum that there is less money to spend on public services (the arm of the social/welfare state).
- This restructuring is forging new opportunities for the private as well as the voluntary/third sectors in what amounts to a state-reconfigured mixed economy. Significantly, the private sector is being presented with opportunities to move into and transform organisational spheres into sites for competitive profit making. For example, in the United Kingdom, the running of prisons through a process of market testing, probation services, police and medical facilities. Specifically, the police are considering outsourcing functions to G4S, a private security company which began as Securicor during the 1930s. Also on 1 March 2012 it was reported that the governor of three prisons in South Yorkshire – Lindholme, Moorland and Hatfield – expelled probation staff after discovering that the local probation trust had formed an alliance with G4S to take over the running of these prisons.
- Correspondingly, and this point should not be overlooked, there are propitious opportunities for the third sector as non-governmental organisations to open up new lines of challenge and resistance, which could facilitate the neoliberal state to reconsider the current direction of travel. Rather than collude with government policy (HM Government 2011), the third sector could launch itself on collision course.

Indubitably, there's something different going on. It is difficult not to notice the neoliberal train gathering speed to punch its way into new operational frontiers. The five principles of neoliberalism which have informed our collective thinking during the last two years can be highlighted by returning to the summation provided by Birch and Mykhnenko (2010):

1. The privatisation of state assets
2. Liberalisation of trade in goods and capital investment
3. Monetarism and the control of inflation

4. The deregulation of labour
5. Marketisation of society through public–private partnerships and a prevailing emphasis upon commercialisation and commodification

Our own distinctive contributions are clearly located within principles 1 and 5 of privatising state assets and marketisation, which provide the evidential supports for the contention that what began over thirty years ago is currently advancing under the weight of economic necessity as neoliberalism smashes its way through the last remaining barriers, penetrating beyond previous lines of demarcation. Accordingly, Cowling analyses the distinctive features of philosophical liberalism, which is followed by an excursus into neoliberalism in the United States and the United Kingdom and the linkages with crime and incarceration. Teague provides a more detailed and richly evidenced exposition of crime, punishment, prison and probation in these two countries. When turning specifically to the prison–industrial complex (Christie 2000; Goldberg and Evans 2009; Soering 2011), this illustrates the pursuit of profit in the criminal justice system of the United States at the expense of justice and rehabilitation (see also Bell 2011; Reiner 2007; Wacquant 2009). Shen and her colleagues journey into China to explore the phenomenon of counterfeit cigarettes and illegal markets precipitated by, and located within, a neoliberal operating environment, before Papanicolaou casts a critical materialist eye over policing within a neoliberal state. Arthur addresses the field of youth justice, which has become increasingly punitive and exclusionary under the neoliberal state formation of New Labour governments between 1997 and 2010. He argues that the state is increasingly absolving itself from its moral responsibility for children and young people appearing before the courts (see the Ministry of Justice (2010) document *Breaking the Cycle* for the latest policy statement on youth justice policy from 2010 to 2015). Next, Crawshaw considers the social marketing of health, where the prevailing governmental discourse emphasises healthy lifestyles through eating properly and reducing alcohol and tobacco consumption, in addition to the exhortation to engage in regular exercise. In other words the atomised individual, existing within a government-at a-distance neoliberal state, must be responsible for his or her own health, rather than governments themselves taking responsibility for the amelioration of the structural determinants of ill health. Abbas, Ashwin and McLean consider two framings of higher education: the first is found in official policy documents where the marketisation of higher education is essential for the production of quality. It views student employment as the key measure of high quality and suggests that disadvantaged students would prefer to undertake degrees that focus on employment training rather than studying academic disciplines. By contrast, the second framing is exemplified by current social science students' empirically grounded accounts of what they value about the education they receive. These students, who are from diverse backgrounds and studying in higher- and lower-ranking universities in England, value the ways that engaging with disciplinary knowledge transforms them personally, empowers them socially and prepares them for employment. On 29 September 2011 a document was published by the United Kingdom Heads of Departments of Sociology Council – *In Defence of Public Higher Education* – which reinforced our pressing concern at the questionable marketisation agenda being pursued within higher education. Additionally, Collini (2012) adopts a critical stance against the crude instrumental reason and associated business mentalities which permeate education. This is anathema for Collini, for whom a university education can be justified through the pursuit of knowledge *for its own sake*, which is of inestimable value, rather than reducing the academic experience to the slick marketing salesman's language of knowledge economy, utility and the student as customer. Similarly, for Žižek, the disinvestment of government, signalled by the shift from grants to fees, turns higher education into a 'market deal between universities and private individuals' (2011, 411). In the penultimate chapter, Whitehead returns to empirical research conducted within the criminal justice system, this time from the standpoint of theorising the *religious question* through the lens of community chaplaincy in Canada and in England and Wales. Religion may have been associated with priests and kings to bolster power at specific historical junctures, but it can also challenge power. It is argued that the voluntary–faith sector could play an unexpectedly important role by which the surging tide of neoliberalism can be challenged by returning to arguments stimulated by ethics, values and justice. It is at this conjuncture that non-governmental organisations can be a source of protest and resistance to the prevailing orthodoxy.

From a theological perspective, Rowan Williams (2010, 20; also see Whitehead's chapter, this volume) asserts that the 'language of customer and provider has wormed its way into practically all areas of social life', as well as colonising previously untroubled organisational domains which operated according to the tenets of a more state-directed, public-spirited rationality (the notion of public services as and for a public good). Moreover contemporary linguistic currency is replete with references to privatisation, markets, commodities and profit, which is re-routing organisations into a configuration of opportunities for capital accumulation. Crouch (2011) reinforces the thesis that neoliberalism is insidiously invading practically all institutions of society by expecting them to behave like business corporations whose rationale is profit generation; and Bell (2011) advances the argument that the function of the state has been transformed from providing public services to that of facilitating market solutions. Accordingly, the boundaries are being blurred between the public provision of services and the role of the private sector, and current debates could culminate in reducing health, education and welfare services to commodities that can be bought and sold in a competitive market place where the moral function of the state has been enfeebled. As we argued in our introductory chapter, we do not accept that this has been inevitable, that what has occurred represents some higher form of development, or that the stage reached by social or personal institutions as they exist at any given moment is the sufficient measure of their excellence (to paraphrase Berlin (1948, 63) when discussing the philosophy of Hegel and Marx). Put simply, we do not accept this, because other political and economic choices are currently available. However, decisions made and the direction of travel being pursued as we complete this book have accorded neoliberalism master status, thus relegating other options under the rubric that there is simply no alternative to what, seemingly out of historical necessity, currently exists and is likely to prevail for the foreseeable future. Rather than use the economic catastrophe of 2007 to dilute neoliberal hegemony, it appears that the central question is how to effect a revivalist crusade to ensure its expansionary survival at all costs.

Lifting our heads to gaze beyond our own blinkered history of the present by standing outside the ephemeral moment, Arrighi (2010) invites us to ponder a 600-year history of what he describes as the long cycles of capitalism. Marx advanced the thesis of the law-like development of the capitalist mode of production, which is always seeking opportunities for capital to expand, relentlessly pursuing new fields of accumulation. Hardt and Negri (2001, 237), after considering the cyclical account delineated by Arrighi, focuses on the accompanying process of crisis followed by capitalist restructuring. Accordingly, the latest crisis that began in 2007 and remains very much with us as we complete this book, is not bringing the neoliberal experiment to an end (no penitential response in sackcloth and ashes from its devotees), but is, in fact, creating opportunities for the survival of the neoliberal compact. Economic turbulence is always close at hand and recent events, from banks that have been lending to bad risks and mortgages supplied to subsequent defaulters (subprime phenomenon), to workers seeing the value of their wages decline and being forced to borrow at interest to make up the shortfall, have all impacted globally upon individuals, families and organisational spheres. At this point, we extend our theorisation of the impacts and effects of what is currently occurring within organisational domains as a consequence of the material basis of the neoliberal dynamic being resurgently put to work:

- The nature and rationale of those organisational spheres discussed in this book is currently the subject of the latest stage of a qualitative transformation that different authors have explored. There *is* something different going on of material significance in the delivery of prisons and probation, adult and youth justice systems, illegal markets and the police function, health, education and welfare provision that we need to acknowledge is creating a new operational landscape and accompanying empirical object requiring further detailed research. The discernible shift is from being above the market to becoming subject to market forces.

- This qualitative shift will stimulate changing organisational coordinates, including understanding the primary task, through the production of a transformed organisational consciousness, which in turn will affect the functioning of, for illustrative purposes, criminal justice, health services, education and welfare.

- The transformative dynamics recounted above will produce new forms of individual worker subjectivity, the creation of an *organisational self* that will be manipulated to fit with neoliberal marketised, competitive, and money-driven expectations. In Marxist terms, this is the production of a form of human consciousness inextricably associated with the material foundations of neoliberalism.

- Indubitably, social relationships *within* these organisations will be transformed and consequently damaged, as well as encounters with those *outside* of the organisation, because neoliberalism fundamentally transmutes the dynamics of social encounters between human beings if the pursuit of profit takes priority over the provision of good service. To put this another way, institutionalising neoliberalism within organisational formations 'reduces all human qualities to quantitative values of exchange' (Giddens 1971, 214).

- A qualitatively different relationship between reconfigured organisations and the state will be established which will continue the process of de-professionalisation and de-personalisation which has been underway since the 1980s, that is, unless current modes of thinking are modified, if not reversed. For example, the case study of probation work by Whitehead (2010), which analyses organisational transformations from the probation officer as social worker exercising therapeutic imagination to the offender manager as a functioning punitive-bureaucratic-risk technician, should serve as a warning.

It is therefore imperative to restate our analytical understanding that the primary objective of neoliberalism is a 'political project to re-establish the conditions for capital accumulation and to restore the power of economic elites' (Harvey 2005, 19). We are being confronted with a phenomenon – vector of class power – which is hermetically sealing off the organisations in question from the possibility of alternative trajectories and potential sources of challenge and resistance. What is being played out in the immediate present, what is acutely affecting social and organisational existence, is the transference of the legitimation of power from the public sphere into a more marketised private domain where capital is the driving force and dominant value. Stated bluntly, it is the transference of power through institutionalising and embedding neoliberalism within organisations which is elevating the interests of profit making before all other human considerations: organisational/professional integrity, ethical consequences (Williams and Elliott 2010), axiological considerations and the demands of criminal justice and social justice. Organisational spaces as social institutions are being re-modelled according to the tenets of the free market within a reconfigured state-finance nexus; it is nothing short of the revaluation of human and social values. These are precisely the issues around which a concerned group of academics have collaborated throughout the chapters in this book, precipitated by the activation of a sociological conscience to reflect upon what is occurring in different parts of the world, to theorise impacts and research effects. Notwithstanding the dominance of the state and the market, one arguably remains confronted with an ethically driven responsibility to formulate responses that will arrest the surging tide of the neoliberal complex notwithstanding the complexity of the oppositional task (Bourdieu 1998; Duménil and Lévy 2011).

Your Planet Needs You: Pugilists against the Rising Tide

Numerous texts respond to global neoliberalism, some of which have been referenced throughout these chapters and seek to offer both critique and challenge. If the collection of papers contained within Williams and Elliott (2010) stimulate a theological-political critique, Chatterton advances the cause of a do-it-yourself politics of change that 'doesn't wait for political leaders, party bureaucracies or elite summiteers to deliver social change' (2010, 188). This do-it-yourself politics includes working collectively, engaging in direct democracy, thinking and acting strategically and making a critical evaluation of one's attempts at transformational activities. Shaoul (2010) delivers a visceral critique of neoliberalism along with a description of the deleterious effects of its economic rationality; Hinojosa and Bebbington (2010) draw attention to the way in which civil society groups have opposed, particularly within Latin America, the damage caused by the depletion of natural resources including environmental damage by (American) companies solely in search of profit (we could substitute the depletion of natural resources with the *depletion of organisational integrity*; environmental damage with *organisational and social damage inflicted upon human beings*). Notwithstanding expressed concerns at the demise of civil society bludgeoned by the combined forces of the state and the market, and the criticism that civil society groups *only* ameliorate rather than wield power to create lasting and necessary change (Harvey 2010), it is possible to advance the view that the third/voluntary sector of non-governmental organisations has a salient role to play in leading the fight against the rising tide of neoliberal effects. Here, we refer again to Hardt and Negri's analysis (2001, 309) when they turn to discuss the pyramid of global constitution, which is constructed according to three discrete tiers. The third tier is of particular interest.

- Tier 1 predominantly refers to the United States as a superpower which possesses the hegemonic global use of force. It also includes an elite group of nations bound together in a series of organisms such as the G7, Paris and London clubs and Davos.
- Tier 2 includes the networks of transnational corporations throughout the world market and networks of capital flows.
- Tier 3 of the pyramid, located at the broad base, comprises those groups that represent the popular interest operating within the parameters of global power structures (tiers 1 and 2). Hardt and Negri (2001, 311) expatiate that located at this third level, 'the global People is represented more clearly and directly not by governmental bodies but by a variety of organisations that are at least relatively independent of nation states and capital'. These are the interstitial structures of global civil society which represent fundamental human needs, desires, and concerns, of which one illustration considered within the scope of this book is community chaplaincy (Chapter 9), located within the interstices of the state's formal criminal justice system of Canada and of England and Wales. There are also many other non-governmental organisations that can oppose the formal structures of the state and the market (18,000 worldwide during the 1990s). It is cogently argued that they do not exist to represent the vested interests of one partial group, that is, some specific factional interest such as elites who wield economic power, but rather to 'represent directly global and universal human interests' (Hardt and Negri 2001, 313) of which the Occupy Movement cited earlier is a recent example.

This pyramidal structure reminds us that the state complex is a site of contradiction and contestation, a shifting balance of forces and interests, notwithstanding the hegemonic status ascribed to political elites advancing the cause of neoliberal market and economic solutions (Coleman et al. 2009; Hall et al. 1978). Even though neoliberalism at every turn seems to tighten its grip, close down oppositional space, bait its trap (Brook 2007) and commit social murder (Chernomas and Hudson 2007) – thus refusing to lie down, accept that it's beaten and quietly expire (Crouch 2011) – arguments rooted in ethical demands, humane values, and social justice continue to provoke the delineation of alternatives. Accordingly, a pressing case remains for the mobilisation of volunteers within civil society, groups of professional bodies within organisational structures, what remains of the trade union movement in health, education and welfare, oppositional political groupings, even student bodies within universities, to work collaboratively and strategically to address those concerns which are analysed within the chapters of this book. Here lies a critical conundrum: it is easier to analyse and diagnose the aetiology of political, social and economic problems, than it is to formulate a coherent and coordinated strategy to engender change which moves the terrain from *what* should be done to *how* this can be achieved. But as we complete this book during the spring of 2012, we continue to observe protests by, of, and for the people in various international manifestations from the Occupation Movement and its tented villages, to trade union officials protesting their disquiet against the privatisation agenda, occasional student rebellions, and, of course, the potential lurking within the Big Society to turn the tables upon their governmentally perceived function (from collusion to collision) by re-moralising the role of the state by putting the interests of life itself before the narrow concerns of economic elites.

The criminal justice, health, education and welfare systems have been and continue to be transformed into commodities which are bought and sold within an increasingly privatised competitive marketplace by and for *Homo economicus*. Nevertheless, the argument is advanced for relocating the prevailing debate from institutionalising neoliberalism within organisational formations, which is attesting to their integration into the circuits of capitalist production as money pursues new opportunities for profitable market exchange, to expanding analysis, debate and critique into the circuits of ethical and axiological contestation which challenges the orthodoxy of the tragic quality of neoliberalism. Loïc Wacquant (2009), whose trenchant critique, within the frameworks of criminal justice and penal policy, takes the bare-knuckle fight to neoliberalism at three levels including words, discourse and critical argument (Daems 2008), to which these chapters contribute. Pierre Bourdieu (1998), in *Acts of Resistance*, agrees that we've heard it stated interminably that there's no alternative to the neoliberal doxa that importunes the land, which, of course, is nothing less than repackaging the old idea of capitalism. Essentially neoliberalism is the elevation of individual self-interest over collective responsibility and social welfare. Therefore, Bourdieu issues a rallying call to 'writers, artists, philosophers and scientists to be able to make their voice heard directly in all the areas of public life in which they are competent' (1998, 9). Finally, Tony Myers (2003), in his introductory text on Slavoj Žižek, explains how the latter conflates Hegelian dialectical methodology with Marxist sociological critique and Lacanian psychoanalysis. It is Lacan's three orders by which mental functioning can be classified – the *Imaginary*, the *Symbolic*, and the *Real* – which are assimilated by Žižek into political activism. Significantly, the *Imaginary* refers to the functioning ego, which, in the postmodern era, stimulates an overabundance of narcissistic self-obsession. By contrast, the *Symbolic order* is the impersonal framework of society as 'the arena in which we take our place as part of a community of fellow human beings' (Myers 2003, 22). The imaginary order has been elevated at the expense of the symbolic order under the doctrine of neoliberalism and its cultural expression in postmodernism, which is currently being allowed to re-code the genetics of organisational structures in such a way that people and the communal interest will be indubitably damaged.

In conclusion, Tom Daems (2008, 238), when expatiating upon the work of Loïc Wacquant, refers to neoliberalism as a 'complete ideological package' in the way that it creates a monochrome political and organisational culture. What is more, Žižek argues that what is happening in the 'latest stage of the post-1968 "postmodern" capitalism is that the *economy itself (the logic of market and competition) is progressively imposing itself as the hegemonic ideology*' (2011, 412; italics in the original). Of course, there are occasional skirmishes into the space occupied by the neoliberal agenda and battles seemingly won. Trade unions turn up the heat on governments by building barricades of protest before receding once again; student voices clamour before falling silent; professional bodies erupt in agitation at the assault on their competencies but can only endure for so long in conditions of conflict. Also, one should not overlook the poignant symbolic moment of the Occupy Movement being evicted from the precincts of St Paul's during the early hours of Tuesday, 28 February 2012 by bailiffs and the police before the bewildered gaze of the established Church of England. The ideological apparatus of the state is being highly successful at convincing us that there is no alternative, particularly when it is supported by the coercive backstop of the repressive state apparatus. Accordingly, the contributors to this book facilitate ongoing debate, stimulate discussion, and contribute to challenging the enveloping structure of neoliberalism, particularly when it encloses organisational spheres within the neoliberal pinfold. We don't sing the neoliberal tune, but strike a discordant note; we don't march in step, but drag two left feet against the spirit of our times; our words clatter into the neoliberal narrative, causing a veritable pile-up. We do these things because there is simply too much at stake to leave the future in the hands of the tireless proponents of neoliberal orthodoxy and, as Žižek (2011) states, inaction could be catastrophic.

References

Arrighi, G. 2010. *The Long Twentieth Century: Money, Power and the Origins of Our Times*. London and New York: Verso.

Bell, E. 2011. *Criminal Justice and Neoliberalism*. London: Palgrave Macmillan.

Berlin, I. 1948. *Karl Marx: His Life and Environment*, 2nd ed. London and New York: Oxford University Press.

Birch, K. and V. Mykhnenko (eds). 2010. *The Rise and Fall of Neoliberalism: The Collapse of an Economic Order*. London and New York: Zed Books.

Bourdieu, P. 1998. *Acts of Resistance: Against the New Myths of Our Time*. Cambridge: Polity Press.

Brook, D. 2007. *The Trap: Selling Out to Stay Afloat in Winner-Take-All America*. New York: Times Books, Henry Holt and Company.

Chatterton, P. 2010. 'Do It Yourself: A Politics for Changing our World'. In *The Rise and Fall of Neoliberalism: The Collapse of an Economic Order*, edited by K. Birch and V. Mykhnenko. London and New York: Zed Books.

Chernomas, R. and I. Hudson. 2007. *Social Murder and Other Shortcomings of Conservative Economics*. Winnipeg: Arbeiter Ring Publishing.

Christie, N. 2000. *Crime Control as Industry: Towards Gulag Western* Style, 3rd ed. London and New York: Routledge.

Coleman, R., J. Sim, S. Tombs and D. Whyte. 2009. *State Power Crime*. London: Sage.

Collini, S. 2012. *What are Universities For?* London: Penguin.

Crouch, C. 2011. *The Strange Non-Death of Neoliberalism*. Cambridge. Polity Press.

Daems, T. 2008. *Making Sense of Penal Change*. Oxford and New York: Oxford University Press.

Duménil, G. and D. Lévy. 2004. *Capital Resurgent: Roots of the Neoliberal Revolution*. Cambridge, MA: Harvard University Press.

———. 2011. *Crisis of Neoliberalism*. Cambridge, MA: Harvard University Press.

Garland, D. 1990. *Punishment and Modern Society: A Study in Social Theory*. Oxford and New York: Oxford University Press.

Giddens, A. 1971. *Capitalism and Modern Social Theory: An Analysis of the Writings of Marx, Durkheim and Max Weber*. Cambridge and New York: Cambridge University Press.

Goldberg, E. and L. Evans. 2009. *The Prison-Industrial Complex and the Global Economy*. PM Press Pamphlet Series No. 0004. Oakland, CA: PM Press.

Hall, S., C. Critcher, T. Jefferson, J. Clarke and B. Roberts. 1978. *Policing the Crisis: Mugging, the State and Law and Order*. Basingstoke: Macmillan.

Hardt, M. and A. Negri. 2000. *Empire*. Cambridge, MA: Harvard University Press.

Harvey, D. 2005. *A Brief History of Neoliberalism*. Oxford and New York: Oxford University Press.

———. *The Enigma of Capital and the Crises of Capitalism*. London: Profile Books.

Hinojosa, L. and A. Bebbington. 2010. 'Transnational Companies and Transnational Civil Society'. In *The Rise and Fall of Neoliberalism: The Collapse of an Economic Order*, edited by K. Birch and V. Mykhnenko. London and New York: Zed Books.

HM Government. 2011. *Open Public Services White Paper*. CM 8145. London: HM Government.

Ministry of Justice. 2010. *Breaking the Cycle: Effective Punishment, Rehabilitation and Sentencing Offenders*. London: Ministry of Justice.

Myers, T. 2003. *Slavoj Žižek*. London: Routledge.

Reiner, R. 2007. *Law and Order: An Honest Citizen's Guide to Crime and Control*. Cambridge: Polity Press.

Shaoul, J. 2010. 'A Marxist International Perspective and Programme'. In *The Rise and Fall of Neoliberalism: The Collapse of an Economic Order*, edited by K. Birch and V. Mykhnenko. London and New York: Zed Books.

Soering, J. 2011. 'How Profit Fuels America's Prison Industry and Keeps our Citizens in Captivity'. *Justice Reflections* 28, article JR196. Lincoln: The Worldwide International Prison Chaplains' Association (IPCA).

Wacquant, L. 2009. *Punishing the Poor: The Neoliberal Government of Social Insecurity*. Durham, NC and London: Duke University Press.

Whitehead, P. 2010. *Exploring Modern Probation. Social Theory and Organisational Complexity*. Bristol: The Policy Press.

Williams, R. 2010. 'Knowing Our Limits'. In *Crisis and Recovery: Ethics, Economics and Justice*, edited by R. Williams and L. Elliott. London: Palgrave Macmillan.

Williams, R. and L. Elliott. 2010. *Crisis and Recovery: Ethics, Economics and Justice*. London: Palgrave.

Žižek, S. 2011. *Living in the End Times*. London and New York: Verso.

NOTES ON CONTRIBUTORS

Dr Andrea Abbas is a sociologist and has worked at Teesside University (UK) since 1999. However, during 2012, she was appointed reader in education at the Centre for Educational Research and Development, University of Lincoln. She has been researching and publishing in the area of the sociology of higher education since 1998 and is currently co-investigator on a three-year ESRC-funded project, Pedagogic Quality and Inequality in University First Degrees.

Dr Georgios A. Antonopoulos is a reader in criminology at the School of Social Sciences and Law, Teesside University. His research interests include the criminality, criminalisation and victimisation of minority ethnic groups and migrants, illegal markets and 'organised crime'. His articles have appeared in the *European Journal of Criminology*; *Crime, Law and Social Change*; *Trends in Organised Crime*; *Global Crime* and *British Journal of Criminology*. He is a member of the editorial board of the *Cross-Border Crime Colloquium* and the journal *Global Crime*. In 2009 he received the European Society of Criminology Young Criminologist Award.

Dr Raymond Arthur is a reader in law at Teesside University and undertakes research on issues related to the delivery of justice for children and families. Published works include *Family Life and Youth Offending Behaviour* (Routledge, 2007) which examines what measures, outside of the criminal justice system, can effectively respond to young people with developing criminal capacities. His latest book is *Young Offenders and the Law* (Routledge, 2010), which critically evaluates the response of the domestic legal system to youth offending in the light of international best practice.

Dr Paul Ashwin is a senior lecturer at Lancaster University in the Department of Educational Research. His research interests are focused on teaching, learning and assessment in higher education. His recent book, *Analysing Teaching-Learning Interactions in Higher Education: Accounting for Structure and Agency* (Continuum, 2012), focuses on ways of conceptualising teaching-learning processes in higher education that support a consideration of both structure and agency.

Professor Mark Cowling, Teesside University, is the author of two books, the most recent being *Marxism and Criminological Theory: A Critique and a Toolkit* (Palgrave, 2008). He is also the editor or joint editor of six collections, four of them in the area of Marxism, one on political issues of the twenty-first century and one on sexual consent.

Dr Paul Crawshaw is assistant dean with responsibility for research and enterprise in the School of Social Sciences and Law, Teesside University, and director of the Social Futures Institute. A medical sociologist by training, since the 1990s he has researched social and political aspects of health and illness with particular emphasis upon risk and governance of health and well-being in health promotion and public health work. He has published widely in these areas. From 2002–11 he has been associate editor and editor of the international, peer-reviewed journal, *Critical Public Health*.

Marin K. Kurti is an adjunct instructor of sociology at Fordham University. He received his BA in sociology from Fordham University and MA in criminal justice from John Jay College of Criminal Justice. His research interests include organised crime and the illegal cigarette trade.

Klaus von Lampe is associate professor at John Jay College of Criminal Justice, Department of Law, Police Science and Criminal Justice Administration in New York City. He has published extensively on organised and transnational crime. His most recent publications include 'The application of the framework of Situational Crime Prevention to "organized crime"' (*Criminology and Criminal Justice*) and 'Re-conceptualizing transnational organized crime: Offenders as problem solvers' (*International Journal of Security and Terrorism*). He is the editor-in-chief of the peer-reviewed journal *Trends in Organized Crime*.

Dr Monica McLean is professor of higher education at the Centre for Research in Higher, Adult and Vocational Education, University of Nottingham. Her research focuses on pedagogy in higher education and comprises two broad interrelated strands. In the first strand she locates empirical data about the everyday experiences of university teachers and student within socio-political contexts (international, national and institutional). The second strand draws on critical theory to investigate learning, teaching, assessment and curriculum in different disciplines and contexts. This work has resulted in a number of invitations to seminars, journal articles and a book entitled *Pedagogy and the University: Critical Theory and Practice* (Continuum, 2006).

Dr Georgios Papanicolaou is a lecturer in criminology at Teesside University. Georgios studied law, penal sciences and criminology at the University of Athens, Greece, and the University of Edinburgh. He works from a materialist theoretical perspective on the history, organisation and role of the police apparatus and his current research interests include the politics of transnational policing and the policing of national and transnational illegal markets. Georgios's book *Policing The Imperialist Chain: Transnational Policing and Sex Trafficking in Southeast Europe* was published by Palgrave Macmillan in 2011.

Dr Anqi Shen is an academic lawyer and senior lecturer in law and policing in the School of Social Sciences and Law, Teesside University. Before coming to the United Kingdom to pursue her PhD she worked in China as a police officer and a qualified lawyer in a Nanjing law firm. Her research interests include comparative law and criminal justice. She has had articles published in both English and Chinese, and her recent work has appeared in the journal *Criminology and Criminal Justice* as well as the *British Journal of Criminology*.

Michael Teague is a criminologist at Teesside University and has published a number of articles on the American criminal justice system. He has also written on the British probation system and is currently completing doctoral research on probation culture in Britain. He is a member of the specialist assessment board for the *Probation Journal* and is on the editorial advisory board of the *British Journal of Community Justice*.

Dr Philip Whitehead is a reader in criminal and social justice at Teesside University. Before taking up his current appointment, he worked for the probation service in the northeast of England for over twenty-six years, during which time he held numerous positions including research and information officer. Since the 1980s he has researched various aspects of probation, criminal and youth justice, which resulted in numerous publications. Recently, he has researched the politics of modernisation in criminal justice, specifically under New Labour, which culminated in *Exploring Modern Probation: Social Theory and Organisational Complexity* (Policy Press, 2010). He is currently researching the religious question in criminal justice in Canada and England and Wales through the lens of community chaplaincy and during the fall of 2011, was a visiting professor at Ottawa University, Canada.

INDEX

Allard, Pierre 204
Althusser, Louis 110
American Probation and Parole
    Association 64
Arrighi, Giovanni 4, 19n, 201, 234

Bannon, A. 62
Bell, Emma 47–8
Berlin, Isaiah 8
Bernstein, Basil
    pedagogic rights 18, 179, 191
Best, Geoffrey 8
Big Society 202, 221, 238
Birch, Kean 12, 231
Black Report (1979) 174
Blair, Tony 33, 47, 67, 69, 72, 141
Blamires, Harry 8
Bourdieu, Pierre 238
Breaking the Cycle (2010) 20n, 232
British Crime Survey 48
Brown, Gordon 33, 47
Bush, George 52, 63

Callaghan, James 27
capitalism 4, 20, 201
    critiques 8
    General Strike (1926) 10
    history of 4
    Industrial Revolution 5
    Keynesian modifications 1, 4, 10–11,
        26, 28, 219
    laissez-faire 5
    modifications 9–10
    nineteenth-century 4–6
    poverty and inequality 5
    private ownership 4
    social problem novels 6, 8, 20n

Castells, Manuel 35–6
Castle, Barbara 27
Children Act (1989) 140
Children and Young Persons Act (1933) 137
Children and Young Persons Act (1969) 137
China 5, 13, 34, 40, 49, 81–104
Change 4 Life 157, 175n
cigarette counterfeiting 81–104
    actors and patterns 91
    business in China 86
    business and corruption 95
    counterfeit production 87
    venues of production 89
Clinton, William Jefferson 47, 72
Communist Manifesto 109
community chaplaincy 18, 203
    Canada 203 7
    England and Wales 208–9
    Ottawa 206–7
crime 38–40
criminal justice system 37, 49, 54, 63, 65,
    69, 202, 208

Dickens, Charles 8
doli incapax 143
Dorling, Danny 14
Duménil, Gerard 4, 201, 231, 236
Durkheim, Émile 212

education 12, 32, 179, 233
    documentary analysis 186
    government policies 180, 183
    pedagogic rights 179, 191
    quality and inequality 180
    research at four universities 184
    student perspectives 185, 191
    undergraduate degrees 179

Eliot, George 6
evangelical religion 7

Faith in the City (1985) 220
Foucault, Michel 3, 12, 17, 19n, 173, 213
Friedman, Milton 26

Garland, David 19n, 47, 49, 51, 105, 202
globalisation 39

Hall, Steve 38, 48
Hall, Stuart: See Policing the Crisis (1978)
Hardt, Michael 234, 237
Harrison, J. F. C. 8, 10
Harvey, David 2, 11, 13, 46, 155, 158,
        173, 215, 219, 235
Hayek, Friedrich 27
Hayman, Andy 115
health 155–77
    choice 167
    environment and lifestyle 158, 170
    research 162
    social marketing 155, 157, 159, 162
Hobbes, Thomas 24
Hobsbawm, Eric 10–11
Human Rights Act 24

ideology 2, 7, 29
International Monetary Fund (IMF) 34
Industrial Revolution 5, 19n

Johnson, Byron 212
justice 8, 215, 219

Keynesianism 1, 4, 10–11, 26, 28, 219

Lacan, Jacques 238
Lawson, Nigel 32
Lévy, Dominique 4, 201, 231, 236
liberalism 6–8, 14, 23–6, 232
Locke, John 23

MacGregor, Ian 30
Maloney Committee (1927) 137
markets 232
Marx 4, 6, 9, 58, 106, 109, 202, 213, 235
Marxism: See Marx
MacDonald, Rob 38

Ministry of Justice 54, 66, 72, 135, 202,
        222, 232
Misspent Youth (1996) 140
Morris, Ian 5
Mounier, Emmanuel 214
Myers, Tony 239
Mykhnenko, Vlad 12, 231

Narey, Martin 53
National Association of Probation
        Officers (NAPO) 66
National Health Service (NHS) 12
National Social Marketing Centre 172
Negri, Antonio 234, 237
neoliberalism 2, 3, 11, 26, 229
    contested category 48
    corporate crime 39
    counterfeit cigarettes in China 81–104
    crime 38, 46, 48
    criminal justice 47, 54, 69, 201
    different countries 33, 35, 48
    health 155–77, 230
    higher education 179–99
    material foundations 35, 106
    policing 105–33
    policy transfer 47
    prisons 36, 49, 50, 53, 65, 68
    privatisation and justice 56, 65
    punishment 46–7
    race 51
    religion 201–28
    United Kingdom correctional system 52
    United States correctional system 49
    Washington Consensus 33
    youth justice 135–53
Newburn, Tim 47
New Deal 11
New Labour 53, 136, 140, 141, 149, 232
News of the World 118
National Offender Management Service
        (NOMS) 53, 222
National Union of Mineworkers (NUM) 30
No More Excuses (1997) 136, 141–2
non-governmental organisations 155,
        209, 237

Obama, Barack 51–2
O'Connor, Tom 210

Occupy Movement 229, 238, 239
Offender Management Act (2007) 66

parental responsibility 147
Parenti, Chritian 49, 57, 126
pedagogic rights 18, 179, 191
personalism 214
Pickett, Kate 14
Polanyi, Karl 6
police and policing 105–33
Policing the Crisis (1978) 124
Poulantzas, Nicos 107, 110, 112, 124
Press Complaints Commission 119
prisons
    USA 49–52, 56–63
    UK 52–6, 65–70
prison–industrial complex 46, 126
Prison Officers' Association (POA) 68
Private Finance Initiative (PFI) 33
privatization 13, 20, 30, 32, 56, 65, 230, 231
public health 156
punishment 36–7, 47–9, 52, 55

Reagonomics 33, 48
rehabilitation revolution 65
Reiner, Robert 45–6, 70, 105
religion 201, 211, 233
    biblical theology 220
    desistance theory 211, 217–19, 224
    justice 215
    personalist philosophy 214
    relationships 218
    sociological theory 212
    typology of religion and crime 216
    unconditional support 217
    value for money 214
restorative justice 144
Rose, Nikolas 136
Roy, Arundhati 230

Sabine, George H. 7, 9
Scargill, Arthur 30

Shildrick, Tracy 38
Smith, Adam 25
social marketing in health 159, 162
Social Futures Institute (Teesside
    University, UK) 230
state 107
    authoritarian statism 109
Stedman Jones, Gareth 9

Tackling Youth Crime (1997) 152
Thatcher, Margaret 2, 27, 28, 29, 30, 31,
    32, 72, 138, 201
third sector 231, 237
tobacco trade 81
Tonry, Michael 48
Toynbee, Polly 31

utilitarianism 7

Wacquant, Loïc 46, 238, 239
Wiener, Martin J. 7
Wilkinson, Richard 14
Wilson, Harold 27
Williams, Rowan and Larry Elliott 236
World Bank 34

youth justice 135–53
    Children and Young Persons Act
        (1933) 137
    Children and Young Persons Act
        (1969) 137
    crime prevention 142
    custody 145
    doli incapax 143
    Maloney Committee (1927) 137
    New Labour (1997–2010) 136, 140
    parental responsibility 147
    restorative justice 144
    since the 1990s 140
    welfare 137

Žižek, Slavoj 2, 229, 233, 238, 239